Anselm Foxell

Her greatest boast, Elizabeth I said, was that she ruled with the love of her subjects. To achieve this, she had to make herself known to them, and it was largely for this reason that almost every summer she went on progress. Progresses also served to satisfy her curiosity about her kingdom and indulge her love of pagentry. Nobles vied with each other in the lavish entertainment of their Queen; they extended their houses for this purpose, or even built anew. Their mansions, such as Burghley, Longleat, Penshurst, Kenilworth, Hardwick, Hatfield, Montacute, Melford Hall, Loseley Park and Parham Park, survive to evoke the vigour and intricacy of that most colourful age.

June Osborne was born in Evesham, Worcestershire, brought up in the New Forest area and read English at Bristol University. Her first career was in art galleries and museums, which brought together her interest in art and history with that in language and literature. She had curatorial posts in Bath, Christchurch and Oldham.

Mrs. Osborne made further study of art history, worked under Sir Ernst Gombrich when he was Professor of History of Art at the Slade School. Then after starting a family, she turned to lecturing, guide-lecturing and writing and has given adult education classes for the Extra-Mural departments of London, Sussex and Kent Universities. Each year she conducts study-tours and lecture-tours in Italy as well as this country and is official guide-lecturer at Hampton Court Palace, the Palace of Westminster and at Knole in Kent.

Entertaining Elizabeth I

Entertaining Elizabeth I

The Progresses and Great Houses of her time

June Osborne

BISHOPSGATE PRESS

For
Ian, Elizabeth,
Jane and Patrick.

© 1989 June Osborne

By the same author
Hampton Court Palace

Osborne, June
   Entertaining Elizabeth I.
   I. England. Elizabeth I, Queen of England,
   1533 - 1603. Royal tours
   I. Title
   942.05'5'0924

   ISBN 1-85219-055-8

All enguiries and requests relevant to this title should be sent to the publisher, Bishopsgate Press Ltd., 37 Union Street, London SE1 1SE.

Printed in Great Britain by the Bath Press, Avon

Contents

Prologue - Elizabeth at Tilbury   11

Introduction — Why Make Progresses?   13

1   Early Years   23

2   Elizabeth becomes Queen   37

3   The Queen Meets the People   43

4   Progresses to the Universities   54

5   Elizabeth and the Aristocrats - I   72

6   Elizabeth and the Aristocrats - II   81

7   An End of Progresses   93

Great Houses of Elizabethan England

Hatfield House   100

Kenilworth   107

Burghley House and Theobalds   117

Longleat   125

Knole   131

Penshurst Place   139

Hardwick Hall   148

Wollaton Hall   158

Kirby Hall and Holdenby   161

Loseley Park   165

Melford Hall   168

Parham Park   173

Montacute House   176

Appendices

Expenses of the Queen's Table, 1576   180

Cost of Entertainment at Lichfield, 1575   182

Extracts from the Household Book of Lord North, 1576   186

New Year's Gifts, 1577-78   190

The Queen at Greenwich, 1598-99   197

The Queen's Wardrobe, 1600   200

ACKNOWLEDGEMENTS

First I should like to say how much I appreciated the kindness and helpfulness I met when visiting the great houses of Elizabethan England, and the willingness to admit me even in the winter when they were normally closed - this I remember particularly at Penshurst, Burghley and Holdenby. Then there was the care and conscientiousness with which the owners and administrators were good enough to vet sections of the text. Here the list is a long one: I should like to thank Viscount De L'Isle of Penshurst, together with the Administrator Group-Captain J.R. Bradshaw, Sir Richard Hyde Parker of Melford Hall, James More-Molyneux of Loseley Park: in addition, Lord Sackville of Knole, and Richard Wakeford the ever-helpful Administrator there; Kate Harris, Librarian & Archivist to the Marquess of Bath at Longleat; Robin Harcourt-Williams, Librarian & Archivist to the Marquess of Salisbury at Hatfield House; I. St.C. Hughes Administrator at Hardwick Hall; Sqn. Ldr. W.D. Brunger, Administrator at Montacute House, Jon D. Culverhouse, Manager of Burghley House, and Mrs Patricia Kennedy, Administrator at Parham Park. I should also like to thank B.M. Morley of English Heritage for very useful notes on Kenilworth Castle, Dr Eric Till for his expertise on Burghley House and Theobalds, and J.H.C. Phelips for his detailed knowledge of Montacute. The informed interest of Miss M.E. Colthorpe of Cambridge was also much appreciated.

When it came to finding illustrations, I continued to meet with great helpfulness; and in this connection I should additionally like to thank Miss Claire Hunter-Craig of the Royal Collection, Charles Manostrocht of Sandwich Guildhall Museum, and the staff of the British Museum, the Ashmolean Museum, the National Portrait Gallery, Woburn Abbey and Corsham Court, also Louise Watts of Girton College, Cambridge.

I am very much indebted to the London Library, for their courtesy and for entrusting me with three plump and precious volumes of Nichols's *Progresses and Public Processions of Queen Elizabeth* to take home and read at my fireside. I must thank too the kind people who drove me to stately homes I might otherwise have found it almost impossible to visit - in particular Leyland Shawe, and Marie and Brian Everett. Graham Tite too has always been ready to share his considerable knowledge. My family has been as helpful as anyone could have wished, especially my son Patrick who assisted me with the section on Elizabeth in Oxford, and my daughter Jane who helped me track down books. My publisher Austen Smith has been invariably genial and understanding; we have almost always seen eye to eye. Finally I should like to thank my valued friend Nigel Foxell for his continuing encouragement and for introducing me to his photographer son Anselm.

June Osborne

March 1989.

PHOTOGRAPHIC ACKNOWLEDGEMENTS

The Marquis of Bath
The Duke of Bedford
Bodleiain Library
Burghley House
Courtauld Institute of Art
Viscount De L'Isle v.c.,
English Heretage
English Life Publications Ltd
Sir Richard Hyde Parker Bart
A. F. Kerstein Esq
Charles Mauostrocht Esq

Lord Methuen
James More-Molyneux
National Portrait Gallery
The National Trust
June Osborne
Patrick Osborne
Readers Digest
The Royal Collection
Lord Sackville
The Marquis of Salisbury
Sherbourne Castle Estate
Mr & Mrs P. A. Tritton

The Armada Portrait of Elizabeth I, attributed to George Gower. (Woburn Abbey)

'Such a Lorde is our greate God, that can frame all things to the best; and suche a Soveraigne Ladye we have, that she can make the crooked paths straighte where she commeth, and drawe the hearts of the people after hyr wheresoever she travels.'

Thomas Churchyard
(On Elizabeth I's visit to East Anglia, 1578)

PROLOGUE

ELIZABETH AT TILBURY

News travelled slowly in the sixteenth century. In the summer of 1588 it seemed certain that the Spanish Armada would join forces with the Duke of Parma at Calais, and that they would sail up the Thames to invade England. In an attempt to counter this, gun-emplacements were planted from the Gravesend Reach to Woolwich, barriers of barges were set across the river both at Blackwall Point and between Gravesend and Tilbury, and at Tilbury there was established a great camp.

Trained troops had been provided by all the counties and cities of the land, and to Tilbury they marched 'with cheereful countenances, coragious wordes and gestures, dauncing and leaping wheresoever they came'.

On 9 August Elizabeth I herself, in stiffened dress with high collar standing up like a halo, rode on a grey horse into the camp and rallied the soldiers with a stirring speech:

'My loving People, we have been persuaded by some, that are careful of our safety, to take heed how we commit ourselves to armed multitudes, for fear of treachery; but assure you, I do not desire to live to distrust my faithful and loving people. Let Tyrants fear; I have always so behaved myself, that, under God, I have placed my chiefest strength and safeguard in the loyal hearts and good-will of my subjects. And therefore I am come among you at this time, not as for my recreation or sport, but being resolved, in the midst and heat of the Battle, to live or die amongst you all; to lay down, for my God, and for my kingdom, and for my people, my honour and my blood, even in the dust. I know I have but the body of a week and feeble woman; but I have the heart of a king, and of a king of England too; and think foul scorn that Parma or Spain, or any Prince of Europe, should dare to invade the borders of my realms; to which, rather than any dishonour should grow by me, I myself will take up arms; I myself will be your general, judge, and rewarder of every one of your virtues in the field. I know already, by your forwardness, that you have deserved rewards and crowns; and we do assure you, on the word of a Prince, they shall be duly paid you. In the mean my Lieutenant-General shall be in my stead, than whom never Prince commanded a more noble and worthy subject; not doubting by your obedience to my General, by your concord in the camp, and by your valour in the field, we shall shortly have a famous victory over the enemies of my God, of my kingdom, and of my people.'

No one present realised that to all intents the victory was already won. The English fire-ships had broken the Armada's formation, and the winds were driving the Spanish ships into the North Sea, past the point of no return, leaving the Duke of Parma stranded, with no means of transporting his men.

So the speech affected the course of the war not a jot, but what was significant about the appearance of the middle-aged Queen on what was thought to be the front line, with her magnificent dress and even more magnificent words, was the effect this produced on all who saw her. To them she seemed even more splendid than Henry V at Agincourt. To them she was not just a queen but a warrior goddess, the Bellona of Roman mythology, and not just a goddess but a virgin saint, a female St George riding out to deliver them from the Spanish dragon. And to her they were her loving people.

INTRODUCTION

WHY MAKE PROGRESSES AT ALL?

Geoffrey Goodman, a young law student, saw the Queen leaving Somerset House in December 1588.

'I did then live in the Strand, near St Clement's Church, when suddenly there was a report (it was December, about five, and very dark) that the Queen was gone to council, and I was told "If you will see the Queen, you must come quickly," Then we all ran, when the Court gates were set open .... and there we stayed an hour and a half, and the yard was full, there being a great number of torches, when the Queen came out in great state. Then we cried: "God save your Majesty!"

And the Queen turned to us, and said, "God bless you all, my good people!"

Then we cried again, "God save your Majesty!"

And the Queen said again to us, "Ye may well have a greater prince, but ye shall never have a more loving prince."

And so the Queen and the crowd there, looking upon one another awhile, her Majesty departed. This wrought such an

Triumphal Procession of Elizabeth I. (Sherborne Castle)

impression upon us ... that all the way long we did nothing but talk what an admirable queen she was and how we would adventure our lives in her service.'

In the Middle Ages most people would not have had the faintest idea what their sovereign looked like. Especially for those living outside the capital city, a crude representation on a coin was probably the only clue they had. Up to the time of Elizabeth I, kings and queens had made very little attempt to come face to face with their subjects. Often in fear of rebellion, they tended to keep themselves remote. The processional ride of Henry Bolingbroke (later Henry IV) through the streets of London, 'Off goes his bonnet to an oyster-wench'[1] was unusual and thought a little undignified.

Two of the kings popularly considered heroic, Richard I and Henry V, spent almost the whole of their reigns abroad. Any loyalty which they may have inspired at home would have been loyalty to a legend — Robin Hood and Robin Goodfellow would probably have seemed more real. Even Henry VIII spent most of his time in one or other of his palaces. He did go to France for the Battle of the Spurs, the Field of the Cloth of Gold, and again as a warrior-king in 1544, and he did take his fifth wife Catherine Howard on a progress to the North Country, but these were exceptions.

The short-lived Edward VI was given little opportunity to test his popularity, which might have been great. At the so-called Siege of Hampton Court, the boy (who at the time was the virtual prisoner of his uncle the Protector Somerset) is said to have waved his dagger and shouted to the people clustering by the Palace gates, 'Will ye help me against those who would kill me?'

'God save your Grace!' they replied, 'We will die for you!' When he was ill with tuberculosis and it was rumoured he was dead, he was propped up by one of the windows of Greenwich Palace to demonstrate that he was indeed still alive; but few would have been there to witness the spectacle, and even fewer would have been prepared to swear that it actually was the King they saw. Mary Tudor discovered increasingly during her reign that the majority of her subjects (those with whom she came in contact) had little love for her, and even less for her Spanish husband, Philip. So anything in the nature of a procession became an embarrassment, and she withdrew more and more from the public eye.

[1]Shakespeare's *Richard II*, Act I, Scene IV.

So the progresses and public processions of the first Queen Elizabeth were virtually without precedent. Equally, they were virtually without successor, at least until the twentieth century. James I (he was already James VI of Scotland) for instance, hardly ever risked them; he had such a fear of assassination, and besides he may have realised that he would cut a comparatively sorry figure. Also he was a Scotsman and felt himself a foreigner south of the border. At Greenwich James had a high brick wall built on either side of the high road that ran through the Palace grounds, and the Queen's House was designed so that his consort could cross from garden to hunting park with no danger of coming into contact with any of the King's subjects. Charles I, whatever his other qualities, lacked the common touch. William III, first and foremost a Dutchman, was always anxious to avoid ceremony. As for the Hanoverian kings, George IV in particular, they were so downright unpopular that anything resembling a progress would have been asking for trouble; it was much quieter and safer to shut oneself away in Brighton. Even Queen Victoria, who as a young woman rejoiced in riding in processions and viewing such spectacles as the Great Exhibition, hardly appeared in public at all in the ten years following the death of her husband. It is not until recent times, when royal tours are constantly undertaken, and the sovereign has developed the delightful habit of 'going walkabout', that we find anything that may be paralleled with the progresses of Elizabeth I.

Broadly speaking, her power was based on the love of her subjects. This at least is what she always maintained. There is a record of a charming conversation she had with the wife of her godson Sir John Harington. How was it, she asked the young woman, that she managed to retain the love of her husband; Sir John was called witty, but not the most solid and stolid of men. The answer was by dealing with him gently, not denigrating or crossing him in any way, so that he became convinced of her love for him. 'Go to, go to, mistress' said the Queen, 'You are wisely bent, I find; after such sort do I keep the good-will of all my husbands, my good people; for if they did not rest assured of some special love towards them, they would not readily yield me such good obedience.'[2]

Elizabeth I believed, constantly and fervently, that this rapport with her people was vital to her sovereignty and to the prosperity of her kingdom. Therefore it was important that she should see and

[2] From Sir John Harington's papers, 1599. He comments, 'This deserveth noting, as being both wise and pleasant.'

be seen by as many of them as possible. Fortunately, she was not only a magnificent orator (her speeches still reverberate in the mind) but had the rare gift of knowing what to say at unlooked-for encounters with individuals.

Not that she was hail-fellow-well-met with the populace at large; yet she knew that it was politic to unbend on occasion. On a Maundy Thursday she would put on an apron and wash the feet of the poor, but she remained every inch a queen. No one was left in any doubt of that.

> 'There's such divinity doth hedge a king
> That treason can but peep to what it would'

wrote Shakespeare[3], no doubt basing his ideas of monarchy on the Queen in whose reign he had been born, brought up and had risen to manhood. Clearly she had about her a unique aura for which divinity seemed hardly too strong a word.

The suppression of the worship of saints and the discontinuation of the observance of saints' days (with few exceptions, such as St George, for England, and St Elizabeth, for the Queen) must have left gaps in people's minds just as they left gaps in the calendar. The lack of holy days, or holidays, meant that people were looking round for something else to celebrate. The Queen's birthday, the Queen's Accession Day, and prolonged feasts at Christmas helped to fill this need; just as, wherever she went, did the progresses.

But there was a deeper need: the desire for a female deity. Since the Reformation the worship of the Virgin Mary, which had been much in the ascendant for the previous hundred years or so, had been eclipsed, and countless statues and paintings of her defaced. In the old faith, the Virgin had been a figure of mercy, more approachable than the Almighty, one who would intercede on behalf of mankind and plead forgiveness for their sins — she was often shown tipping the scales in scenes of the Last Judgement. Without her, religion seemed cold and hard, and redemption less likely.

Those who had the benefit of a classical education (which was much in vogue in the sixteenth century) might have been aware of a prophecy voiced in both Virgil and Ovid. The concept described in Ovid's *Metamorphoses*, Book I, was that there had been four ages of man — the Golden Age of Saturn, a time of peace, leisure and everlasting spring; then the Silver Age of Jove, when the pattern of

[3] *Hamlet* Act IV, Scene V.

the seasons and agriculture began; then the sterner Age of Brass; followed by the wicked, mercenary and warlike Age of Iron. In this final age the virgin Astraea, daughter of Pan and Syrinx, is described as being the last of the immortals to leave the blood-soaked Earth. In Virgil's Fourth *Eclogue* appears the prophecy that Astraea will return, and bring back with her the Golden Age of Saturn.[4]

Elizabeth, it was suggested, might be the reincarnation of Astraea; a pagan deity yet with religious overtones. The whole idea is encapsulated in *Hymn to Astraea I* by Sir John Davies of Hereford. (Note the initial letter of each line.)

> **E**arly before the day doth spring
> **L**et us awake my Muse, and sing; and sing;
> **I**t is no time to slumber.
> **S**o many joyes this time doth bring
> **A**s Time will faile to number.
>
> **B**ut whereto shall we bend our layes?
> **E**ven up to Heaven, againe to raise
> **T**he Mayd, which thence descended,
> **H**ath brought againe the golden dayes
> **A**nd all the world amended.
>
> **R**udeness itselfe she doth refine,
> **E**ven like an Alchymist divine;
> **G**rosse times of yron turning
> **I**nto the purest forme of gold;
> **N**ot to corrupt, till heaven were old,
> **A**nd be refined with burning.

As well as Astraea, the Queen was referred to as Oriana, Gloriana, Pandora (signifying hope), Cynthia (goddess of the moon), Belphoebe (beautiful goddess of the sun), and she was also often associated with Diana, classical goddess of hunting, the moon and chastity. Shakespeare is thought to have been referring to Elizabeth as 'a fair Vestal, thronéd by the West' in *A Midsummer Night's Dream* (Act II, scene I); impervious to Cupid's dart, '... the imperial Votaress passed on, / In maiden meditation, fancy free.' If she had ever married, the spell would have been broken.

[4] For a much fuller exposition, see Frances A. Yates *Astraea: the Imperial Theme in the Sixteenth Century* (Routledge & Kegan Paul, 1975).

A whole cycle of madrigals were written in her praise, entitled *The Triumphs of Oriana,* of which this, by John Bennet, is a characteristic example.

> All creatures now are merry, merry minded,
> The shepherds' daughters playing,
> The nymphs are fa-la-la-ing,
> Yon bugle was well winded.
> At Oriana's presence everything smileth,
> Music the time beguileth,
> The flowers themselves discover,
> Birds overhead do hover.
> See where she comes, see where she comes
> With flowery garlands crownéd,
> Queen of all queens renownéd.
> Thus sang the shepherds and nymphs of Diana
> Long live fair Oriana.

The flattery and music together must have delighted the Queen's ear, and this was the kind of flowery, artistic compliment which frequently greeted her on her progresses. Its visual equivalent is the Procession picture at Sherborne Castle, showing an idealized Elizabeth born in triumph amongst her courtiers.[5] Politic she may have been, aware of the requirements of the time and the people's desire for a figurehead she certainly was, but if she had not personally enjoyed her progresses, it is unlikely she would have undertaken them.

She seems to have had a genuine desire to travel and to meet people, of whatever station of life. She was full of curiosity, and of confidence, for wherever she went she was sure she would be welcomed. She loved pageantry; music and poetry were meat and drink to her. She loved fine clothes (the inventory of the Queen's Wardrobe made in 1600 (see page 200) includes '99 robes, 102 French gownes, 67 rounde gownes, 100 loose gownes, 126 kirtells, 136 forepartes, 125 petticcoates') and she delighted in any excuse to wear them. She was equally fond of beautiful jewellery, as is apparent from almost every one of her portraits. She loved to be given presents and they were showered on her wherever she went. She enjoyed entertainments of every kind — dancing, masques, plays, pageants, jousting and bear-baiting, as well as sports, particularly hunting. And her vigour was virtually inexhaustible.

---

[5] For a full analysis of this painting, see Roy Strong's *The Cult of Elizabeth.* (Thames & Hudson, 1977).

There were also practical reasons why the Queen went on progresses. Her palaces were hardly adequate for the kind of state she liked to keep; at Nonsuch, for instance, there was not enough room for all her servants and some were forced to camp outside. The Court being also the centre of government, it had always been necessary for the monarch to move from palace to palace every few weeks. With so many hundreds of people occupying them, and sanitation rudimentary at best, the buildings had to be emptied and 'sweetened' before they were fit for use again. So some moving about was necessary. Her father, Henry VIII, had acquired Whitehall and Hampton Court from Cardinal Wolsey, and had enriched them lavishly. He had improved Eltham, taken over Oatlands, and had built Nonsuch. He had spent money at such a rate that when his children came to the throne the royal coffers were much depleted. Elizabeth built no palaces herself. If some of her subjects were prepared to extend or even erect magnificent mansions in order to entertain her, why should she prevent them?

Her progresses were nearly always in the late summer, a time when plague, which was endemic anyway, was likely to be at its worst. Elizabethan physicians knew little about the causes of plague, but it was generally understood that it was more likely to rage in large cities such as London than anywhere else. This was a good reason for getting out of town at this time of year. Fearful, however, of jumping out of the frying-pan into the fire, Elizabeth always had enquiries made on this point, and would never venture to any place where cases of plague were currently reported. Although at least one occasion the Royal Progress left plague behind it — a sad legacy for Norwich in 1578. (see page 52.)

Entertaining the Queen was regarded by some of the aristocracy as an imposition and an expense. The expense could certainly be enormous. Sir William Cecil, whose house, Theobalds, she visited twelve times, sometimes for a month or more, reckoned it cost him two to three thousand pounds a visit — an astronomical sum in sixteenth-century terms. Some nobles preferred to opt out for this reason; others because they felt it wiser to keep away from the Court circle and live quietly in the country, perhaps because they were Roman Catholics or perhaps because there was some past event they did not wish to be remembered. The Phelips family of Montacute, for instance, would not have wanted the Queen to be reminded that one of them had been surveyor-general to Lady Jane Grey's father, the Earl of Suffolk, who had been executed for his part in the Wyatt Rebellion. They found it better to avoid both the expense and the limelight.

Equally, however, there were many nobles eager for the honour of entertaining her. For every one relieved at being able to avoid it, there was probably another equally disappointed because she did not favour him with a visit. This must have been infuriating, to say the least, if one had gone to the trouble of rebuilding one's house for this very purpose.

The esteem in which the Queen was held could indeed verge on idolatory. Today it is a hackneyed phrase to say, when someone admires a woman to distraction, 'he thinks the sun shines out of her'. But of Elizabeth I, people spoke as if this were actually true. The Rainbow portrait at Hatfield shows her resplendent, all-seeing, grasping a rainbow, and bears the inscription, '*Non sine sole iris*' — 'No rainbow without the sun'.

In Cecil's view the costly undertaking was well worth while. The Queen even received ambassadors at his house and at his expense; he arranged for them 'rich shows, pleasant devices, and all manner of sports that could be devised, to the great delight of her Majesty and her whole train'. There were, however, other less altruistic reasons for wishing to entertain her. Noblemen might desire it in hopes to better themselves; a short but successful visit to one's house could be a very effective push up the ladder of advancement. Or, if out of favour (as the Earl of Hertford was for marrying against the Queen's wishes), they might regard it as a means of buying their way back in. Robert Dudley, Earl of Leicester and Master of the Horse, staged the most elaborate entertainments for the Queen at Kenilworth (see page 74), including fireworks, hunting, morris-dancing, bear-baiting, an Italian acrobat, a play performed by actors from Coventry, a bride-ale, and a pageant on the lake with floating islands and an eighteen-foot (5.5 metres) long mermaid. If the weather had been kinder there would have been even more — all commissioned in hope of the ultimate in royal favour, marriage with the Queen.

When Elizabeth I visited a city or a town not only did she provide the people with a very special sort of travelling circus, together with a certain amount of temporary employment, she could also put that particular locality on the map. Frequently progresses were made with the primary object of increasing the prosperity of a place; her visits to Norfolk, Suffolk and Gloucestershire, for instance, were made largely to give a boost to the wool trade. They might also stimulate others to good works. When the Earl of Warwick came with the royal party to Worcester, he observed, 'This is a proper citie; hit is pitty it shudde decay and become poore; and for my part I will devise some way to do it good.'

The visits to Oxford and Cambridge, while they were made partly as compliments to Dudley and Cecil, at the same time demonstrated the value the Queen set on learning and the arts, and gave new stimulus to the universities.

After the defeat of the Armada in 1588, Elizabeth came to be regarded as a heroic figure, Queen of a new Troy, and personification of the country's greatness. She gave her name to an age in a way that no monarch had before her time, and very few since. Her progresses aided her considerably in perhaps the most notable of her achievements, the gaining and keeping of her people's affection.

While still a young woman she visited Coventry in 1565 and was presented with a purse containing £100 in gold angels. 'It is a good gift', said the Queen, 'One hundred pounds in gold; I have but few such gifts.'

'If it please your Grace,' observed the Mayor of Coventry, 'there is a great deal more in it.'

'What is that?'

'It is the hearts of all your loving subjects.'

'We thank you, Mr Mayor,' replied the Queen, 'it is a great deal more indeed.'

CHAPTER 1

EARLY YEARS

'A very wittye and gentyll yonge Lady.'

(William Thomas, Clerk of the Closet to Edward VI)

'The Princess Elizabeth is greatly to be feared; she has a spirit full of incantation.'

(Simon Renard, Ambassador to Emperor Charles V)

Elizabeth's progresses and processions may be said to have began with her christening.

In the sixteenth century royal births were the cause of far greater celebration than royal marriages. Certainly Henry VIII was bitterly disappointed that after all the trouble he had had in divorcing his first wife, Catherine of Aragon, in order to free himself to marry his second wife, Anne Boleyn — thereby also severing himself and his country from the Church of Rome — their baby turned out to be a girl. He longed for a male heir and thought his first marriage was accursed with still-born and short-lived children (apart from his daughter Mary) due to him having married the child-wife of his late brother, Arthur. More likely it was due to the in-bred nature of the House of Aragon. The idea of a queen ruling in her own right, he would have considered ludicrous. Still, the fact that his new queen had been brought to bed of a healthy child, even though it was a girl, made him confident that boys would follow — Anne being young and lusty, and he himself already the father of an illegitimate son. So Elizabeth's birth was worth celebrating.

It took place on 7 September 1533, a Sunday, between three and four in the afternoon at the royal palace of Greenwich. This Palace, also known as Placentia, was a cluster of red brick buildings and towers on the banks of the Thames, where the Royal Naval College now stands. It had been founded by Duke Humphrey of Gloucester, regent during the minority of Henry VI, on the site of Bella Court, the home of Margaret of Anjou. Elizabeth's father was also born here, and it became one of her favourite palaces, despite the fact that it was also the scene of her mother's arrest and her brother Edward's death. To celebrate the birth, bells were rung, bonfires were lit, and the 'Te Deum' sung continually in thanks for the Queen's happy delivery.

The christening was arranged for the following Wednesday. It seems astonishing what elaborate ceremonial could be whistled up at three days' notice, but it is likely that everything was at least half-ready in hopeful anticipation of the birth of a prince. The ceremony was in the Friars' Church adjoining the palace. This was hung with tapestry, as were all the walls between which the procession would pass on its way from the royal apartments. The Mayor and aldermen of London in their scarlet gowns and gold chains, the city councillors and forty of the chief citizens, arrived by barge to join the assembly of lords, knights and gentlemen at the palace. The font was of silver and stood under a canopy of crimson satin. Around it were stationed gentlemen wearing aprons, with towels round their necks, ready to ensure that 'no filth shoulde come to the fonte'. Then the procession arrived; walking two by two, first the citizens, then the gentlemen, esquires and chaplains, then aldermen, the Mayor, members of the King's Council and the Chapel Royal, the barons and earls, including the Earl of Essex carrying gilt bowls, the Marquis of Exeter with a taper, the Marquis of Dorset carrying a salt, and Lady Mary Norfolk bearing the jewelled chrisom, or christening cloth. The child, wrapped in a purple velvet mantle with a train of ermine, was in the arms of the widowed Duchess of Norfolk, while her son walked on her right and the Duke of Suffolk on her left. The long train of the baby's mantle was carried by the Earls of Wiltshire and Derby on either side, and the Countess of Kent at the end. A rich canopy was held over the child by four lords, and many ladies and gentlemen brought up the rear of the procession. At the church door they were met by the Bishop of London and other clerics.

The godmothers were two aged widows, Mary Howard, Duchess of Norfolk and Margaret Grey, Marchioness of Dorset, while the godfather was Thomas Cranmer, Archbishop of Canterbury. The baby was brought to the font and baptised, then Garter King of Arms cried, 'God of his infinite goodness send prosperous life and long to the high and mighty Princess of England ELIZABETH!' With a fanfare of trumpets she was brought to the altar where the Gospel was read. Immediately afterwards the child was confirmed, and this time the Marchioness of Exeter was godmother. (It may seem strange that a child should receive confirmation at only three days old — a practice doubtless due to the fear of infant mortality).

Baptismal gifts were a gold standing cup from the Archbishop of Canterbury, another such cup ornamented with pearls from the Duchess of Norfolk, three pounced gilt bowls from the

Marchioness of Dorset, and three engraved gilt bowls from the Marchioness of Exeter. Then a plentiful supply of refreshments and hippocras (wine) was provided. The procession reassembled and made its way back by the light of more than five hundred torches to the door of the Queen's chamber.

For a short while the infant Princess was dressed in fine clothes and treated with the ceremony felt appropriate for a King's daughter. While Anne was still in the ascendant, Elizabeth was the only child recognised as legitimate, although this did not mean she was recognised as heir to the throne. Henry had an illegitimate son the Duke of Richmond and, until his death in 1536, it seemed likely that he was next in line. At the age of three months she was given her own separate household at Hatfield, under the care of Lady Bryane. Her half-sister Mary, aged seventeen, was sent to wait on her — disinherited by King Henry because she would not agree to the legitimacy of his marriage with Anne Boleyn, and maintained that her mother, Catherine of Aragon, was still the King's true wife.

By the time the little girl was three, the tables were turned. Anne miscarried of a male child. This was her death knell, and once she was cast aside and disgraced, it was Elizabeth whose legitimacy was in doubt. The shrewd little girl noticed the difference at once. 'How haps it?' she asked, 'Yesterday my Lady Princess, today but my Lady Elizabeth.' (Anne Boleyn was executed in May 1536 on a probably trumped-up charge of adultery and incest.) It is not recorded how and when Elizabeth learnt that her mother had been beheaded by order of her father, but the doubtfulness of her position was immediately reflected in the provision made for her. Children's clothes — at least those of the rich — were made to fit exactly and doubtless she had grown out of the fine clothes she had worn at court. Now Lady Bryane, at her wit's end, wrote to the King's chief minister, Thomas Cromwell, requesting clothes for her, 'for she hath neither gown, nor kirtle, nor petticoat, nor no manner of linen, nor smocks, nor kerchiefs, nor rails [robes], nor body stitchets [corsets], nor biggens [nightcaps] ... beseeching you my lord, that ye will see that her grace may have that which is needful for her, as my trust is that ye will do.' (It is interesting to compare this sad list with the inventory of the Queen's Wardrobe made in 1600.) (see page 200).

Uncertain of her charge's standing, she asked to know 'what is in the king's grace's pleasure and yours, that I shall do in everything?' She complained of John Shelton who had assumed control of the household and who insisted that Elizabeth should dine at high table, which arrangement seemed unsuitable to Lady Bryane and made it impossible for her to supervise the little girl's diet.

Finally she reported on the child's welfare, and apologised for spoiling her a little,

'God knoweth my lady hath great pain with her great teeth, and they come very slowly forth, which causeth me to suffer her grace to have her will more than I would. I trust to God an' her teeth were well graft, to have her grace after another fashion than she is yet; so as I trust the King's grace shall have great comfort in her grace. For she is as toward a child and as gentle of condition, as ever I knew any in my life. Jesu preserve her grace!'

Almost immediately after the execution of Anne, Henry married Jane Seymour who had been her lady-in-waiting, and Jane produced the son he had been waiting for all these years. The baby was born at Hampton Court, and the two Princesses, Mary and Elizabeth, were brought to the palace to figure in the infant's christening procession, as stately an affair as Elizabeth's own had been. Mary was godmother, and her little sister's task was to carry the jewelled chrisom cloth; but since it was heavy, Edward Seymour, the baby's uncle, carried her. Henry himself did not attend, perhaps because there was plague about. The procession wove its way through the state apartments to the newly completed Chapel Royal where a silver-gilt font had been provided. After the christening, which was again performed by Archbishop Cranmer, Garter King of Arms proclaimed long life to the 'right high, right excellent and noble prince, Prince Edward'. Then the procession reassembled and made its way back to the Queen's bed chamber, where King Henry was waiting, with tears of joy in his eyes. But within three days Queen Jane developed a fever, and within a fortnight she was dead.

Mary was chief mourner at her stepmother's funeral, then she and Elizabeth returned to a quiet country life in Hertfordshire, under the eye of Lady Bryane. Edward was given a suite of lodgings at Hampton Court, but most of the time he too was at Hatfield or Hunsdon. Elizabeth was fond of him, and despite her dislike of needlework, made him a cambric shirt. And young though she was, she may have felt it politic to make much of her little brother; it was the only way to the heart of the father she idolised.

By the time Edward was six, and she was ten, they were having

Elizabeth as Princess, aged about thirteen. Artist unknown. (Royal Collection; Windsor Castle)

lessons together at Hatfield. Elizabeth's governess was Katherine, or Kat, Champernowne (after her marriage, Kat Ashley), and she developed a great and lasting affection for her. The children followed a curriculum which was both broad and deep; had they

27

The Old Palace, Hatfield.

not been the highly intelligent, talented and industrious children that they were, they would have found it daunting. They studied not only the classical languages and scripture that were the mainstay of most Tudor schooling, but in addition modern languages, mathematics, science, history, geography and music — in short, a true Renaissance education. Elizabeth's tutor was, in the first place, William Grindal, a pupil of Roger Ascham, and later Ascham himself. Ascham's methods (such as double translation) were exacting and thorough, yet not beyond the ability of these very precocious children. Elizabeth developed early her love of music and enjoyed learning the lute and viol. Equally she enjoyed physical exercise — riding, hunting, archery and dancing. Indeed all the tastes and predelictions, all the music, poetry and pageantry that delighted her on her progresses when she was Queen, were presaged by the width of her education and interests as a child. Or almost all; her young brother was already more sober and puritan in his tastes, and a love of luxury was not encouraged in either of them. Edward called her his 'sweet sister Temperance'; Elizabeth was no doubt feigning a puritanism that was not part of her true nature. For she was also learning to be wily, and to watch which way the wind was blowing.

Henry VIII's last queen, Catherine Parr, was a scholarly yet vivacious woman who took a kindly interest in her step-children.

To her Elizabeth dedicated her translation into Italian of *The Queen's Prayers and Meditations,* and to her wrote, also in Italian, a fluent and mature letter asking her to intercede for her and convey her good wishes to her father — Henry in his later years had grown so irascible that she dared not approach him directly.

After King Henry died and was succeeded by young Edward VI, the boy's elder uncle Edward Seymour, Duke of Somerset, acted as Protector, and virtually ruled for most of the reign. The boy's younger uncle, Thomas (known as the Lord High Admiral, though he had no connection with the sea) meanwhile married the late King's widow. Catherine Parr had probably loved him for a long time, but she was really his second choice. A swashbuckling fellow, he was hungry for power and, had he been allowed to, would much rather have married Elizabeth. Meanwhile Elizabeth, now in her teens, was sent to live with Catherine Parr and, being fond of her stepmother, was probably quite well pleased with this arrangement. On the other hand, it made it difficult for her to avoid the amorous advances of the Lord High Admiral. He obtained a key to her bedroom, and more than once came bouncing in in his nightshirt, slapped her bottom, and tickled her (at one time assisted by Catherine, who doubtless felt this was the best way to make light of the whole thing). On another occasion he caught her in the garden and, while his wife held her, cut her black dress to ribbons. In the end, however, Catherine, pregnant and no doubt jealous, sent Elizabeth away and she established her own household at Cheshunt. A few months later the poor mistreated Catherine died in childbirth at Sudeley Castle.

The irrepressible Kat Ashley remarked to the Princess that the Lord High Admiral was now free to marry her. Elizabeth blushed and said no, but her governess persisted that she would agree if the Lord Protector desired it. Exactly what were Elizabeth's feelings we shall never know. She seems to have been flattered by Seymour's attentions, and on several occasions sent her treasurer, Thomas Parry, to speak with him. On the other hand, she was only fifteen and he a great lusty fellow of thirty-eight. Probably she was just dazzled and, once she was away from him, regained her usual composure and caution.

The reckless Seymour meanwhile set about trying to undermine his brother's authority and ingratiate himself with young King Edward. He stole by night into the King's apartments at Hampton Court and foolishly shot the boy's lap-dog, which aroused the whole palace. Seymour was arrested and sent to the Tower — not so much for that, but really for conspiring to marry Elizabeth.

Parry and Kat Ashley were also taken to the Tower to be questioned about their part in the affair.

Elizabeth immediately realised the danger she was in; when the Lord Protector sent a courtier, Sir William Tyrwhitt, down to Hatfield to question her, she denied everything. Although her servants at the Tower disclosed all the details of the amorous horseplay between Thomas Seymour and herself, she still stood her ground, and Somerset found he could prove no case against her. For a while, to Elizabeth's disgust, he sent Tyrwhitt's wife to Hatfield to be her governess in place of Kat Ashley. She protested so vehemently, consistently denying any implication in Thomas Seymour's plots, that after a while her former governess and treasurer were restored to her. Seymour, on the other hand, was much less astute, and refused to answer the charges against him. On 20 March 1549 he was beheaded by the order of his brother. Elizabeth commented drily, 'There died a man with much wit and very little judgement.' In January 1552 Somerset was executed in his turn. Edward noted laconically in his diary, 'The Duke of Somerset had his head cut off upon Tower Hill between eight and nine o'clock in the morning.'

Elizabeth had survived, but the strain of the Seymour affair affected her health and for the following year she was not robust. The episode may have been enough to put her off matrimony for life; it certainly increased her natural wariness. She lived in self-conscious sobriety, which pleased her brother Edward so much that he gave her Hatfield as a present. She continued with her academic education under Roger Ascham.

In his book *The Schoolmaster,* Ascham describes her as an outstanding pupil, one who 'shines like a star' among all the most learned ladies of the time.

'The Lady Elizabeth has accomplished her sixteenth year; and so much solidity of understanding, such courtesy united with dignity, have never been observed at so early an age... No apprehension can be quicker than hers, no memory more retentive. French and Italian she speaks like English; Latin, with fluency, propriety and judgement; she also spoke Greek with me, frequently, willingly and moderately well. Nothing can be more elegant than her handwriting.'

Meanwhile her brother's reign was drawing to its close. At the age of twelve, according to his diary, he had measles and smallpox at the same time; certainly he was very ill and his general health was undermined. At about the time of Somerset's execution he was beginning to show symptoms of tuberculosis. Somerset's position as Lord Protector was taken over by John Dudley, Duke of Northumberland. He , ambitious for his family, and even more for himself, tried to persuade the dying Edward to settle the crown on Lady Jane Grey who was Edward's cousin and Northumberland's daughter-in-law. But although Edward's will was altered (whether by him or by Northumberland) the plot failed, Northumberland was killed, Lady Jane Grey and her husband, Lord Guildford Dudley, sent to the Tower (where they were later executed), and Mary Tudor came to the throne as the first queen regnant of England.

Elizabeth, who had been unaware that her brother was terminally ill, wisely kept away during the Lady Jane Grey episode. But it now being clear that Mary was Queen, she met her at Wanstead and joined in her ceremonial ride into the City. The shouts of 'God save Queen Mary' were interspersed with 'God bless the Lady Elizabeth!' All who saw the Princess remarked on her noble bearing and her red-gold hair — truly her father's daughter. 'Her figure and face are very handsome', commented Simon Rénard, ambassador to Emperor Charles V,' and such an air of dignified majesty pervades all her actions that no one can fail to suppose she is a Queen.'

In time Mary was to become jealous and suspicious of her half-sister, but for the present she was all leniency. She even considered pardoning Lady Jane Grey, and she had the Marchioness of Exeter and her son, Edward Courtenay,[1] released from the Tower. Edward had been imprisoned there by Henry VIII in 1538 when he was only twelve years old, simply because his right to the throne was stronger than Henry's own (he was the great-great grandson of Edward IV). He was now a good-looking young man of twenty-seven. It may be that Mary, ten years his senior, was attracted to him, while he appeared to prefer Elizabeth, and this sparked off her antagonism towards the Princess. Added to this was the question: was she or was she not a heretic?

Mary had lost no time in reinstating Roman Catholicism, both at Court and in the country. It was not a matter of choice but of state

[1] Edward Courtenay, Earl of Devonshire 1526(?)-56. Much of his imprisonment in the Tower was in solitary confinement. After his release (3 August 1553), he was created Earl of Devonshire and Knight of the Bath. He carried the Sword of State at Mary's coronation, and received the Spanish ambassadors when they came to London (2 January 1554). After the Wyatt Rebellion he was put back in the Tower, then sent to Fotheringay. At Easter 1555 he was released but exiled; he travelled first to Brussels, then to Italy, dying suddenly in Padua in 1556

religion. At first Elizabeth, together with Anne of Cleves, held back and pointedly did not attend mass. Mary very much feared that her sister would marry Edward Courtenay and together they would seize the crown. Her attitude to her became so unfriendly that Elizabeth realised the danger she was in. She decided to conform, outwardly at least; but by the end of 1553 she was finding the whole situation too difficult and she left the Court and went to live at Ashridge in Hertfordshire.

It was Mary's determination to marry Philip II of Spain that again turned the tide of events. She could hardly have made a more unpopular choice; it was not so much that Philip was also a Catholic, but that he was a foreigner. Fear of Spanish domination sparked off a rebellion, led by Thomas Wyatt of Kent. The plan was that Mary should be deposed, and Elizabeth, married to Edward Courtenay, should rule in her stead. These two beautiful young people, both thoroughly English, might have proved far more popular than Mary and Philip. But Edward's character had not been improved by his years of incarceration in the Tower; he was weak, vacillating and not to be relied upon. Wyatt's uprising was intended to have his backing in the West Country, and that of the Duke of Suffolk in the Midlands, but this support failed to materialise. Wyatt was captured and put in the Tower where he was tortured and ultimately executed.[2] Mary summoned Elizabeth to London. Elizabeth protested she was ill and could not come (she was indeed unwell), but finally agreed to travel in easy stages of not more than eight miles a day. When she was carried into the capital she was wearing a pure white dress and rode in an open litter; onlookers commented on her defiant and princely bearing. Even in adversity, Elizabeth would turn a journey into a progress.

On her arrival Elizabeth was kept alone for two weeks, then questioned by Bishop Gardiner. She swore there had been no correspondence between her and Wyatt. Nevertheless she was sent to the Tower. She wrote to the Queen protesting her innocence, asking that she should not be condemned without proof, and begging for an interview. In the Tower she was attended at first by only three men and three women, all servants of the Queen. Before he died, however, Wyatt denied that Elizabeth had been in any way implicated in the plot, and conditions for the Princess improved somewhat. She was allowed ten of her own servants and permitted to walk, first in the Queen's Lodgings, then in a small garden. There is a charming story of a small boy who brought her flowers

[2] The Wyatt Rebellion was similarly the death-knell for Lady Jane Grey and her husband.

every day while she was in the Tower — until this was disallowed, and his father was rebuked by the Constable. Mary considered Lord Chandos too lenient as Constable of the Tower, and he was replaced by Sir Henry Bedingfield of Oxburgh, Norfolk, who brought with him a guard of a hundred soldiers. Princess Elizabeth, very much aware all this time that her life was in danger, enquired if 'Lady Jane's scaffold was yet taken away?'

At the end of May 1554 Elizabeth was taken (by Bedingfield and Lord Williams of Thame) from the Tower to Woodstock. The journey was done by stages: she spent the first night at Richmond, closely guarded by soldiers with none of her own attendants present — she was very much afraid she would be put to death. On to Windsor the next day, where she was lodged in the Dean's house; then to Lord Williams's house at Ryecote where, to Bedingfield's disapproval, she was 'very princlie entertained both of knights and ladies'. Finally they reached Woodstock, where she was kept in the Gatehouse until the end of April the following year.[3] According to Holinshed, she engraved with a diamond on the window,

> 'Much suspected by me,
> Nothing proved can be,
> Quoth Elizabeth prisoner.'

Elizabeth was allowed the use of four rooms, and could walk in the garden and the orchard; the room with the inscription had a carved arched roof of Irish oak, coloured blue and gold. Nevertheless she felt herself a captive; Holinshed also says in his *Chronicles* that when she heard a milkmaid singing, she would sigh and say she wished she were one too. She wrote to Mary's vice-chamberlain, once more protesting her good intentions towards the Queen, 'look into the bottome of my hart, whether my innocencie have not alwaies dreaded only to conceave so muche as an ill thought of her.'

King Philip interceded on the Princess's behalf. He was shrewd enough to realise that if she were executed, the heir to the throne would be Mary Queen of Scots, allying England and France against Spain. Meanwhile Elizabeth was sent from Woodstock to Ryecote, from there to Wing in Buckinghamshire, then to an inn at Colnebrook, and finally to Hampton Court. This was at the time of

---

[3] Princess Elizabeth's Lodgings at Woodstock were demolished by Sarah, Duchess of Marlborough, during the building of Blenheim Palace.

Mary's pseudo-cyesis (false pregnancy); she had shut herself away in the palace to await forlornly the birth of a baby that never was. Meanwhile Elizabeth had stitched a set of baby clothes (they may still be seen at Hever Castle). After Elizabeth had been imprisoned for a week in the Water Gallery at Hampton Court, Mary agreed to see her, while Philip, who had doubtless engineered the meeting, hid behind an arras.

Reluctantly the Queen was forced to admit that she would in all probability be childless, and to recognise the sister as heir. She gave her a ring worth 700 crowns and allowed her to return to Hatfield. The household was supervised by Sir Thomas Pope, the founder of Trinity College, Oxford. As well as being interested in scholarship he seems to have been a genial fellow. At the risk of offending the Queen, he commissioned quite an elaborate masque for the Princess's entertainment at Shrovetide 1556 (see page 103).

The question of Elizabeth's marriage was once more under discussion — it was certainly assumed she *would* marry. No one envisaged her being a virgin queen. At this stage Philip wanted her to marry the Duke of Savoy. He attempted to send the duchesses of Lorraine and of Parma to bring Elizabeth to Flanders; but the Queen would not allow them to go to Hatfield, so they went back without the Princess. The courtship of Eric of Sweden also began, but the Princess's reply was a plea 'to remayne in that estate which of all others best lyked or pleased me'. With Mary's example before her, she realised the dangers of foreign marriages.

After Edward Courtenay died so mysteriously in Padua, at the age of thirty, Elizabeth was once more invited to Court. She made quite a procession through London,

'The xxviiith daye of November, came ryding thrugh Smythfeld and Old Balee, and thrugh Fleet-Strret, unto Somersett-place, my good Lade Elisabeth's Grace the Queenes Syster; with a grate company of velvet cotts and chaynes, hir Graces Gentyllmen: and aftyr, a grate company of her men, all in redd cotts gardyd with a brod gard of blake velvett and cutts...'

(Vitell. Mss Cott.F.S.)

She stayed at Somerset House, but after only a week returned to Hatfield. It was at Hatfield she was based during the last four years of Mary's reign, years of comparative calm for Elizabeth. Ascham was allowed to return as her tutor. Discreetly she kept out of state affairs and spent her time reading Greek, making translations from the Italian, embroidering, writing letters, and playing the lute and the virginals — quite a pleasant way of life. With permission from the Queen, she made various excursions, including a ceremonial hunt in Enfield Chase. She rode escorted by twelve ladies in white satin and twenty yeomen in green, and was met by fifty archers in scarlet boots and yellow caps. One of them gave her a silver-headed arrow winged with peacock's feathers. Having killed a buck, the Princess was allowed the doubtful privilege of cutting its throat. This was in April 1557. In the same month the Queen came to see her at Hatfield. They went to mass in the morning, bear-baiting in the afternoon, and after supper saw a play performed by the choristers of St Paul's. One of them was a sweet-voiced boy called Maximilian Poynes; he sang and Elizabeth accompanied him on the virginals.

In the summer she visited the Queen at Richmond, and made this the occasion of a water-procession. She travelled from Somerset Place in the Queen's barge, together with Sir Thomas Pope and four ladies. The barge was festooned with garlands of artificial flowers and covered with a green silk canopy embroidered with eglantine (wild roses) and gold flowers. Six boats followed, carrying her attendants who were dressed in russet damask and blue embroidered satin with silver spangles and cloth-of-silver caps with green feathers. The Queen received her in a rich pavilion set up in the garden maze; it was made in the form of a castle and decorated in chequer-pattern with silver lilies and gold pomegranates. Here they consumed a fine banquet, including an elaborate dish or 'subtlety' in the form of a pomegranate tree bearing the arms of Spain.

Elizabeth also spent Christmas with the Queen and Philip at Hampton Court. She supped with them in the Great Hall which was lit with a thousand lamps. After the meal she nibbled comfits, but demurely retired before the masques and revels began. On St Stephen's (Boxing) Day, dressed in white satin and pearls, she attended mass in the Queen's Holy Day Closet next to the Chapel; and three days later joined their majesties in watching jousting in the Tiltyard — half the contestants being dressed as Germans and half as Spaniards.

Deserted by Philip, childless, bitterly unhappy and prematurely aged, Mary died on 17 November 1558. Elizabeth was at Hatfield. To Hatfield, therefore, came a deputation of lords to announce to her that she was Queen. They found Elizabeth sitting under an oak tree reading a Greek testament. Immediately she knelt and said,

'*Dominum factum est et mirabile in oculis nostris*' ('God has done it and it is wonderful in our eyes'). Then without delay she selected her chief counsellors, with Sir William Cecil as Principal Secretary, and held her first council in the Great Hall before leaving Hatfield for London on 23 November.

At last she was her own, and her kingdom's mistress.

CHAPTER 2

ELIZABETH BECOMES QUEEN

'She was of admirable beauty, and well deserving a Crown; of a modest gravity, excellent wit, royal soul, happy memory, and indefatigably given to the study of Learning; insomuch as, before she was 17 years of age, she understood well the Latin, French, and Italian tongues, and had an indifferent knowledge of the Greek. Neither did she neglect Music so far as it became a princess, being able to sing sweetly, and play handsomely on the Lute.'

(Camden, *Annals of Queen Elizabeth*)

How did Elizabeth appear to her people? We have already seen that she was formidably well educated, and of her accomplishments there is no doubt. But her appearance is more elusive, despite the many portraits of her that survive. She was extremely particular about the way she was portrayed. When she first sat to Nicholas Hilliard, the miniature painter, he relates that she chose to sit 'in the open alley of a goodly garden, where no tree was neere, nor anye shadowe at all, save that as the heaven in lighter than the earthe soe must that littel shadowe that was from the earthe.' As a young woman she had a fair complexion and yellow hair; as she grew older, she covered her face with a mask-like make-up and her hair appeared more reddish. As an elderly woman she undoubtedly wore a wig over her own sparse grey locks. She had a narrow Roman nose, high forehead and dark, quick piercing eyes, 'a majestic look to dash strangers out of countenance'.[1] When she first came to the throne she was slim, lively, erect and imperious.

Sir James Melville, sent by Mary Queen of Scots in 1564 to meet her, reported with commendable tact that Elizabeth was the fairest queen in England and Mary was the fairest queen in Scotland. Elizabeth pressed him further, asking whether she or her cousin was the taller. He had to admit that Mary was. Then, said the Queen, she is too tall, for she considered herself exactly the right height.

As Elizabeth approached sixty, less was written of her beauty, at least in the commentaries of unbiased onlookers, and during the last years of her life the maids-of-honour turned the mirrors to the wall. But she retained her beautiful hands, with exceptionally long, slender fingers.

[1] Fuller, *Holy State.*

With these she accomplished the most lovely italic handwriting, and played the virginals as well as stringed instruments. Lord Melville describes how he listened to her secretly at the chamber door; she played extremely well, he thought, but as soon as she realised he was there, she left off. With her hand raised as if to strike him, she said she was not used to playing before an audience, but played when she was alone 'to shun melancholy'. But one cannot help doubting her apparent artlessness; she probably had every intention of letting Melville hear her play, since she did it far better than Mary Queen of Scots.

She was very self-aware and full of vanity. This was apparent not only in the richness of her dress and the lavishness of her jewels, but in her attitude. She would brook no competition. For this reason she strongly discouraged her gallant young courtiers from marrying; and should they be ill-advised enough to do so, then their wives must know their place. In a letter to Lord Leicester at the Hague, dated 11 February 1586, Thomas Dudley writes,

'It was told her Majesty that my Lady [Leicester] was prepared presently to come over to your Excellency, with such a train of Ladies and Gentlemen, and such coaches, litters, and side-saddles, as her Majesty had no such, and that there should be such a Court of Ladies, as should far surpass her Majesty's Court here. This information (though most false) did not a little stir her Majesty to extreme choler and dislike of all your doings there, saying with great oaths, she would have no more courts under her obeyance but her own; and revoke you from thence with all speed.'

He advises Leicester to spend two or three hundred crowns on some rare thing, to send as a peace-offering to the Queen. (Leicester was very well aware what etiquette demanded. When he celebrated St George's Day in Utrecht with a feast, he sat on a stool, and had a chair of state provided for the Queen, even though she was not there.)

Although she insisted on deference being paid to her at all times, she could on occasion be considerate of other people, especially a tried and trusted courtier. Normally no one was allowed to sit while the Queen was standing; but the elderly Lord Burghley was lame, and on one occasion she broke off in the middle of her speech to order that a stool should be provided for him. She came to visit him in his town house in the Strand when he was ill with gout in 1591. That day she was wearing a very tall head-dress, higher than

William Cecil, Lord Burghley. (National Portrait Gallery, on show at Montacute House)

the lintel of the door. Burghley's servant said, 'May your Highness be pleased to stoop.'

The Queen replied, 'For your Master's sake I will stoop, but not for the King of Spain's.'

From the moment of her accession she appeared supremely self-confident. The day before her coronation she rode in procession from the Tower of London through the City to Westminster. 'And entrying the Citie', so it was reported (by Richard Tothill, presumably an eye-witness),

'was of the People received marveylous entirely showing in all sorts of ways their love and loyalty. Her Grace, by holding up her handes, and merie countenaunce to such as stode farre off, and most tender and gentle language to those what stode nigh to her Grace, did declare herselfe no less thankfullye to receive her People's good wyll, than they lovingly offered it unto her. To all that wyshed her Grace well, she gave heartie thankes, and to such as bade God save her Grace, she sayde agayne God save them all, and thanked them with all her heart; so that on eyther syde there was nothing but gladnes, nothing but prayer, nothing but comfort.'

The impression she made on her people could hardly have been surpassed; they noticed especially that if quite humble people offered her flowers or had a request to make, she would stop her carriage to thank them or to listen to what they had to say.

When she came to Fenchurch Street there was a platform with musicians, and a child prepared with an oration to welcome the Queen on behalf of the City. But the noise of the crowd was so great she could hardly hear what he was saying. So she made the whole procession stop while she listened attentively; observers noticed in her 'a marvelous change in loke' as the child's words, and the people's acclamation, appeared to touch her heart.

By the Eagle Inn in Gracious Street, the City had prepared an elaborate pageant portraying the Tudor succession — somewhat selective family tree (direct line only), with Henry VII shown in a red rose and his wife Elizabeth of York in a white rose, the roses intertwined. Above them appeared Henry VIII and Anne Boleyn, and finally at the top was represented Elizabeth I. A child made a speech expounding that the pageant signified the uniting of the houses of York and Lancaster, but the Queen could hardly hear him because of the noise of the crowd. Again she had the procession stopped and silence requested, here and at each pageant, because she did not want to miss a word that was said to her.

The procession moved on to Cornhill for the second pageant. This represented the virtues — Religion, Love of Subjects,

Wisdom and Justice, trampling on the vices, Superstition and Ignorance, Rebellion, Folly and Bribery. Again a child had prepared an oration; the Queen made sure she came close enough to hear him, and publicly promised to do her best to maintain those virtues and suppress the vices.

The third pageant, accompanied by music, showed the eight beatitudes. On then to Cheapside where the city waits performed at the door of St Peter's Church. The streets were lined with members of the city companies, all in their best array. She was presented with a crimson satin purse containing 1,000 gold marks. The Queen's speech of thanks was brief and to the point,

'I thank my Lord Mayor, his Brethren and you all. And whereas your request is that I should continue your good Lady and Queen, be ye ensured, that I will be as good unto you as ever Queen was to her People. No will in me can lack, neither do I trust there shall lack any power. And persuade yourselves, that for the safety and quietness of you all, I will not spare, if need be, to spend my blood. God thank you all.'

The next pageant was of Good and Bad Government, the latter showing how the rule of a wise and good woman could bring prosperity to the state. Then there was a speech in Latin by a pupil of St Paul's School. Poor women offered her bunches of flowers or rosemary, which she accepted graciously. Elizabeth was constantly attentive, constantly appreciative of all that had been done to welcome her as the new Queen. But perhaps the most significant moment was when a child representing Truth gave her a Bible in English — she took it, kissed it, and laid it to her breast. 'Be ye well assured,' she promised, 'I will stand your good Queen.'

The Queen's supremacy was confirmed by her coronation on 15 January 1559. As has always been the custom, it took place in Westminster Abbey. Before the ceremony she dined in Westminster Hall, and into the hall rode Sir Edward Dimmock in full armour as her champion. He threw down his gauntlet and challenged anyone who would deny her right to the throne. Elizabeth drank his health from a golden cup, which he was afterwards given for his fee.

The anointing and crowning was followed by the homage of the bishops, signifying that she was defender of the faith in England. The Epistle and Gospel were read, first in Latin and then in English, and her title was proclaimed, 'The most high and mightye Princesse our dread Soverayne Lady Elizabeth, by the Grace of

41

God, Queene of England, France and Irelande, defender of the true auncient and Catholic faithe, most worthy Empresse from the Orcade Isles to the Mountaynes Pyrenei.'

The next day the coronation was celebrated with jousting, and on 25 January she held her first parliament. The Speaker lost no time in bringing up the question of her possible marriage. As for many years she was to continue to do, she prevaricated. If she was to change from her single state of life, she said, she would never 'in the matter conclude anything that shall be prejudicial to the Realm: for the weal, good and safety whereof I will never shun to spend my life.'

CHAPTER 3

THE QUEEN MEETS THE PEOPLE

23 April 1559

'The same day the Queen in the afternoon went to Baynard's Castle, the Earl of Pembroke's Place, and supped with him, and after supper she took a boat, and was rowed up and down on the River Thames; hundreds of boats and barges rowing about her; and thousands of people thronging at the water-side, to look upon her Majesty, for the trumpets blew, drums beat, flutes played, guns were discharged, squibs hurled up into the air, as the Queen moved from place to place. And thus continued till ten of the clock at night, when the Queen departed home. By these means shewing herself so freely and condescendingly unto her people, she made herself dear and acceptable to them.'

(Quoted in John Nichols's *Progresses & Public Processions of Queen Elizabeth,* Vol. I, p.67)

Elizabeth lost no opportunity of letting herself be seen by her subjects and from time to time meeting them face to face. Once when she was on progress in Huntingdonshire, an ordinary man came up to her coach. 'Stay thy cart, good fellow,' he said to the driver, 'Stay thy cart, that I may speak to the Queen.' And the coach was stopped while Elizabeth, highly amused at the man's presumption, spoke to him, thanked him for his loyalty and gave him her hand to kiss.

Impromptu encounters were one thing, but as soon as a town or a city received notice that the Queen intended to visit it, tremendous preparations were set in train. The general state of the roads — rutted, potholed, often a morass of mud — presented an almost insuperable problem. There had been some attempt to improve them during the reign of Mary I. In 1555 a statute was drawn up allotting responsibility for repairing them to the parishes through which they passed. Each parish appointed a surveyor whose task it was (on pain of being fined 40 shillings) to gather up and oversee a local work-force. This effected some improvement, but apart from the old Roman roads, the common highways had never been properly constructed or drained — they were no more than trackways — so the efforts of local surveyors were no more than temporary palliatives. When it was known the Queen was coming, these efforts were redoubled. When she went to St

James's on 8 September 1561, 'From Islington thither the hedges and ditches were cut down to make the next way for her. There might be ten thousand people met to see her, such was their gladness and affection for her.'

What is seldom reported is how the highways looked afterwards, when the ten thousand people had finished trampling about, and the Queen's procession had passed.

The Queen herself sometimes rode on horseback, especially in her younger days. A good many changes of horse might be needed if the day's travel were long, and there was usually a stop made just outside the town she was to visit, for the changing and refreshing of her horse, herself or both. Increasingly, however, the Queen took to riding in coaches. Coaches had been introduced into England by William Boonen, a Dutchman, and in 1564 Boonen became the Queen's coachman, after which 'divers great ladies ... made them coaches and rid in them up and down to the great admiration of all beholders.'[1] But however magnificent the coaches looked, they were unsprung and doubtless extremely uncomfortable. Lubold von Wedel, one of the foreign travellers who wrote accounts of visits to England towards the end of the sixteenth century, described the Queen's coaches which he saw at Greenwich. One was made of red leather studded with silver gilt nails, one 'so small that only two persons can sit in it; but so contrived that both the fore and hind wheels are attached far from the body'; another was supported by no less than twelve wheels. No doubt these last two were so constructed in an attempt to minimise the jolting. A contemporary illustration of Elizabeth in the grounds of Nonsuch Palace shows her riding in a low-slung, open-sided carriage drawn by two horses; only suitable, one would imagine, for short journeys in dry weather.

The royal procession might typically be formed up as follows; first the Queen's servants and two of her guardsmen, then the equerries and chamberlains, then some of the members of the Privy Council, and the Archbishop of Canterbury with his own train of about fifty horsemen. Then Burghley and Walsingham rode in front of the royal coach, where Elizabeth rode alone. Behind her was her Master of the Horse, Robert Dudley, and more of the Privy Councillors. Then rode twenty-four elegant maids of honour, followed by about fifty more of the Yeomen of the Guard, and two empty coaches. This was for a procession to Westminster, so there was no baggage train. When the Queen travelled through

[1] Edmund Howes, *Annals,* a continuation of Stow's *Chronicle.*

the countryside she was followed by three or four hundred carts, bearing among other things her state bed (taken to pieces to be reassembled on arrival), her hip-bath, clothes and jewellery, and linen in canvas bags. After the carts came three hundred or more pack-horses and mules. They covered ten or twelve miles (16-19 km) in a day. The route was planned in advance to make sure of the necessary stopping-places. Obviously few houses could accommodate such a train, and it was common for many of the lesser folk to be billeted or to have to camp out in tents. Assuming that the Queen had given sufficient notice of a progress, all this would be pre-checked by the gentlemen-ushers. There might, however, be sudden changes of plan; when the Queen intended to visit Kent in mid-July 1573, she was informed by Lord Cobham that there was plague in Sandwich, and both plague and smallpox at Canterbury, so she postponed her trip until the end of the month, when the weather was cold and wet.

When she did arrive at Sandwich, the Queen found that all the streets had been covered with gravel, and 'strewed with rushes, herbs, flags and suche lyke, every howse having a nombre of grene bowes standing against the dores and walls, every howse paynted whyte and black'.[2] After a fortnight in Canterbury, by invitation of the Archbishop, the Queen spent two days in Faversham, which cost the townspeople £44 19s. 4d., including a silver cup worth £27 2s. This does not seem unreasonably expensive; but what did rouse the people's ire was the extortion perpetrated by some of the purveyors and the difficulty in obtaining payment for goods. (The purveyors had the habit of coming to the City of London and laying hands on the first carts they saw, which deterred countrymen from bringing provisions into the town; so it was ordered that the carts should serve the Queen no more than four times a year. This was enforced by the governors of Christ's Hospital.) Apparently such abuses were particularly bad in Kent. A countryman came up to the royal party at Greenwich and enquired,'Which is the Queen?'

'I am your Queen,' Elizabeth replied, 'What wouldst thou have with me?'

'You', he said, 'are one of the rarest women I ever saw, and can eat no more than my daughter Madge, who is thought the properest lass in our parish, though short of you, but the Queen Elizabeth I look for devours so many of my hens, ducks and capons, as I am not able to live.' Susceptible to this flattering

---

[2] Quoted in Nichols's *Progresses and Public Processions of Queen Elizabeth,* Vol.I, p.337.

Warwick Castle

approach, the Queen looked into the man's complaint, enquired who the purveyor was, and had him hanged.

Some of the Queen's progresses were principally to towns and cities, rather than the homes of noblemen; this was especially notable in the 1570s, when she visited Warwick, Bristol, Worcester and Norwich.

Her visit to Warwick was in 1572. Although she stayed at the castle, it was mainly a civic affair. She arrived at Ford Mill Hill, just outside the town, at about three in the afternoon, sharing a coach with Lady Warwick, and with her came the usual train: Lord Burghley, Lord Howard of Effingham, the Earls of Sussex, Oxford, Warwick, Huntingdon, Rutland and, of course, Leicester. The Queen had her coach opened as widely as possible so that everybody could see her. The Bailiff and the burgesses fell to their knees and remained kneeling during an immensely long and fulsome speech by the town recorder, with many references to classical and medieval history. He said he had been dazzled by the splendour of her majesty's countenance, and ended by giving her, as a present from the town, a purse with £20 in gold sovereigns. The Queen accepted it graciously. A mite, she said, from their hands was worth a thousand pounds from some others. Then she spoke to the recorder, 'Come hither, little recorder. It was told me that you would be afraid to look upon me or to speak boldly; but you were not so afraid of me as I was of you,' and she turned to the burgesses, 'I most heartily thank you, my good people.' She always knew exactly what to say.

Having listened patiently to the long oration, however, she was anxious to be off, and when she was given a paper with Latin verses, she handed it to Lady Warwick, observing, 'If it be any matter to be answered, we will look into it.' Enough was enough.

A ceremonial entry was made into the town. The bailiff in scarlet and the principal burgesses in 'gownes of puke [a fine woollen cloth of inky colour] lyned with satten and damask' accompanied her right up to the castle. 'A well favoured and comely company' she remarked, perhaps with irony.

After two nights at the castle, the Queen made an impromptu visit to Kenilworth with the Earl of Leicester, enjoying 'princely sports'. She stayed there from Wednesday to Saturday. On her return she found various entertainments had been prepared. Country dancing took place in the castle courtyard, and the Queen watched with great pleasure from her bedroom window. Then in the evening there were fireworks. A mock fort and a mock castle had been constructed of canvas on a timber framework. The fort was manned with townsfolk, pretending to be soldiers, and the canvas castle by the Earl of Oxford, Edward de Vere, a colourful but dissolute character who had married Anne, younger daughter of Lord Burghley. With him he had about two hundred men. The contestants were armed as far as possible, mortars and battering-rams had been procured from the Tower of London by the Earl of Warwick, and a mock battle was enacted with squibs and fireballs. It was an exciting spectacle, 'the wildfyre falling into the Ryver Aven, wold for a tyme lye still, and then agayn rise and flye abrode, casting forth many flashes and flambes, whereat the Queen's Majesty took great pleasure.'

But a great ball of fire fell on a house at the end of the bridge and set it alight. In the house was a man called Henry Cowper, asleep in bed with his wife. Immediately the Earl of Oxford, Sir Fulke Greville and others set about rescuing the couple and attempting to put out the fire which had spread to the adjoining houses. These they managed to save, but Henry Cowper's house was burnt to the ground, together with all his possessions. Eye-witnesses were surprised that more harm was not done, for the fireballs and squibs were falling all over the town 'some on houses, some in courts at baksides, and some in the streete, as farre as almost to St Mary's Churche, to the great perill, or else great feare, of the inhabitants of this Borough'. Four houses were reported to be on fire at the same time. The pyrotechnics had got thoroughly out of hand, and the display was transformed to a rescue bid.

In the morning the Queen had the now destitute Henry Cowper and his wife brought before her. Not only did she offer her sympathy, she ordered a whip-round amongst the courtiers and raised £25 12s. 8d. as compensation before she went off to enjoy more 'princely sports' at Kenilworth.

The Warwick episode does not seem to have put Elizabeth off mock forts and mock battles, and two years later they were again provided for her entertainment, this time at Bristol. She had been unwell earlier in the summer, 'sad and pensive', and perhaps she needed something to cheer her up. She arrived in Bristol on 14 August 1574, and was greeted in verse by a boy representing Fame. No sooner was it known that she was coming to Bristol, he said, than ...

'babes in street gan leap:
The youth, the age, the rich, the poor came runnyng all on heap,
And clapping hands, cried maynly out 'O blessed be the hour,
Our Queen is commyng to the Town, with princely trayn and power.'

Three more boys were at the next gate, representing Salutation, Congratulation and Obedient Goodwill. Appropriately enough, Obedient Goodwill did not prolong his speech,

'But since the time is short, and Prince to lodging goes,
I say, God bless the Queen, that gives the White and fair, Red Rose.'[3]

The Queen stayed at the house of Sir John Young; she was escorted there by three hundred soldiers. A large mock fort had been built, and in this was staged first a dialogue between Dissension and Peace. This was followed by the storming of a smaller fort called Feeble Policy. Then came the storming of the main fort with a great show of fireworks. The Queen left by torchlight and the

[3] The Tudor rose, combining the white rose of York and the red rose of Lancaster.

mock-battle was resumed the following day. She was so delighted with the combat and spectacle that she gave 200 crowns so that the soldiers could have a banquet. At her departure a gentleman of the city spoke a 'Doleful Adieu', regretting that her stay had been so short.

The Queen's visit to Worcester the following year was to promote the declining cloth industry, for the city was not prosperous. Despite this, the civic authorities made elaborate preparations. It was laid down that all 'myskyns', or dunghills, should be removed from the city, and the streets strewn with gravel. The four city gates were to be painted a discreet shade of grey, and the royal arms set up on both sides of them; also the people's houses were to be decorated with lime-wash in white and colours, and the front of the Guildhall refurbished with the Queen's arms picked out in gold. A new layer of gold was to be put on the four civic maces and the aldermen's staff. Scarlet gowns lined with black satin were made for the bailiffs, the rest of the civic party were to be dressed in violet or 'murrey' (mulberry colour). The freemen from the various guilds should wear their livery gowns, but all their gowns were to be inspected in advance to make sure they were 'comely and decent'. A fine silver-gilt cup was bought in London for £10 17s. 2d., and £40 in sovereigns and gold angels collected to put in it, as a present for the Queen. Two stages were set up, one at the Grass Cross and the other by St Helen's Church. A levy totalling £212 was imposed to pay for the visit: £20 from the city treasury, £96 from the civic dignitaries, and £96 from the citizens. (The actual cost proved to be £198 16s. 4d.)

On Saturday 13 August the streets were lined with people as the Queen entered Foregate Street, riding on her palfrey, and she was delighted with the verses and speeches of welcome delivered by the boys from the stages, and the crowd shouting 'God save your Majesty!' She managed to stay looking cheerful despite the weather which turned so wet that she called for her cloak and hat. She entered the cathedral porch where Christopher Fletcher, a scholar from the King's School, made a Latin oration. She received another gift (£20 in a crimson velvet purse) and walked into the church itself to the accompaniment of cornets, sackbuts and voices. She looked at the tombs of King John and Prince Arthur (her uncle, elder brother of Henry VIII), and from there walked into the Bishop's Palace.

In view of the weather, it was not surprising that the next day the Queen decided to ride by coach to service in the cathedral. But she kept both sides of the coach open so that the crowds in the streets and churchyard could have a good view of her as they shouted out, 'God save your Majesty! God save your Grace!'

'I thank you, I thank you all,' she replied many times.

On the Tuesday she rode out of the city in order to dine with her cofferer, Thomas Habingdon. The civic dignitaries went with her as far as the city boundaries, and there they were about to dismount and kneel, but as the road was extremely muddy with the recent rain, the Queen stopped them, 'I pray you, keep your horses and do not alight.' At eight in the evening she returned to the city lit with candles and torches, riding on horseback despite the appalling weather — and still kept her 'cheerful princely countenance', turning her horse from side to side and speaking to the people.

On the departure of the royal party, two gallons (nine litres) of hippocras were given to the Earl of Leicester. Speaking no doubt for the Queen as well as himself, he said, 'I assure you 'tis a city I love with all my heart; and if I may any way do it good, you shall find me willing and ready.'[4]

When Elizabeth visited Norwich during her progress to East Anglia in 1578, her motives were much the same as they had been at Worcester. Norwich was also primarily a cloth-town, and the industry was in decline. The city was given about two months' notice, so it was possible to spruce it up considerably. The market-cross was painted in timber-colour and white. The pillory and cage used to punish malefactors were removed, and the 'muck-hill at Brazen Doors' taken away, so that the Queen would not come into contact with anything unpleasant. The churchyard wall of St John's, Maddermarket, was taken down so as to widen the street; the road was also widened at St Giles's Gate. It was forbidden for any cows to be brought into the city during the Queen's visit, and every innkeeper was instructed to have a horse always ready for use as a post-horse. Thomas Churchyard, who frequently wrote and directed entertainments for the Queen's delight, arrived three weeks in advance of the royal party, and had three boats made into barges for a water-pageant. The city borrowed £400 or £500 to defray the expenses.

After dinner on Saturday 16 August, the Queen and her train, including ambassadors from France, set out from Beacon Ash, five miles away from Norwich. She was met by the Mayor (Sir Robert Wood) and, walking two by two, sixty of the handsomest young men of the city — all attired in black satin doublets, black hose, black taffeta hats with yellow bands, and sleeveless coats of purple

[4] The Earl of Warwick is reputed to have said much the same thing.

taffeta. With a speech in Latin, the Mayor gave her a silver-gilt cup containing £100 in gold — a generous gift, considering the city's financial straits. 'Princes', she said, 'have no need of money ... we come for the hearts and the allegiance of our subjects.' Nevertheless she took it and handed it to one of her footmen.

According to legend the city of Norwich was founded by King Gurgunt, who built a castle called Blanche Fleur. So along with the handsome youths, rode a man representing Gurgunt. He was dressed in full armour and a black velvet hat with white feathers. He had a speech all ready to greet the Queen when she reached St Stephen's Gate. But it was pouring with rain so he never had a chance to deliver it. She entered to music by the city waits. In St Stephen's parish a stage had been set up (measuring 40 x 8 feet/12 x 2m) and on it were weavers with models or pictures of looms illustrating different weaving techniques. Weaving was still a cottage industry, so there were no factories for the Queen to visit. A small boy dressed in a robe of white taffeta with a crimson scarf and garland of flowers on his head, represented the Commonwealth of the City. The Queen was delighted with his speech, and as he flung the garland into the air, exclaimed 'This device is fine!'

A second and even larger pageant greeted her when she reached the entrance to the market. On the stage were five people dressed as women, representing the City of Norwich, the biblical heroines Deborah, Judith and Esther, and 'Martia', described as sometime Queen of England. Music sounded and each of the five addressed the Queen in verses, such as Martia's,

'Here cometh the Pearl of Grace.
Here comes the Jewel of the World, her people's whole delight,
The Paragon of present time, and Prince of earthly might.'

Elizabeth stayed at the Bishop's palace while she was in Norwich. She may have been surprised when she looked out of the window on the Monday morning to see Mercury down below, dressed in blue satin lined with cloth of gold. He had come in a cloud-like coach to tell her that there were entertainments ready at any time she wished to go out and see them.

But the weather was wet, so she stayed in until the next day when she saw a masque concerning Cupid (Love) and his encounter with Chastity and her waiting-maids Modesty, Temperance, Good Exercise and Shamefastness. These ladies set upon Cupid with some ferocity and overcame him. Then Chastity gave Cupid's bow to the Queen, saying that she could shoot at whom she pleased.

On the Wednesday Elizabeth and the French ambassadors dined at the Earl of Surrey's house. Churchyard had everything ready for an entertainment called *Manhode and Dezarte,* but there was no space for it at the Earl of Surrey's, so he took the cast by boat to a landing-stage. They waited three hours but the Queen did not come. Meanwhile, on her return to the city the Queen was met by Stephen Limbert, master from the grammar school. He had a speech in Latin ready but seemed nervous. 'Be not afraid,' she reassured him, and told the French ambassadors to pay attention. When he had finished his oration (comparing the Queen's goodness with the fertilizing effect of the River Nile, in that it made the land flourish), she told him it was the best speech she had ever heard and gave him her hand to kiss. (Unfortunately the Queen's visit was to have had another effect that no one wanted, being followed by an outbreak of plague in Norwich — it was said that the infection had been brought by the royal baggage-train. The epidemic raged a year and three-quarters (August 20 1578 to February 19 1580). It was reported that 2,335 English and 2,482 foreigners died of it — amongst them ten of the aldermen who had welcomed the Queen to the city.)

The Lord Chamberlain told Churchyard that the Queen would be riding out next day and he should have some show ready. Having some idea of the route she would take, Churchyard's preparations included having a large pit dug by the river-bank. He covered this in canvas painted green with at the top a drawstring running through curtain rings; when this was released it would look as if the earth were opening. Into the bag he put twelve golden-haired water-nymphs (actually boys) clad in white silk with head-dresses of ivy and moss, and a consort of 'broken music'. The idea was to have the subterranean sound of music playing in harmony, then the twelve nymphs should leap from the hole and dance with tambourines (which were a novelty at the time). Nearby the cast of *Manhode and Dezarte* stood in readiness — all men except for a boy representing Beauty.

Just as the Queen was about to arrive, however, there was a thunderclap and a downpour of rain. The actors ran for shelter. All their costumes were ruined. 'Although some of us in a boate stode under a bridge,' reports Churchyard, 'We were all dashed and washed, that it was a greater pastime to see us looke like drowned rattes, then to have beheld the uttermost of the shewes rehearsed.' This, he concluded, was the peril of arranging open-air entertainments.

Nothing daunted, though, he set about planning some device for the following day, when the Queen was due to leave. He decided to turn the water-nymphs into land-fairies; at least it might make the Queen laugh. There was very little time and the frolic was largely improvised. Seven of the twelve boys should dive through the hedge and surprise the Queen with hastily conned verses, then Churchyard himself, masquerading as Queen of the Fairies, should lead his bedraggled troupe in a dance. It was a real farce, but Elizabeth applauded heartily. She did not leave the city until about seven in the evening, though she still had five miles to ride.

In their efforts to entertain the Queen, the people of Norwich had spared neither trouble nor expense. Yards of silk, satin, velvet and cloth-of-gold had been used to make the costumes, now largely ruined by the rain. But the loss was accepted philosophically and they hoped she would come again. As for the Queen, she left the city with tears in her eyes. 'I have laid up in my breast such good will', she said, 'as I shall never forget Norwich.'

Although it was strange, observed Churchyard, that ordinary people living far from the Court, should behave with courtesy, generosity and friendliness, yet such was the effect of a visit by their Queen. And this was the recipe he recommended for the continuing allegiance and goodwill of her subjects.

CHAPTER 4

PROGRESSES TO THE UNIVERSITIES

'Where I have come, great clearkes have purposed
To greete me with premeditated welcomes;
Where I have seene them shiver and looke pale,
Make periods in the midst of sentences,
Throttle their practic'd accent in their feares,
And in conclusion, dumbly have broke off,
Not paying me a welcome. Trust me sweete,
Out of this silence yet I pickt a welcome:
And in the modesty of feareful duty
I read as much, as from the ratling tongue
Of saucy and audacious eloquence.'

(Shakespeare, *A Midsummer Night's Dream*,
Act V, Scene I, Theseus to Hippolyta)

Quite early in her reign, Elizabeth decided to make progresses to the universities of Oxford and Cambridge, the first being to Cambridge in 1564.

Her reasons for this were at least twofold. Partly the expeditions were undertaken as a compliment to individuals she favoured and respected; but there was also her love of scholarship for its own sake, her estimate of its importance and therefore her desire to promote it. To numerous grammar schools she gave charters, and to the universities recognition.

CAMBRIDGE, 1564

The High Chancellor of the University of Cambridge was Sir William Cecil, Lord Burghley, the most valued and trusted of her ministers. 'My Spirit' she called him. He had been a student at St John's, Cambridge at the age of fourteen; and from the same college had stemmed her tutors Roger Ascham and William Grindal. She was very much aware of her debt to all three.

She gave the University surprisingly little notice. The letter to Cecil from the Bishop of London, advising him of her intention, is dated 15 July and was received at Cambridge on the 17th; the Queen's visit was timed for 8 August. She expected to be greeted, he said, with 'all manner of scholastical exercises' — sermons, disputations, comedies and tragedies, orations and verses, and almost all in Latin or Greek.

From the University doctors were sent to discuss arrangements

King's College Chapel, Cambridge.

with Sir William Cecil, the Bishop of London, the Master of Requests and the Dean of Westminster. From the Court to Cambridge came officers to enquire if any people had died of the plague there recently; doubtless the visit would have been cancelled if there had been. Meanwhile quantities of beer, ale and wine were sent to King's College, and it was ruled that every inhabitant of the city should provide enough sand to cover the streets when the Queen came. Cecil arranged (perhaps not very willingly, for he never liked him) that Robert Dudley should act as intermediary and master of the ceremonies. Throughout Cecil was nervous, apprehensive and troubled with pain in his leg. Dudley, on the other hand, was genial and reassuring. He put himself, he said, entirely at the service of the University of Cambridge, offering his friendship, his purse, and himself. If they were worried that the visit would go awry, he dismissed their fears. The Queen, he said, 'doth esteme goodwill above any other gifts... nothing can with better will be done by youe, than yt will be graciously accepted of her.'

55

But Cecil was still anxious. When he arrived by coach with his wife on 4 August (troubled with an 'unhappy greefe' in his foot), he instructed that members of his university should show their uniformity both in their dress and their religion. The Vice-Chancellor, Dr Hawford, thanked him on behalf of the University, and invited him to stand with them when the Queen came. Cecil was presented with two pairs of gloves, two sugar-loaves and a marchpane (marzipan).

The next day Robert Dudley arrived. Cecil met him at King's College and he inspected the lodging prepared for the Queen. Then he was received at Trinity College, where over two hundred people had gathered in the Hall, and was likewise given two pairs of gloves, two sugar-loaves and a marchpane. From there he went to St John's College where he saw Cecil in his chamber; together they reviewed the arrangements for the Queen's entertainment.

1. The Choristers' School was made the Buttery.
2. The Pantry and Ewry were two Chambers in the King's College.
3. The open Kitchens and Skulleryes were raised against St. Austin's wall.
4. The Celler, in the Provost's Buttery.
5. The Councell Chamber, in the South Vestry.
6. The Guard Chamber, was the Lower Hall of the Provost's Place.
7. The Chamber of Presence, the Lodging over that.
8. The Gallery and Other Chambers served for the Queen's Lodging.

The nobles, etc., were accommodated as follows:

1. The Earl of Warwick and the Lord Robert were lodged in Trinity College.
2. The Duke, at Mr Ray's, Alderman.
3. The Lord Chamberlayn and the Lord Clinton, at Trinity Hall.
4. The Lord Hunsdon, at Clare Hall.
5. The Earl of Sussex, at Katherine Hall.
6. The Earl of Oxford, the Earl of Rutland, and the Secretary, at St. John's College.
7. The Cofferer, the Masters and other Officers of the Household, at Queen's College.
8. Mr Doctor Haddon, the Lady Strange, and divers

other Ladies, in the Fellows Chamber in King's College.

9.   The Maids of Honour and the Physitians, at Gonvil and Caius College.

The Vice-Chancellor went on to the Duke of Norfolk's lodging, gave him two pairs of gloves, *one* sugar-loaf and a marchpane, and then to the Earl of Suffolk — who only got one pair of gloves and no edibles.

A great 'falling-gate' was set up at the corner by Queen's College and Martin Gill's house, and the lane between there and King's College was strewn with rushes and adorned with flags, draperies, branches, and verses pinned up on the walls.

On the day of the Queen's arrival the whole University assembled by King's College — first the scholars, then the Bachelors of Arts and the Bachelors of Law, then the 'Master Regents', the 'Non Regents' and Bachelors of Divinity. Then stood the doctors in their gowns and hoods, and the Vice-Chancellor, accompanied by three beadles, by the west door.

The Queen was greeted by the Mayor at Newnham, and he handed her the mace, and a cup worth £19 containing twenty gold angels. She changed horses and entered the city to a fanfare of trumpets, wearing a black velvet gown and a gold-spangled hat with feathers.

As she passed by, the scholars fell to their knees and shouted, *'Vivat Regina!'* Two of them presented her with written orations, one in verse and one in prose. Two Bachelors and two Masters of Arts did likewise.

King's College Chapel was decorated with tapestry, fine hangings were set on the pulpit and communion-table, and the unpaved floor strewn with rushes. Between the vestry door and the alter a 'traverse' or partition of crimson velvet was set up for the Queen, and by the chancel a closet where she could rest if she wished. Where she was to tread the floor was covered with Turkey carpet. A prie-dieu covered in cloth-of-gold was provided, with a Bible in Latin, and a red velvet chair for her to sit in while she listened to the oration 'if she had forsaken her horse'.

At the west door Elizabeth was welcomed by Sir William Cecil, on his knees despite his bad leg. He handed to her the beadles' staves, which she handed back, trusting that Cecil and the other magistrates of the University would be honest in their administration. 'Although the Chancellor did halt,' she added, 'she

57

trusted that justice did not halt.'

A speech of welcome was made by the Orator (William Master of King's College), praising the Queen's virtues — which she modestly disclaimed — and the antiquity of the University. Then she was given four pairs of gloves trimmed with gold, and six boxes of comfits 'which she thankfully took, and so went to her chamber'.

Next day was Sunday, and the Queen attended a service in King's College Chapel. She entered by the north door, four of the most senior academicians bearing a canopy over her. She sat in the crimson velvet 'traverse' to listen to the sermon by Dr Perry. It lasted an hour; nevertheless the Queen sent to congratulate him afterwards. After supper she watched a Latin play, Plautus's *Aulularia* (*The Comedy of the Little Pot*), performed by members of the University, though not from King's College.

The next afternoon, Elizabeth attended disputations in philosophy and science in the university church of St Mary. After supper there was another play, this time performed by the students of King's College — a tragedy in Latin hexameters called *Dido*. On the following day (the 8th) they acted a play in English, *Ezechias*.

On 9 August the Queen made a tour of the colleges, listening to orations in Greek and Latin at each one. She was given a beautifully bound book containing the verses spoken to her, and a book listing all the colleges, their founders, number of students, and revenues. After dinner she attended further disputations in Latin in St Mary's Church, this time concerning theology and law. (The latter had to be cut short for lack of time.) Then the Queen herself delivered a speech, also in Latin. She said that her goodwill towards the University had overcome her feminine modesty. She did not wish to disappoint them by remaining silent, and she was anxious to do all she could to promote learning. 'Ply your studies diligently,' she advised them. She said she regretted that she had not added yet to the University buildings put up by her ancestors. However, Rome was not built in a day, and she was young enough yet to remedy this and leave some monument behind her. She spoke apologetically of her own lack of learning (!), and ended by saying, 'It is time then that your ears, which have been so long detained by this barbarous sort of an oration, should now be released from the pain of it.'

Her speech was acclaimed with shouts of '*Vivat Regina!*' ('Long live the Queen'). '*Taceat Regina,*' the Queen replied ('Let the Queen shut up') and in great good humour went back to her lodging.

The University, however, was disappointed that she said she

was too tired to watch a tragedy by Sophocles (*Ajax*) they had been rehearsing — she had stayed up late watching the other plays. Now it seemed she had had enough. She made up her mind to leave Cambridge early the following morning, and ride to Ely in time to take her midday dinner with the Bishop. That morning various noblemen, including Robert Dudley, were made Masters of Arts. Meanwhile the Queen heard in private a speech by a Mr Preston (he had spoken in the disputation on philosophy), which pleased her so well that she dubbed him her Scholar and gave him eight gold angels.

OXFORD, 1566

'Her sweet, affable and noble carriage left such impressions in the minds of scholars, that nothing but emulation was in their studies, and nothing left untouched by them whereby they thought they might be advanced by her, or become acceptable in her eye.'

Anthony Wood on The Queen's Entertainment at Oxford 1566

It was only to be expected that Elizabeth's progress to Cambridge, honouring Cecil, should be followed by one to Oxford, honouring Dudley, who had been made Chancellor of the University on 29 September 1564. But there was another aspect to this visit, more grave than the paying of compliments. The Earl of Leicester took his responsibilities seriously and had found initially much to criticise in the University where less than a decade before, Cranmer, Ridley and Latimer had been burnt at the stake.

'The disorders, not muttered of, not secretly informed here and there in corners, but openly cried out upon continually and almost in every place, are such as touch no less than your religion, your lives and conversation, and the whole estate of your Universitye, Professions and Learning... The chiefest points are the want of instructing your youth in the Principles of Religion, and the little care that Tutors have that waye, and most especially the suffering of secret and lurking Papists amongst you...'

Part, at least, of the Queen's intention was to see how things were being run, to rout out recusants, and to make sure that the university, as well as the city, recognised her as head of the Church in England.

Elizabeth made her first state visit to Oxford during her progress of 1566. She left Greenwich Palace and passed Northamptonshire, visiting Stamford, on her way to Oxfordshire where she stopped first at Woodstock, the old palace where she had been so long imprisoned. The dons rode out from Oxford to greet her; then she, they and the nobility rode together to the city. Within half a mile of it they were met by the Mayor and aldermen. After the usual ceremony of presenting and returning the mace, the custom was for the distinguished visitor to receive five oxen, five sheep, five calves, five lambs and five sugar-loaves. As some of these presents might have caused problems, the Queen was given instead a silver-gilt cup worth £10, containing £40 in gold.

She entered the city by coach at five or six in the evening of 31 August. At Carfax (then known as Quatrevois — four ways) she was greeted by the scholars. '*Vivat Regina!*' they cried.

'*Gratias ago, gratias ago,*' she replied ('I give thanks, I give thanks'). Then she listened to a speech in Greek by Mr Lawrence, King's professor of Greek at Oxford, and this delighted her just as much. She thanked him, in the same language, and said it was the best oration in Greek she had ever heard. She invited him to speak with her further in her lodgings.

When she came to the door of Christ Church, the students of that college, standing in their surplices, acclaimed her again, '*Vivat Regina!*', and there was another speech, this time by Mr Kingsmill, Orator of the University. She thanked him, but somewhat tersely, 'You would have done well, had you good matter.' Then she proceeded into the church for a service, walking under a canopy held up by Doctors Kennall, Humphrey, Thomas Whyte and Richard Barber, to a 'traverse' which had been made for her on the right-hand side of the choir. Dr Godwyn the Dean gave thanks for the Queen's safe arrival in Oxford, and she listened with pleasure to a 'Te Deum' sung to the accompaniment of cornets. After the service she returned to her lodgings, possibly noticing as she went the verse in Latin and Greek pinned to the gates and walls — for instance, this by James Calfhill, one of the canons,

'Famous virgin Elizabeth, the glory of her sex
And wonder of her kind, and Queen of the people of Britain,
You come welcome to us, and you bring perfect joy,
Following the unfinished memorials of your father.'[1]

[1] The Latin reads:
'*Inclyta foeminei Virgo, quae gloria sexus*

Et generis decus, et gentis Regina Britannae,
Grata venis nobis, perfectaque gaudia portas,
Imperfecta tui subiens monumenta parentis. '

The next day was Sunday, and Dr Overton of Magdalen College preached a sermon in English in Christ Church Cathedral. The Queen, however, did not attend. She said she was not well. Instead she received in her privy chamber 'a very pretty boy' called Peter Carew (son of the late Dean of Christ Church), who spoke to her an oration in Latin, followed by two verses in Greek. She was so enchanted by this that she had him repeat it all over again for Lord Cecil to hear. Dr Overton's reactions are not recorded.

In the afternoon she followed the official schedule, and sat in the 'traverse' provided while she heard a sermon by Thomas Harris of New College. Perhaps she had thought one sermon a day was enough. A large platform had been set up in the Hall at Christ Church. In the evening it was illuminated with wax candles, and performed in front of the nobility and the Spanish ambassador was a Latin play *Marcus Geminus.* Again the Queen did not attend, but the Spanish ambassador spoke so highly of the performance that she promised not to miss any more of the events planned for her entertainment.

The next morning (2 September) there were lectures and debates, which the ambassador and various of the noblemen attended; then there were two orations by Bachelors of Arts at New College, one by Gregory Coryat (for which he was given a half-sovereign) and the other by William Reynolds. It was hoped to hold further disputations at Christ Church in the afternoon, but they had to be cancelled because the stage was taking up too much room. So the Queen kept to her lodging, and there Thomas Neale, Professor of Hebrew, gave her a book of the prophets, which he had translated, and a book in Latin verse describing all the colleges of the University, and listing their founders and the dates of their foundation.

In the evening she attended the first part of a play in English, *Palamon and Arcite,* written by Richard Edwards for this occasion,[2] but now, unfortunately, lost. It was performed in the

[2] Richard Edwards 1523-66, of Christ Church, was Master of the Children of the Chapel Royal. *Palamon and Arcite* was written on the same theme as the Knight's Tale in Chaucer's *Canterbury Tales.* Palamon and Arcite, prisoners of Theseus, King of Athens, both fell in love with Emilia, sister of Theseus's wife Hippolyta (Queen of the Amazons). They enter a tournament to contest for her hand. Arcite defeats Palamon, but at the moment of victory is thrown from his horse and dies. After mourning Arcite, Palamon and Emilia are married. From the *Tesseida of Boccaccio.*

61

The Hall, Christ Church College, Oxford

Hall at Christ Church. The play was much applauded, although at the beginning part of the stage collapsed and three people were killed (Walker, a student from St Mary's Hall, Penrice a brewer,

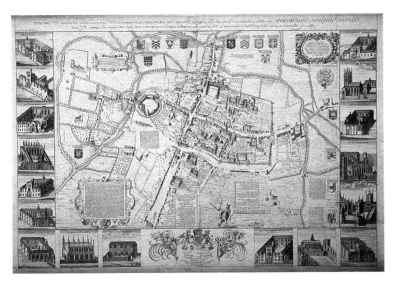

Oxford in 1578, map by Ralph Agas, engraved by Robert Whittlesey, 1728.
The south is shown at the top. (Bodleian Library)

and John Gilbert, cook of Corpus Christi College) and five injured,
to whom the Queen immediately sent the Vice-Chancellor and her
own surgeons, to see what could be done for them. As for the play,
it was well acted, she laughed heartily and thanked the author in
person.

After dinner on the Tuesday the Queen walked to St Mary's
Church to hear disputations in Latin on natural and moral
philosophy, which lasted from two till six. Verses in Latin, Greek
and Hebrew were set up on the doors and walls — it can hardly be
supposed that she ever had time to read them — together with a
map of Oxford with all the colleges marked, and a descriptive verse
under each one. She took a lively interest in the debates; when
Edmund Campion of St John's College said, 'There is a God who
serves Your Majesty, in what you do, in what you advise,' she
turned to the Earl of Leicester with a smile, and suggested he was
referring to him.

The next day there were disputations in natural and moral
philosophy in the Hall of Merton College. The Queen dined at
Christ Church, and her Council at Magdalen; then she went to St
Mary's and stayed there for four hours listening to disputations in
civil law.

In the evening she attended the second part of *Palamon and
Arcite* (the two parts should have been performed on the same day,
only the disputations at St Mary's went on too long). Apparently it

63

was a very lively performance. It included a scene of Theseus hunting a fox with hounds who were heard baying from the quad —the young scholars were so much taken up with the action that they shouted out, 'Now, now! — there, there! — he's caught, he's caught!'

'O excellent!' declared the Queen, 'These boys, in very truth, are ready to leap out of the windows, to follow the hounds.'

After the performance Elizabeth called for Richard Edwards to congratulate him on his play. 'By Palamon,' she said,

> 'I warrant he dallieth not in love when he was in love indeed; by Arcite, he was a right martial knight, having a swart countenance and a manly face; by Trecatio, God's pity, what a knave it is; by Perithous throwing St Edward's rich cloak into the funeral fire, which a stander-by would have stayed his arm with an oath, Go, fool, he knoweth his part, I warrant.'

The part of Emilia, described as gathering spring flowers and singing in a garden, was almost certainly performed by Peter Carew — in any case the young actor was given a reward of eight angels in token of the Queen's pleasure.

The nobles, some of whom had seen the last part of the play before, were equally delighted. They said it was even better than the same writer's *Damon and Pythias,* and so funny that if he wrote another play before he died it would drive him mad with laughter. In fact he did die, only a few months later, and this was the last he wrote.

The next day, Thursday, there were more disputations in St Mary's Church, this time in physick. They ended at about six. Then the Queen, having first invited the Spanish ambassador, the Earl of Leicester and Lord Burghley to speak in her stead (which they courteously declined), made her own oration in Latin. Those who do things badly, she began, hate the light; in the same way, she shunned the light of her audience's learning. However, she felt she must speak some words in praise of the University or she would be thought churlish and contemptuous, for, she said, they deserved praise. Since she had come to Oxford, she told them, she had watched and listened to many things, and approved them all. The second part of her speech concerned Oxford as a seat of learning; she had had excellent tutors herself but, she said, she was sterile and infertile ground (!). Her wish was that learning should prosper greatly in her lifetime, and receive a benefaction after her death.

Her speech was loudly applauded, and as she left St Mary's Church she was handed by Mr Edrick (who had been Greek Reader of the University) a book of Greek verses praising the noble acts of her father. The playwright Edwards was standing by and he remarked to the Queen, 'Madam, this man was my master,' (he had had him for his tutor when a student at Corpus Christi College). The Queen replied — with a wink, one guesses — 'Certainly he did not give thee whipping enough.'

After supper Elizabeth and her courtiers watched a Latin tragedy called *Progue* (by James Calfhill, canon of Christ Church) performed in Christ Church Hall. It met with polite approbation, but nothing like the enthusiasm that greeted *Palamon and Arcite*.

At nine o'clock the next morning there was a convocation and the following gentlemen were made Masters of Arts:

Edward de Vere, Earl of Oxford
William Howard, Baron of Effingham
Thomas Butler, Earl of Ormond
Ambrose Dudley, Earl of Warwick
Henry Lord Strange (son of the Earl of Derby)
Edward Stafford, Lord Stafford
John Sheffield, Lord Sheffield
Sir William Cecil, Secretary of State
.... Rogers, Comptroller
Sir Francis Knollys, Captain of the Halberdiers
Sir Nicholas Throckmorton
John Tamworth of the Queen's Privy Chamber.

The Earl of Leicester presided in his capacity as Chancellor of the University — certain of the recipients must have had to lower their pride to receive their degrees at the hands of the man they still thought of as Master of the Queen's Horse. After they had taken an oath to observe the statutes, liberties and privileges of the University, a sermon was preached in the Cathedral by Dr John Piers. The Queen, however, worn out with hours of disputations and the previous night's Latin tragedy, did not attend. Then the Vice-Chancellor and the proctors presented her with six pairs of very fine gloves (one wonders if she ever got around to wearing them all) and some of her courtiers were also given one or two pairs. She left Christ Church after dinner; as she did so a Mr Toby Mathew made a speech to her which she liked so much she made him a Queen's Scholar.

From Christ Church she went to the Carfax and took the East

Robert Dudley, Earl of Leicester. (National Portrait Gallery)

Gate road from the city, escorted by senior members of the University and the civic dignitaries. As she passed the scholars once more shouted out '*Vivat Regina!*'; and on the walls of St Mary's Church, All Souls and University Colleges there were sheets of verses bemoaning the Queen's departure. At Magdalen Bridge she was told by Sir Francis Knollys, Steward of the City, that that was as far as the civic liberties extended — she turned and thanked the Mayor and his train and said goodbye to them.

About two miles from Oxford, in the Forest of Shotover, the Earl of Leicester told her that that was as far as the University's jurisdiction extended. Roger Marbeck took the opportunity of making an eloquent speech to her, saying how learning had been in decline, but there was now every sign that it would be revived under so learned a monarch as she was. When he had finished she gave him her hand to kiss, and thanked all the representatives of the University who were with her. 'Farewell,' she said, 'the worthy University of Oxford; farewell, my good subjects there; farewell, my dear scholars, and pray God prosper your studies; farewell —farewell.'

OXFORD, 1592

> '..Phoenix doth like Phoebus shine, and lends the
> world great light'

> (Thomas Churchyard, 'Few Plaine Verses... made when
> the Queen's Majesty was last at Oxenford', 1592)

Plague struck the University in 1577, and there was no college left unaffected. During the second half of July a hundred scholars died. Some of the plague-stricken were so maddened by pain that they ran around the streets or flung themselves in the river. Almost all the dons and heads of colleges fled from the city. Small wonder that Elizabeth gave the place a wide berth at this time.

In 1592, however, the Queen decided to revisit Oxford to see what changes had been made in the last twenty-six years. Meanwhile she had remained concerned about any lingering traces of Roman Catholicism — not so much on purely religious grounds, but because too many undiscovered pockets of this faith might endanger her throne — and in 1567 her High Commissioners wrote a letter to All Souls College on the subject of 'superstitious books' they held there.

Her beloved Dudley died in 1588. He was succeeded as Chancellor of the University by her even more devoted admirer Sir Christopher Hatton. When he too died (1591), the office was taken over by Sir Thomas Sackville, Lord Buckhurst (see page 134). Buckhurst was a literary man (his blank-verse tragedy in English *Gorboduc*, held to be the earliest work of its genre, had been acted in Elizabeth's presence in 1561, and it was his suggestion that prompted this second state visit.

Arriving with a fine retinue at Woodstock on 22 September, she was met on the way to Oxford by the Vice-Chancellor, three beadles, the heads of colleges and the dons in scarlet robes, the proctors and about eighteen Masters of Arts. She replied in Latin to their speech of welcome — fortunately the latter was brief, for the weather was appalling. The civic dignitaries met her at the end of St Giles, and she was given a silver-gilt cup with sixty angels in it.

The procession moved on to Carfax, where Henry Cuff, a Reader in Greek, made a Greek oration. She replied in the same language. Then an undergraduate made a speech and recited verses in Latin, and she with her usual fluency replied in Latin. Then they moved on to the gate of Christ Church, where the graduates and students acclaimed her, shouting, '*Vivat Regina!*' In Christ Church quad she was met by the University Orator — he had been given that post for life in 1564. Then she was escorted into the cathedral by four dons bearing her canopy; inside a 'Te Deum' was sung, giving thanks for her safe arrival.

The next day was a Saturday. In the afternoon the Queen went into St Mary's Church to listen to a debate in philosophy; the speeches tended to go on rather long, and at the end she was thanked 'for her great patience in hearing'. On the 24th, Sunday, and the 26th, Tuesday, she attended performances of comedies. The first was *Bellum Grammaticale,* and the second *Rivals;* Philip Stringer, a Cambridge onlooker, described both as 'meanely performed', but the Queen was her usual courteous self.

At 8 a.m. on the Monday there was a sermon, followed at 9 a.m. by a lecture on divinity (which was not well attended). Then the Warden of Merton, Dr Savile, invited the Privy Council, about sixty people in all, to dinner, followed by a disputation on the topic 'Whether dissension among the people can be useful to the state'.

The next day there was a further debate on 'Which changed a man most, the air he breathed or the food and drink he consumed?' One of the doctors in the faculty of Physick was an enormously fat man. He stripped to demonstrate how his body had been changed by what he ate and drank, and challenged all present to show him a body that had been changed so much by air. However, the Moderator of the disputation concluded that air had the greater power.

On 27 September various nobles, together with the French ambassador, were given the honorary degree of Master of Arts.

They were:

In the morning:
Edward Earl of Worcester
George Clifford, Earl of Cumberland
Henry Herbert, Earl of Pembroke
Sir John Wingfield, Knight
Sir Thomas Coningsby, Knight
Sir William Knollys, Knight, afterwards Earl of Banbury
Michael Stanhope, Esquire, brother to Lord Stanhope of
    Harrington
Thomas Knevet, Esquire
Edward Darcy, Esquire
John Stanhope, Esquire
William Poinyz, Esquire
Richard Brackenbury, Esquire
Thomas Lake, Esquire
Anthony Ashley, Esquire
Henry Noel, Esquire.

In the afternoon:
Monsieur Beauvoys la Noude, the French Ambassador
Monsieur Mauditor
Sir Edward Stafford, Knight.

Then there was another disputation in St Mary's as to whether it could be lawful to dissemble in the matter of religion. The Bishop of Hereford concluded the debate with a long oration which the Queen found tedious — or perhaps too near the bone, remembering her predicament in the time of Mary Tudor. Twice she asked him to cut it short, as she herself was to make a speech; but he would not, so her speech was postponed to the next morning.

That was 28 September. Elizabeth, speaking in Latin, said that the merits of the University were such that her hesitation to use a language she had not studied for thirty-six years was overcome. If she had a thousand tongues instead of one, she would not be able to express the thanks due to the University. Half-way through her speech she noticed that Sir William Cecil — who always did have trouble with his legs — had been left standing and was looking most uncomfortable. She ordered a stool to be provided for him before she continued. 'If I have always undertaken the care of your bodies,' she said, 'shall I neglect your minds? God forbid.' Requiring them to continue orthodoxy in their beliefs and not to tolerate dissension, she left

Oxford in the afternoon, going by Fish Street, Carfax and East Gate, and was accompanied by the dons as far as Shotover Hill. There they made their farewell orations and she looked back wistfully towards the city, saying (in Latin), 'Farewell, farewell, dear Oxford, God bless thee, and increase thy sons in number, holiness and virtue.' Then she went on towards Ryecote.

AFTERMATH

The cost to the colleges was listed as follows:[2]

'The Old Rents of every College in Oxford, according to which they were taxed for the Entertainment of Queen Elizabeth, in the 34th Year of hir Reign, were reckoned as followeth:

1. Christ Church	£2000	10. Exon College	£200
2. Magdalen College	1200	11. Oriel College	200
3. New College	1000	12. Trinity College	200
4. All souls	500	13. Lincoln College	130
5. Corpus Christi College	500	14. University College	100
6. Merton College	400	15. Baliol College	100
7. St. John's College	400	16. Jesus College	70
8. Brazen Nose College	300	17. Wadham Coll. *	100
9. Queen's College	260	18. Pembroke Coll. *	100

As for the University, the Queen's visits seem to have had a sobering effect. Shortly after he became Chancellor in 1564, the Earl of Leicester had complained not only of the lack of religious instruction, but the 'Excesse in apparell, as silke and velvet, and cutt dubletts, hose, deepe ruffs and such like', the 'Haunting of the Towne, that the streets are every daye and all day longe more full of Schollers than Townsmen', and that the students spent their time gambling and tippling in the ale-houses.

By the end of the century (1598) Paul Hentzner in his *Journey into England* was able to report: 'The students lead a life almost monastic; for as the monks had nothing in the world to do, but when they had said their prayers at stated hours, to employ themselves in instructive studies, no more have these.'

---

[2] From Gutch's *Collectanea Curiosa*. *At that time not founded.

The previous year, Dr Thomas Bodley had written to the Vice-Chancellor offering to found, at his expense, the library that still bears his name. If Hentzner's description was accurate, there was fit material to profit from it.

CHAPTER 5

ELIZABETH AND THE ARISTOCRATS - I

'For her lyking of this house, I assure you, I think she never came to a place in her lyfe she lyked better or commended more ... her own lodgings specyally. She thinks the cost well bestowed, she sayth, if it had been five times as much; but I wold her Majesty wold bestowe but half as much more, and then I think she should have as pleasant and comodyus a house as any in England.'

(Letter from the Earl of Leicester to Lord Burghley, June 1575)

It was not exactly cheap, entertaining the Queen, but it was certainly fashionable. 'When it pleasesth her in the summer season to recreate herself abroad, and view the estate of the country', observed William Harrison in his *Description of England,* 'every nobleman's house is her palace.'

The pattern was set by such men as William Cordell. Described in his epitaph as 'great by his birth, but greater by his brain', Cordell was a lawyer; he had been made Master of the Rolls by Queen Mary, and was astute enough to retain this office until his death twenty-three years into the reign of Queen Elizabeth. He received the Queen at his house, Melford Hall, during her progress in East Anglia in 1578. It was said that 'he was one of the firste that beganne this great feasting, and did lighte such a candle to the reste of the shire, that many were glad bountifully and franckly to follow the same example, with such charges and cost as the whole trayne were in some sort pleased therewith.'

From Long Melford the royal party went on to Hawstead, where, according to tradition, Elizabeth dropped a silver-handled fan into the moat. If she did, perhaps it was with astonishment at the extraordinary fountain that had been erected in her honour. She would have crossed a triple-arched bridge and come to a little wicket-gate. Through this was visible a full-length stone figure of Hercules, holding a club in his right hand and urinating into a basin. It is not recorded what the Queen's reaction to this was. With all her oft-acclaimed virginity, she could swear like a trooper and perhaps was not easily shocked. In fact her amazement may have been greater at seeing the pyracanthus shrubs that covered the walls of the inner court where the statue stood, for pyracanthus, with its white flowers and scarlet berries, was then a plant of extreme rarity.

When the Queen first visited Sir Nicholas Bacon (Lord Keeper, father of the essayist) at Gorhambury, she found the house elegant enough but criticised its lack of size. 'You have made your house too little for your Lordship,' she remarked.

'No, Madam,' Bacon replied, 'but your Highness has made me too big for the house.'

Gorhambury had been built on lands which had belonged to St Albans Abbey. As the Queen saw it then, it presented a plain gabled façade, 115 feet (35 metres) in length, with a central archway. Two towers and a belfry provided a vertical accent, and the walls were rendered in white plaster. Embellishment was not to be found until one entered the main courtyard, where the traditional Gothic (as in the Great Hall) mingled oddly with the fashionable Italianate (as in the Renaissance porch). The house had taken five and a half years to build, and was completed in 1568, at a total cost of £3,177 11s. 9½d.

Though Gorhambury had style, its dimensions were modest. The Hall was decorated with paintings of the feasts of the gods, yet it measured a mere 35 by 20 feet (11 x 6 metres). Bacon took the Queen's criticism to heart, and by the time she paid her second visit, five years later (27 May 1577), he had doubled the size of his house, incorporating a Tuscan colonnade and over it a fine new west gallery 120 feet (37 metres) in length.

Bacon frequently referred to his friend Lord Burghley for advice when it came to entertaining the Queen and his establishment at Gorhambury became a byword for elegance. 'At every meale, according to the season of the year, he had his table strewed with Sweet Herbes and Flowers... When his Lordship was in his Country-house at Gorhambury, St Albans seemed as if the Court were there, so Nobly did he live.'[1]

Gorhambury was particularly famous for its lovely gardens. The gateway to the orchard was adorned with a figure of Orpheus, together with an inscription recording how barbarous the place had been, full of prancing satyrs and howling wild beasts, until tamed by the coming of the god of music. In the orchard was a small banqueting-house (banquets were not then great feasts but delicate and fanciful repasts, such as Capulet's 'trifling foolish banquet' in *Romeo and Juliet* for which his guests did not bother to stay). This was a pretty little building with the Liberal Arts depicted on the walls — much more tasteful, it sounds, than the crudity of Hawstead.

The Queen's visit of 1577 lasted for five days. Bacon had

[1] John Aubrey, *Brief Lives.*

brought in twelve cooks from London for the occasion, paying them an average of £1 each. Sixty sheep, eight oxen, eighteen calves, thirty-four lambs and ten kids were provided, and Bacon laid out an extremely large sum on buying birds for the royal table:

'*Achates in Fowls* Item, Capons of all kinds 206, £16. 5s. 4d. Pullets of all kinds, 21s. Chickins 31 dozen and 8, £6. 6s. 8d. Geese 10 dozen and 6, 12s. Herons 12 dozen and 8, £26. 13s. 4d. Bitterns 8 dozen and 10, £17. 4s. 2d. Ducklings 12 dozen, £3. 13s. Pigeons 19 dozen and 7, 42s. 10d. Birds of the West 18 dozen and 7, 18s. 7d. Godwittes 2 dozen, £4. Dotterds 14, 9s. 4d. Shovelerrs 13, 43s. 4d. Pheasants 2 dozen and 5, £3. 12. 6d. Partridges 14, 11s. 8d. Quails 16 dozen and 9, £8. 7s. 6d. Maychicks 17 dozen, £3. 8s. Malards 23, 15s. 4d. Teals 12, 4s. Larks 3 dozen and 9, 2s. 6d. Curlews 3, 4s. Knots 1 dozen, 4s.'

The total cost of the visit was £577 6s. 7½d. — not an unreasonable sum for such open-handed hospitality.

Bacon's expense at Gorhambury was paltry compared with that of the nineteen-day extravaganza staged by the Earl of Leicester at Kenilworth in 1575. The entertainment at Kenilworth was so remarkable that it was the subject of a detailed account by Robert Laneham,[2] his gentleman-usher. Laneham seems to have been a colourful character, not without education and accomplishments. He went to St Paul's School, then became a merchant-venturer, trading with France and Flanders. He was a fair linguist, enjoyed music, dancing and stories. He may also have been an actor or a writer. Impressed with all this talent, the Earl took him into his service. 'I now go in my silks,' wrote Laneham, 'that else might rustle in my cut canvas.' During the royal visit, he was 'always amongst the gentlewomen', and was nicknamed the Black Prince.

The Castle of Kenilworth, Laneham considered, had two great advantages: a large lake curving round to the south and west, and to the north and west an extensive chase, well stocked with red as well as fallow deer. Diana herself might have hunted in it, he remarked. The lake was spanned towards its northern tip by a well-built timber bridge, 14 feet (4 metres) wide and 600 feet (183 metres) long, linking the chase with the castle.

The Queen arrived on Saturday 9 July, and was met by Leicester

---

[2] It is in the form of a letter to Master Humphrey Martin. Two copies are in the Bodleian Library.

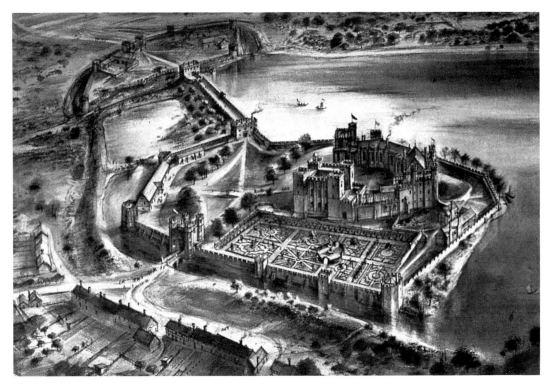

Kenilworth Castle, a reconstruction of its appearance at the time of the Queen's visit in 1575.

at Long Itchington, seven miles away from Kenilworth. Long Itchington was also one of his properties. After dinner they spent the afternoon hunting[3] and arrived at Kenilworth at 8 p.m. At the first gate of the castle Elizabeth was greeted by a sybil clothed in white silk, and at the Tiltyard Gate by a ranting giant of a porter, trudging to and fro, who at the Queen's coming gave up his keys and club, knelt and begged her forgiveness. This granted, he ordered the six trumpeters to sound a welcome. The real trumpeters were concealed behind huge pasteboard figures eight foot (2.5 metres) high, with trumpets 5 foot (1.5 metres) long. The Queen rode on into the Base Court and here she was greeted by the Lady of the Lake (much of the entertainment at Kenilworth being based on Arthurian legend). She and her attendant nymphs had reputedly arrived on a movable island (presumably a raft) from the middle of the water. She made a speech about the history of the

[3] George Turberville's *Book of Hunting* illustrates her picnicking at Long Itchington.

castle, and told how she had been guardian of the lake since Arthur's time, and was now offering it to Elizabeth. Her comment was that she thought it was hers already.

To the sound of oboes, shawms and horns, the Queen moved on to the castle gate. A bridge had been constructed there, seventy feet (21 metres) in length with side-rails and seven pairs of posts. On the first pair were wire cages full of live birds, purporting to be a gift from Sylvanus, god of birds and woods; on the second, silvered bowls of fruit and nuts (allegedly from Pomona); on the third, bowls of wheat, barley and oats (from Ceres, goddess of corn); on the fourth, grapes and wine (from Bacchus). The fifth pair of posts supported trays of fish (from Neptune); the sixth, two ragged staves with arms and armour (from Mars, god of war), and the last all sorts of musical instruments — lutes, viols, shawms, cornets, flutes, recorders and harps (from Phoebus Apollo, god of music).

There was a further welcome from a poet dressed in blue silk and crowned with bay. Then, to the sound of flute music, the Queen was escorted to her lodgings. Even then all was not quiet; guns and fireworks were shot into the night, audible twenty miles away.

On the next day, Sunday, after morning service in the parish church, the afternoon was spent in listening to 'excellent music of sundry sweet instruments' and in dancing. In the evening there were more fireworks, blazing and thundering till past midnight.

The Monday was hot and sultry, so the Queen stayed indoors until five, when she went hunting. Returning by torchlight at nine o'clock, she was met by a '*Hombre Salvagio*' (wild man or woodwose) covered in moss and ivy and carrying an oak tree. This was George Gascoigne,[4] the author of the entertainments. He spoke, in verse, a dialogue with Echo. Is the rejoicing for a king or a queen, he asked. 'Queen,' Echo replied.

'And who gave all these gifts? I pray thee, Echo, say; Was it not he who (but of late) this building here did lay?'

'Dudley,' answered Echo.

As a gesture of submission to the Queen, the woodwose broke his tree in two; the top flew off and almost hit the head of her horse. 'No hurt, no hurt,' she said, to everyone's relief.

More hunting took place the next day — a deer was caught, de-eared, but allowed to go free — and on the Thursday bear-baiting. Leicester had thirteen bears in the inner court, and to these were unleashed 'bandogs' or small mastiffs; a 'sport very

---

[4] George Gascoigne's *Princely Pleasures at the Court of Kenilworth* was first published in 1576, and gives the full text of the entertainments.

pleazaunt' declared Laneham. It seems extraordinary that the Queen — in most other respects a woman of sensibility - could take pleasure in it. In the evening there were spectacular fireworks, which appeared to continue burning even under the water, and an Italian acrobat who impressed everyone with his 'goinges, turninges, tumblinges, castinges, hops, jumps, leaps, soomersauts, caprettiez and flights'. So flexible was he, Laneham said, that it seemed his backbone was made of lute-strings.

Wet and windy weather precluded outdoor events for the next two days. After that, on the Sunday (feast of St Kenelm) the Queen went again to service in the parish church. In the afternoon a country wedding, or bride-ale, was celebrated in the castle grounds. The clownish bridegroom was somewhat lame as he had broken his leg playing football. He was wearing his father's tawny worsted jacket, a straw hat and harvest gloves, with an inkhorn at his back and a muffler hanging from his belt. He and his sixteen friends tried their skill at a quintain[5] which had been set up. Then there was morris-dancing, with six dancers, a Maid Marian and a fool. In came three girls carrying spice-cakes, and a simpleton (much pestered by flies) brought the bride-cup. At last came the bride, thirty-five years old and rather ugly, accompanied by twelve bridesmaids. The festivities in the courtyard continued with a pageant-play performed by men of Coventry. The Queen watched from an upstairs window, and asked to see the play in its entirety the following Tuesday. After supper there was another play, and after that an 'ambrosial banquet' (though the Queen, it was noticed, ate little or nothing) and a masque.

Five gentlemen were knighted the next day and nine people were touched for the King's Evil, or scrofula, which was said to be cured by the monarch's touch; but because of the hot weather Elizabeth did not emerge from her lodgings until about five when she went hunting. On her return she was greeted with a water-pageant, including an eighteen-foot (5.5 metres) mermaid, the Lady of the Lake, a wicked Knight called Sir Bruce Sans Pitee, and Arion riding and singing on a dolphin twenty-four feet (7 metres) long and containing a consort of six instruments.

The purpose of all this lavish entertainment — from which Leicester's finances never recovered — was to be made clear in the open-air performance planned for the Wednesday, the last full day of the Queen's visit. Leicester had commissioned George

---

[5] Quintain: post set up as mark and often provided with sandbag to swing round and strike unskilful tilter (*Oxford Illustrated Dictionary*).

George Gascoigne, poet and dramatist, presenting one of his works to Elizabeth I.

Gascoigne to write a masque of Diana and her nymphs along the following lines: Diana, hunting with her companions, remembers how it was that seventeen years ago she lost one of her favourite nymphs, Zabeta. ('Zabeta' is based on the last part of the Queen's name and clearly refers to her.) One of the nymphs suggests that Zabeta is now a follower of Juno, goddess of marriage, although Diana (goddess of chastity as well as hunting) maintains that she is still loyal to her. They search for Zabeta. Meanwhile there is an interlude in which a man covered in moss says he is the son of the woodwose who appeared on the Monday of the previous week; he says his father lies languishing and will continue to do so unless the Queen removes the film from his eyes. He sends Mercury in a cloud to comfort her and bring her to him since the nymphs can find no sign of Zabeta. Diana (Chastity) invokes the aid of her father, Jupiter. Diana thinks she has won. But Iris, goddess of the rainbow, is sent by Juno to tell the Queen (Zabeta) that she should not be carried away by Mercury's or Diana's fine words, and that she will find more reason for following Juno rather than Diana. Diana, she reminds the Queen, did nothing to help her when she was imprisoned as a princess.

The purpose of the whole masque was to persuade Elizabeth that it was the general wish that she should not stay single but marry the Earl of Leicester.

George Gascoigne had rehearsed the show and kept it in readiness for two or three days, with all the actors in their costumes. They intended to stage it at Wedgenall, about three miles away from the castle, and a 'fair pavilion' had been set up for the purpose. But, unfortunately, the Wednesday was hopelessly wet, and the Queen kept indoors. Even worse, she had decided to leave the following day, so the entertainment was never performed. 'The cause whereof', notes Gascoigne,' I cannot attribute to any other thing than to lack of opportunity and seasonable weather.'

Leicester, by now desperate that Elizabeth might have missed the point of all his fabulous extravaganza, quickly commissioned George Gascoigne to write and perform a suitable farewell. Gascoigne, accomplished in improvisation, dressed himself as Sylvanus, god of the woods, and offered to accompany the Queen as she went. He described to her the joy of all who welcomed her at Kenilworth, how at her coming 'the trees florish in more than ordinarie bravery, the grasse growes greener than it was wont to do, and the deer went tripping ... in extreme delicacie and delight', even though they were about to be killed. The recent storms, he said, were made by the gods weeping at the Queen's imminent departure.

Perhaps she found him tedious, but Gascoigne was untiring in his efforts. He told her there was no need for her to slacken her pace on his account — he would ride beside her and continue his tale for twenty miles yet. He said he would rather be Her Majesty's footman in this world than a god on horseback in the next. One of Diana's nymphs, he informed her, was called Ahtebasile (meaning ah, thou queen), otherwise known as Completa or Complacide. There were two brothers who served her, Due Desert and Deepe Desire; Due Desert was changed into a laurel tree, and Deepe Desire (meaning Leicester) into a holly bush, 'now furnished on every side with sharp pricking leaves, to prove the restlesse prickes of his privie thoughts'.

At this point they came to a holly bush, and out of it stepped a man representing Deepe Desire. Never was such grief, he maintained, as at the Queen's departure. He begged her to prolong her stay at Kenilworth,

'Live here, good Queen, live here; you are amongst your friends.
Their comfort comes when you approach, and when you part it ends.'

He continued in song, accompanied by a consort of musical instruments, and culminating in a series of paradoxes:

'Oh farewell life, delightful death, farewell.
I die in heaven, yet live in darksome hell.'

The Queen rode on regardless.

So concluded the last and most famous of the Queen's visits to Kenilworth. Leicester had virtually staked his all in attempt to persuade her to relinquish her single state and marry him; and he had failed. It was about this time that he began to console himself with the rival charms of Lettice Knollys, Countess of Essex. Three years later he was to entertain the Queen again, this time in his property at Wanstead in Waltham Forest. No less a writer than Sir Philip Sidney was invited to devise an entertainment (this concerned a May-Lady, who was courted by two rivals, a forester and a shepherd — the Queen was to decide which was the more deserving). The visit lasted four or five days, and proceeded with the splendour and expense everyone was accustomed to expect. But less than a month later Leicester entered into a secret marriage with Lettice Knollys — the hope of a royal alliance, which had prompted the merry-making at Kenilworth, finally abandoned.

CHAPTER 6

ELIZABETH AND THE ARISTOCRATS - II

'Her Highness hath done honour to my poor house by visiting me, and seemed much pleased at what we did to please her. My son made a fair Speech, to which she did give a most gracious reply. The women did dance before her, whilst cornets did salute from the gallery; and she did vouchsafe to eat two morsels of rich comfit cake, and drank a small cordial from a gold cup. She had a marvellous suit of velvet borne by four of her first women attendants in rich apparell; two Ushers did go before, and at going up stairs she called for a staff, and was much wearied in walking about the house, and said she wished to come another day. Six drums and six trumpets waited in the Court, and sounded at her approach and departure.'

(Sir Robert Sidney, in a letter to Sir John Harington describing a visit from the Queen in 1600)

Whether the Queen should marry, and if so whom, was a question which continued to concern her subjects, especially her immediate circle of courtiers. Elizabeth was aware that if she married a foreign prince, there was a danger that the country from which he came would one day have too much sway in her kingdom; if he were a Roman Catholic the problem would be exacerbated by religious differences. Yet if she married one of her own subjects, that would give him and his family quite extraordinary power. In either case, what would happen if she should pre-decease her husband?

Eric of Sweden had tried to soften her heart by sending her eighteen large pied horses and two shiploads of treasure; but the gift left her unmoved and she maintained that she preferred a single life. What her true feelings were about love and marriage is not easy to ascertain; a poem ascribed to her may give some clue:

When I was fair and young and favour graced me,
Of many was I sought their mistress for to be,
But I did scorn them all and answered them therefore,
Go, go, go, seek some other where,
Importune me no more.

How many weeping eyes I made to pine with woe,
How many sighing hearts I have no skill to show,
Yet I the prouder grew, and answered them therefore,

> Go, go, go, seek some other where,
> Importune me no more.
>
> Then spake fair Venus' son, that proud vicorious boy,
> And said, fine dame since that you have been so coy,
> I will so pluck your plumes that you shall say no more
> Go, go, go, seek some other where,
> Importune me no more.
>
> When he had spake these words such change grew in my breast
> That neither day nor night since that I could take any rest,
> Then lo, I did repent of that I said before,
> Go, go, go, seek some other where,
> Importune me no more.

There is little doubt that she was genuinely attached to Leicester, and had it not been for the suspicious circumstances surrounding the death of his first wife, Amy Robsart (who was found dead at the bottom of the stairs at Cumnor Place), she might have been tempted to marry him. This would have been in spite of the Earl's unpopularity with almost all the other lords, and in particular Lord Burghley, whose opinion she greatly respected.

Burghley was in favour of her marrying the Duc d'Alençon, whom Elizabeth referred to with affectionate condescension as her 'little frog' — she was about twenty-five years older than him. It was in connection with the little frog's wooing that the French ambassadors were in London at Whitsuntide 1581, and they were royally entertained at Whitehall, with a show probably devised by Sir Philip Sidney.

At the end of the tiltyard was a gallery where the Queen would sit, and this was called the Fortress of Perfect Beauty. As a prelude to the performance, a boy announced to her as she came from chapel that some of her gallant knights would beseige the castle on 24 April (at the Queen's request this was postponed until 1st May), 'they will attempt anie thing for thy sake, and service of that earthlie and yet ... most heavenlie sun.'

The principal challengers were the Earl of Arundel, Lord Windsor, Philip Sidney and Fulke Greville. They called themselves 'The Foster Children of Desire'.

On the appointed day they entered the tiltyard in turn, each accompanied by trumpeters, pages, grooms and yeomen. They made a brave show, Sidney for instance:[1]

---

[1] The account is by Henry Goldwell, or Goldingham.

'Then proceeded Maister Philip Sidneie, in very sumptuous manner, with armour part blew, and the rest gilt and engraven, with four spare horses, having caparisons and furniture verie rich and costlie, as some of cloth of gold imbrodered with pearle, and some imbrodered with gold and silver feathers, laied with gold lace and hats of the same with gold bands and white feathers, and each one a paire of white buskins. Then he had thirtie Gentlemen and yeomen, and four Trumpetters, who were all in cassocke coats and Venetian hose of yellow velvet, laied with silver lace, yellow velvet caps with silver bands and white feathers, and everie one a paire of white buskins...'

On the first day each of Desire's Children ran six courses attempting to beseige the fortress. On the second day, worn out by their exertions, they entered the tiltyard in a chariot, seated round a lady representing Desire, and accompanied by a consort of musicians playing doleful strains. The horses drawing the chariot were caparisoned in white and carnation silk, the colours of desire. A herald requested the Queen (Beauty) to watch the attempts of Desire's Children, who were carried wherever Desire took them. More jousting followed. Then, in the evening, a boy in ash-coloured clothes with an olive-branch in his hand fell flat on his face in front of the Queen. He told her of the Foster Children of Desire's submission to Beauty; Virtue, he said, stands guard over her and is not to be overcome by Desire.

The meaning all this pageantry attempted to convey was that the Queen should remain virgin. Beauty had continued unassailable despite all the efforts of the gallant knights, and the implication was that the Duc d'Alençon would have no greater success.

He did not. He arrived full of hope at Michelmas, and left, honoured but disappointed, at Christmas.

Towards the end of her life, Elizabeth's principal favourite was Robert Devereux, Earl of Essex. An annual excuse for celebration was the anniversary of the Queen's accession, 17 November, and in 1595 the Earl provided an elaborate entertainment. 'There is great preparation for these triumphs,' wrote Rowland White to Sir Robert Sidney, 'and such Devices promised as our age hath not seen the like.'

Before the tilt the Queen sent her glove to the Earl in token that he was her champion. Francis Bacon was responsible for the allegorical part of the entertainments. The Earl, when he arrived, was met by a Hermit, a Secretary of State, a Soldier and a Squire.

Robert Devereux, Earl of Essex. (National Portrait Gallery)

The first three tried to persuade him to give up his vain love for the Queen and turn instead to meditation, matters of state, or warfare. But the Squire said that the knight will never forsake his love for his mistress, but give up his life to her service. For once the Queen seems to have had enough of flattery; she declared that if she had known there would be so much said about her, she would not have come.

The lords, nevertheless, continued to vie with one another and went to great lengths to impress her. She visited Sir Francis Carew at Bedington in Surrey during the month of August (1599). Sir Francis had a particularly fine cherry-tree; but cherries are generally over by July. So he had a canvas tent made to retard their ripening, and managed to postpone their fruiting season until the Queen came.

Her enthusiasm for progresses had not flagged, nor had her subjects' flair for ingenious flattery diminished. In August 1591 she visited Lord Montague at Cowdray Castle, just outside Midhurst in Sussex,[2] arriving at about 8 p.m. on Saturday the 15th. The approach to the grey stone castle was by a bridge over the River Rother and along a tree-lined avenue. Music sounded as she came, and she stopped her coach on the bridge to listen to a speech by a man dressed in armour, with a club in one hand and a key in the other. He was standing between two porters carved out of wood. He told her that they had been put to sleep by a spell, and that there was a prophecy that the walls of Cowdray would shake and the roof totter until it was visited by the wisest, fairest and most fortunate of beings. Now, of course, this moment had arrived; he greeted her with fulsome epithets and handed her the key. Getting down from the coach, the Queen embraced Lady Montague and her daughter, then retired to her lodgings.

There was a great feast the next day, and no less than three oxen and a hundred and forty geese were provided — for breakfast! But there is no record of other entertainment being provided until the Monday. Elizabeth and her courtiers rose early to go riding in the park, and there they found an elegant bower had been constructed. Musicians performed; one dressed as a nymph sang and gave the

[2] Cowdray Castle was a courtyard house built for William FitzWilliam Earl of Southampton during the reign of Henry VIII. On Southampton's death in 1543, it passed to his half brother, Sir Anthony Browne. Browne was proxy for the King at his marriage with Anne of Cleves; another of his delicate missions was the arrest of his cousin, Margaret, Countess of Salisbury. Another Anthony Browne, Viscount Montague, succeeded in 1592 at the age of twenty-four. The chief feature of the castle's interior was the Buck Hall, adorned with eleven carved oak bucks. This, and almost all the rest of the castle, was destroyed by fire in 1793.

Elizabeth I by Marcus Gheeraerts the Younger

Banquet and masque from the Memorial Picture of Sir Henry Unton,
c.1596. The masque of Diana and her nymphs is accompanied by a 'broken'
consort of musicians; masque presented on royal occasions are likely to have
been more elaborate than this, yet the inclusion of the crowned figure of
Diana, goddess of the moon, hunting and chastity, may be a reference to the
Queen herself. (National Portrait Gallery)

Queen a crossbow. Rather than have all the deer running wild in
the grounds, where she might very well have missed them, thirty or
forty had been rounded up into a paddock. Of these she killed three
or four, and the Countess of Kildare tactfully restricted herself to

87

one. They rode back to the castle for dinner, then, at about six, went up into one of the turrets to watch sixteen bucks being pulled down by greyhounds. These bloody and somewhat unedifying sports had been arranged by Lord Montague's third son, Henry, who was Ranger of Windsor Forest.

The next day, after dining at the priory, the Queen went to view 'my Lord's walks'. There she met a Pilgrim dressed in russet velvet, with scallop-shells of cloth of silver on his hat. After a flattering speech he led her to an oak-tree hung with coats-of-arms of the nobility and gentry of the county. A woodwose (or wild man) clothed in ivy appeared on the scene and explained that the deeply rooted oak symbolized the Queen herself. Three more bucks were killed by hounds before she went back to the castle for supper.

On the Wednesday there was a magnificent picnic. A table 24 yards (22 metres) long was set up in the 'walks'. Having dined there, the Queen and her courtiers walked to a 'goodly fishpond'. There stood an angler. He had had no luck, he said, he had been there two hours and caught nothing. There was another fisherman drawing his nets near where the Queen stood; he told her of an old saying that you can catch fish only when the water is calm and the sovereign virtuous. Then he drew in his net and deposited a huge pile of fish at Elizabeth's feet.

The weather seems to have held fine for this visit and it was possible for the Queen to have another alfresco dinner the next day; this time the table was 48 yards (44 metres) long. In the evening she enjoyed watching country people dancing to tabor and pipe. When she left on the Friday, she passed through an escort of six gentlemen[3] whom she knighted. They left their escutcheons hanging with the others on the oak-tree.

A month later the Queen enjoyed perhaps the most extra-ordinary of all the receptions prepared for her. Edward Seymour, the Earl of Hertford, was anxious to buy his way back into her favour. He had made a secret marriage to Catherine, the younger sister of Lady Jane Grey. This alliance was felt by the Queen to be not merely imprudent but very possibly traitorous, and he was penalized by a nine-year period of imprisonment and a fine of £15,000. Consequently, when it came to entertaining Elizabeth, he felt he should make an exceptional effort and outdo his peers.

Hertford's house at Elvetham, near Odiham in Hampshire, was neither large enough nor grand enough for the purpose. So he

---

[3] Sir George Browne (Lord Montague's son), Sir Robert Dormer, Sir Henry Goring, Sir Henry Glenham, Sir John Carvell and Sir Nicholas Parker.

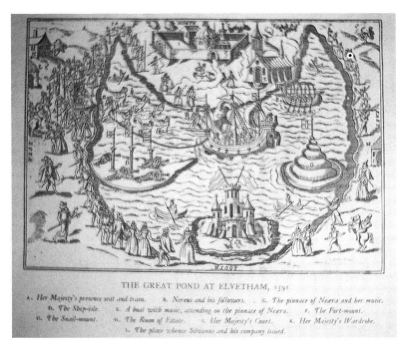

THE GREAT POND AT ELVETHAM, 1591

A. *Her Majesty's presence seat and train.*   B. *Nereus and his followers.*   C. *The pinnace of Neæra and her music.*
D. *The Ship-isle.*   E. *A boat with music, attending on the pinnace of Neæra.*   F. *The Fort-mount.*
G. *The Snail-mount.*   H. *The Room of Estate.*   I. *Her Majesty's Court.*   K. *Her Majesty's Wardrobe.*
L. *The place whence Silvanus and his company issued.*

Entertainment provided for the Queen's visit to Elvetham, 1591. (From Nichols's Progresses and Public Processions of Queen Elizabeth).

employed three hundred workmen to make a suitable setting ready for the Queen's visit in 1591. The new buildings were put up on a hillside in the park at a little distance from the house. They seem to have been exhibition architecture, rather than permanent structures. A state-room was erected; the outside walls were covered with branches and clusters of hazelnuts, the roof with ivy, the interior with tapestries, and the floor with sweet-smelling rushes and herbs. At the end of it a withdrawing chamber was provided for the Queen. Near this were put up the service rooms — spicery, larder, wine-celler, pantry, ewery, and chandlery where candles were kept. Then there was a great hall for the use of the knights, ladies and gentlemen, accommodation for the Queen's footmen 'and their friends', a guardroom, a room for Lord Hertford's steward and another for the gentlemen who waited at table. Nearby was set up a buttery, a pitcher-house, a bake-house with five new ovens, some of them fourteen foot (4 metres) deep, a main kitchen with four ranges and a place for boiling meat, and another kitchen with just one long range. Then there was a boiling-house, a scullery, and a room for the cook. These last were all temporary buildings, roofed with timber or canvas.

Between all these and the Earl's house, he had a large half-moon pond dug. This contained three man-made islands: one in the shape of a Ship a hundred feet (30 metres) long with three trees for masts, a Fort twenty feet (6 metres) square and surrounded with willows, and a Snail Mount with spiralling green hedges rising from a base forty feet (12 metres) across to a height in the centre of twenty feet (6 metres). Between the islands were moored various boats which could hold musicians, notably a fine pinnace complete with masts, rigging, snails, anchors, gaily coloured flags and pennants.

The Queen was expected at supper-time on Monday 20 September. In the morning the Earl gathered all his servants together and reminded them of their duties. Then after dinner he rode out, with two hundred or more men in his train, to meet the Queen as she came out of Odiham Park and escort her to Elvetham. Half-way between the park gate and the house she found herself greeted by a Poet dressed in green and wearing a laurel-wreath. He addressed her on his knees, and refused a cushion offered to him by a boy, saying 'For now we kneel to more than usual saints.' His verse-speech expressed how all living things rejoiced at her coming, 'the milke-white heifer wantons with the bull'. Only Envy was displeased and had laid obstructions in the Queen's path. These were symbolically removed by six virgins, who represented the Three Graces and the Three Hours; then they accompanied Elizabeth to the house, strewing the way with flowers and singing a six-part madrigal with the refrain,

> 'O beauteous Queen of second Troy
> Accept of our unfeigned joy.'

She dismounted at the door and was welcomed by the Countess and her ladies. Whatever the Queen may have thought about her previously, she now embraced and kissed her, so it seemed all was forgiven. Before supper, guns fired a salute from the Ship Isle and the Snail Mount, and afterwards the Earl, knowing his sovereign's excellent taste in music, had provided a consort of six musicians to perform for her. They played a pavane which had been composed by Thomas Morley when he was organist at St Paul's. The piece pleased her so much that she allowed it to be renamed after her.

The next morning was wet and stormy, but by dinnertime it had cleared up. The Queen dined in the newly constructed state room, while a consort of music sounded. Afterwards, at about four, there was a water-pageant. She sat under a canopy of green satin trimmed with silver lace, which had been set up at the edge of the pond. Opposite was a bower containing characters connected with the sea — Nereus the sea-prophet, five tritons and the gods Neptune, Oceanus, Phorcus and Glaucus. They waded or swam across towards her, drawing with them the pinnace on board which were singers, musicians and the Nymph of the Sea Neaera. Meanwhile lurking in the woods was Sylvanus, in love with Neaera. Rival orations between Nereus and Sylvanus culminated in Sylvanus being toppled into the water, to the great glee of the sea gods. Sylvanus scrambled up the bank, crying vengeance. However, Nereus declared that in the Queen's presence all this squabbling should cease. The entertainment ended with a speech by Neaera who presented her with a fan-shaped jewel, and the Queen named the pinnace the *Bonadventure*. She was delighted with the water-pageant, and rewarded the actors handsomely.

When the Queen opened her casement window next morning, she was serenaded by three excellent musicians. They sang a pastoral song about Corydon and Fair Phyllida so well that she commanded an encore. Then, after dinner, ten of the Earl of Hertford's servants (all Somerset men) played a game they called 'bord and cord', rather like five-a-side volley-ball. The Queen watched them for over an hour and a half. After supper fireworks were let off from the three islands in the pond, 'fire-wheels, pikes of pleasure, and balles of wilde fire, which burned in the water'. Meanwhile a torch-lit banquet of about a thousand dishes was served in the lower gallery in the garden.

The next day, Thursday, Elizabeth had no sooner appeared at her window than the Fairy Queen and her maidens came dancing across the garden. They sang a song in six parts, accompanied by a sextet consisting of lute, pandora, bass-viol, cittern, treble-viol and flute. The music was composed by Edward Johnson, and the words ran:

> Elisa is the fairest Queene
> That ever trod upon this greene.
> Elisa's eyes are blessed Starres,
> Inducing peace, subduing warres.
> Elisa's hand is crystal bright,
> Her wordes are balme, her lookes are light.
> Elisa's breast is that faire hill
> Where Virtue dwells, and sacred skill.
> O blessed be each day and hour
> Where sweet Elisa builds her bower.[4]

---

[4] A modern recording is in *Elizabethan Lute Songs* (James Bowman, counter-tenor, with lute and viols), E.M.I- (EMX 2101).

The Queen was so pleased that she had them repeat the song three times, and gave a generous reward to the performers.

It was a fitting ending to a reception which had excelled in spectacle and music. As she left, going through Elvetham Park, she passed the characters from the shows - Nereus and the sea gods, Sylvanus and his men of the woods, the Three Graces and the Three Hours, all in attitudes of woe because of her departure. It was pouring with rain, appropriately enough, as the Poet pointed out in his farewell speech, 'For how can Summer stay, when Sunne departs?'

An intricate duet, 'Come Again, faire Nature's Treasure', accompanied by a consort of instrumentalists, was sung as she reached the park gate. Despite the weather, the Queen stopped her coach to listen, and took off her mask to thank the musicians. To the Earl of Hertford she promised she would never forget her stay at Elvetham, where so many ingenious and exquisite things had been provided for her delight.

CHAPTER 7

AN END TO PROGRESSES

'She was a Lady adorned with Majesty, Learning, Languages, Wisdom and Piety; yet fearful of death, for she hated any word that tended to it.... Roger Lord North, when carving one day at dinner, the Queen asked what the covered dish was; he lifting up the cover replied, 'Madam, it is a coffin'; a word which moved the Queen to anger. 'And are you such a fool', said she, 'to give a pie such a name?' This gave warning to the Courtiers not to use any word that mentioned her death.'

(Sir Edward Peyton, *Divine Catastrophe of the Kingly Family of the House of Stuarts,* 1652)

Not stopping to request an audience, nor even to wash, the Earl of Essex burst into the Queen's bed chamber. He had arrived back from a disastrous campaign in Ireland and had ridden headlong to Nonsuch. But more than the failure of that campaign, which has cost £300,000 and the lives of 12,000 men, what sealed the Earl's downfall was his extraordinary presumption. He found the Queen in a state of undress, her red wig still on its stand, her face bare of the elaborate make-up behind which it was now habitually concealed, and her grey hair in wisps around her temples.

It was an entry so tactless that she never forgave him. Had she known what she actually looked like, retribution might have come even more swiftly; but for years now she had seen her face only in a distorting mirror that flattered. Therefore she did not hesitate to present it on progresses and to relish the compliments perpetually bestowed on her. Meanwhile her continuing energy and enthusiasm became to her courtiers a source of wonder, and sometimes of exasperation.

On 23 June 1600, very shortly after Essex's downfall (at this time he was under house arrest; he was beheaded on 25 February 1601), the Queen attended the wedding of Lord Herbert to Anne Russell at Blackfriars. Elizabeth rode in a litter carried by six knights. After supper the celebrations continued with a masque of eight ladies. They were dressed in cloth of silver with mantles of crimson taffeta. After their performance, the leader among them went up to the Queen and invited her to take part as well. Elizabeth asked what role she was to play. 'Affection', was the reply. 'Affection,' said the Queen, remembering with bitterness the Earl of Essex, 'is false.' However, she rose to her feet and danced.

There was talk of a progress into Wiltshire later that summer, then of a week's visit to Farnham Castle. On 12 August she finally set off, but only as far as Nonsuch, going via Tooting, and from there — having been so regally entertained on her last visit — to the Earl of Hertford's seat at Elvetham. 'The Lords are sorry for it,' was the comment,[1] 'but her Majesty lets the old stay behind, and the young and able to goe with her. She had just cause to be offended, that at her remove to this place she was so poorly attended, for I never saw so small a train.'

She visited Bedington, dined with the Archbishop of Canterbury at Croydon, returned to Nonsuch, and before the end of the month was at Oatlands near Weybridge. 'The Court is now given over to hunting and sports... on Thursday her Majesty dines and hunts at Hanworth Parke; upon Tuesday she dines at Mr Drake's; and this day she hunts in the new lodge in the forest. God be thanked she is very merry and well.'

The Master of the Sports was Lord Nottingham. On 12 September the indefatigable Queen was still hunting, 'Every second day she is on horseback, and continues the sport long; it is thought she will remayne in Oatlands till fowle weather drives her away.'[2]

There was something frenetic about all this activity. Nor did it slacken in the winter. On St Stephen's Day (Boxing Day) having watched two galliards performed by Mrs Mary Whyte and a celebrated dancer called Mr Palmer, she could not refrain from joining in herself, and stepped with Mr Palmer into a coranto.

Even more than before, the Queen was showered with allegorical compliments. Mary, Countess of Pembroke wrote a verse dialogue in praise of her as Astraea; Richard Vennard an equally adulatory poem *The Miracle of Nature,* and a flattering masque called *A Lottery* was performed in front of her at Sir Thomas Egerton's York House. This last was introduced by a Mariner, and the theme was the same as had been presented to her at Cowdray: no fish can be caught unless the sea is calm and the sovereign virtuous.

Elizabeth's last progress seems to have been in July 1602. She had intended to go via Sir John Fortescue's house in Buckinghamshire and Elvetham once more, and then on to Bath and Bristol, but this ambitious itinerary was abandoned. To the

[1] *Sidney Papers,* Vol. II.
[2] *Sidney Papers,* Vol. II.

Elizabeth I in old age. (Corsham Court)

customary ringing of church bells, she moved from Greenwich to
Chiswick, and then on to Harefield Place near Uxbridge, the
country seat of the Lord Keeper, Sir Thomas Egerton and his wife,
the Dowager Countess of Derby. The Countess was a literary lady
(celebrated in verse by poets from Spenser to Milton), and she
seems to have taken charge of the entertainments.

The Queen was met by a Dairymaid called Joan and a Bailiff.
Joan tells the Bailiff how she has been kept awake all night by 'the
chatting of the pyes [magpies] and the chirkinge of the frisketts'
[crickets?], and these noises foretell the coming of a stranger. In
case the stranger is someone important, even the Queen herself,
they decide to prepare all sorts of dainties — possets, fruit,
syllabubs, cheese and clotted cream — and they have two jewels to

95

present, in the form of a rake and a fork. It is all very reminiscent of the rustic feast in Shakespeare's *A Winter's Tale*.

After the Queen had dismounted (she still rode, it seems), she was greeted by two actors, one dressed to resemble a brick house, representing Place, and the other with yellow hair, wearing a green robe and carrying an hour-glass, representing Time. The hour-glass was stopped, not running, to signify that time stood still at the Queen's coming. They had come together, they told her, to welcome the Goddess of the Sun. Both Time and Place are full of joy at her visit, and they have a diamond jewel in the shape of a heart to present to her that is 'mistress of all the hearts in the world'. On the Monday (St Swithun's Day) Elizabeth, Lady Walsingham gave her a robe of rainbow colours, and called the ageing queen (she was now sixty-nine),

> Beauty's Rose and Virtue's book,
> Angel's mind and Angel's look.

Even if St Swithun had sent the rain, she told her, Iris the goddess of the rainbows would come. No rainbow without the sun, she implied (the inscription on the Rainbow portrait of Elizabeth at Hatfield).

As the Queen was leaving, Place, now wearing widow's weeds, made a doleful speech of farewell, 'Time can go with you, Persons can go with you; they can move like Heaven; but I, like dull Earth, must stand unmoveable. I could wish myself like the enchanted Castle of Love, to hold you here for ever', but must now stay forsaken and desolate. The Queen was asked to forgive the fact that it had rained so much during her visit — the responsibility was not Place's, she was assured, but St Swithun's.

Persistent rain deterred Elizabeth from going on any further progress and she stayed at Oatlands, moving on 8 October to Richmond. Despite the weather, she seemed well enough. 'The Queen's health and disposition', wrote Sir Fulke Greville to the Countess of Shrewsbury, 'I assure you, is excellent good; and I have not seen her every way better disposed these many years.' But smallpox was rife, and this, together with the weather, made her put off another visit to Lord Hertford's at Elvetham. She was back at Whitehall in November for the customary Accession Day tilts, but ultimately her health gave way.

'No, Robin, I am not well,' she confided to Sir Robert Carey when he came to pay his respects. She sighed deeply many times, and told him of the heaviness that had come over her during the last ten or twelve days.

Elizabeth had been ill, on and off, since the middle of January 1603. She had been warned by her astrologer, Dr Dee, not to remain at Whitehall, and so, during one of her periods of comparative health, she moved to Richmond.

Indomitable to the last, the Queen struggled against her final illness. For four days she lay on cushions, refusing to take any nourishment, go to bed, or see any of her physicians. The ladies in waiting, not being allowed to go to bed either, drooped with fatigue. Elizabeth, whose beauty was still extolled, but who had grown lined and raddled, her teeth blackened with eating too many sweetmeats, had not for the last twenty years seen her face in a true looking-glass. Now she asked to see one, and burst into a storm of rage over all those who had praised her with such empty flattery.

Death-mask of Elizabeth I. (Penshurst Place)

97

But by Wednesday 23 March she had lost the power of speech. When James VI of Scotland was named as her successor, she put her hands to her head as if in the act of crowning, and this was taken as signifying her assent.

At about six in the evening she made signs for Archbishop Whitgift and her chaplains to come to her. He questioned her concerning her faith; she replied by raising her eyes and lifting up her hands. The old Archbishop continued long praying upon his knees until, stiff and weary, he blessed her, hoping he might now be free to rise and go. But the Queen made a gesture with her hand signifying that he should go on praying, which he did for half an hour more, then tried again to leave her, but the almost exhausted Archbishop was forced to pray fervently on his knees for another half-hour. The Queen showed herself to be much comforted by this, and everyone except her ladies was allowed to go. It was not long after, at about three o'clock in the morning, that she breathed her last.

Her body was embalmed, wrapped in lead covered with velvet, placed in a strong coffin, and brought to Whitehall to lie in state. Yet it was reported that it burst, and broke open the cerecloth, lead and timber with a loud crack, and the coffining had to be done all over again.

Just as Elizabeth's first public progress may be said to have been her christening, her last was her funeral. It took place over a month after her death.[3] A long and elaborate procession was lined up, comprising not only the wealthy and influential, but also quite humble people. In the front of the cortège were fifteen poor men and 260 poor women, as well as all manner of servants — children who worked in the woodyard, scullery, pantry, scalding-house and larder, grooms, yeomen, clerks and sergeants from various offices, the Queen's chief cook, her physicians and musicians, the Gentleman and Children of the Chapel Royal dressed in surplices and singing as they went. Then came the gentlemen-ushers, the Cofferer, the Clerk of the Wardrobe, the Queen's chaplains and French and Latin secretaries. Between these groups were carried heraldic standards — the Dragon, the Greyhound and the Lion, the Portcullis, the Rouge Dragon and the Rouge Cross, the Banner of Cornwall.

Then walked the civic dignitaries, the Masters of the Revels, the Tents and the Jewel-house, the Knights Bachelor, the Lord Chief Justice, the Gentleman of the Privy Chamber, the Gentlemen

[3] These particulars are taken from a description by Henry Petowe.

Pensioners holding poll-axes head downwards and draped in black.

The Lord Mayor of London followed, then the Controller and Treasurer of the Royal Household, the Master of Requests; there were barons, bishops (including the Bishop of Chichester who was to preach at the funeral), earls, earls' eldest sons, marquesses, the Lord Keeper, the Archbishop of Canterbury, the French ambassador, and various heraldic kings-at-arms. Earl and viscounts carried the banners of the realm: Wales, Ireland and finally England.

The climax of the procession was the Queen's coffin. It was carried in a chariot draped in black and drawn by four horses. Six knights held a canopy over it, and it was escorted by six earls, twelve noblemen, and the gentlemen-ushers carrying white rods. The Earl of Worcester, as Master of the Horse, led Elizabeth's palfrey, accompanied by two squires and a groom. After Garter Kings-at-Arms came the chief mourner, the Marchioness of Northampton, then the Lord Treasurer, the Lord Admiral, more earls, countesses, viscountesses and Ladies of Honour. Aloft were borne twelve great banners illustrating the Queen's lineage, from Henry II and Eleanor of Aquitaine to Henry VIII and Anne Boleyn, all of them carried by noblemen.

But what moved spectators most was the sight of the figure lying on the coffin. Sculpted in wax, it showed the Queen in her parliamentary robes, crowned, with the orb and sceptre in her hands. The streets of Westminster were thronged with people as the procession moved slowly towards the Abbey. They crowded the rooftops, they clung to gutters and craned out of windows. As the coffin passed, reports Stow in his *Annals,* 'there was such a generall sighing, groning, and weeping as the like hath not been seene or knowne in the memorie of man, neyther doth any historie mention any people, time or state, to make like lamentation for the death of their Soveraygne.'

In death, as in life, she had drawn the hearts of her people after her.

GREAT HOUSES OF ELIZABETHAN ENGLAND

HATFIELD HOUSE

'The King lately went to see his bastard daughter, who is twenty miles away, and the princess with her.' So wrote the ambassador Eustace Chapuys to his master the Emperor Charles V. By bastard he meant Elizabeth, and by princess, Mary; the setting was at Hatfield and the date 17 January 1534. The infant Elizabeth was aged sixteen months; Henry VIII had gone down to the old palace to dandle her on his knee. Mary was seventeen, and had been deputed to act as her baby sister's lady-in-waiting. The King refused to see his elder daughter because she would not recognize her mother's divorce or renounce her own title as heir to the throne. He had sent Cromwell to try to persuade her otherwise, but he failed and Henry ordered that she should be granted no access during his stay. Mary asked leave at least to come and kiss his hand, but he was adamant. As he was departing, however, it was reported that she ran up to a balcony to catch a glimpse of him. The King turned to see her kneeling with her hands clasped together. He touched his hat and bowed to her before he rode away.

The part of the old palace where this episode is said to have taken place still stands at Hatfield; Chapuys describes it as a 'terrace at the top of the house', and it would have overlooked the main courtyard. For originally the palace was a four-square building with this court in the centre. It was constructed in brick and housed the bishops of Ely; Cardinal Morton completed it in 1497. Acquired by Henry VIII at the time of the Dissolution of the Monasteries, he used it as a quiet country residence for his children. It remained a royal palace until the time of James I. The single range of buildings which survives today includes the kitchen and the Great Hall, with its magnificent timber roof of oak and chestnut.

It was mainly in this Old Palace at Hatfield that Elizabeth was brought up. Her superior status to her sister was shortlived; with the downfall of her mother, Anne Boleyn, the little girl found she was no longer being treated as a princess, and was inadequately supplied with clothes (see page 25). Then came the comparatively tranquil period when, together with her young brother, she received at Hatfield the kind of education thought proper for Renaissance princes.

Young Edward VI gave Hatfield as a present to Elizabeth, 'his sweet sister Temperance'; and there she continued her education under Roger Ascham. She was now maintaining her own household. It was administered by her cofferer, Thomas Parry, who kept precise accounts of the expenses of each department. They begin with basic matters of bread and drink, and finish with sundry payments to actors, musicians and the bringers of gifts:

The Accompte of Thomas Parry, Esquyer, Cofferer to the Verie Excellent Princess the Ladie Elizabeth her Grace the Kinge's Majestie's most Honorable Sister, with all somes of money received by him for the Provision of her Grace's Household Expences:-

The Bakehouse and Pantrye

	£. s. d.
Paid to John Newman, for 24 quarters and four bushels of wheat	16. 6. 8
Paid ditto, for the like quantity	16. 6. 8
Paid ditto, for 24 quarters of wheat	12. 0. 0
Nicholas Saunders, for 5 quarters of wheat	5.18. 6
Edward Smith, for 2 quarters, 4 bushels	2.18. 6

The Buttery and Cellar

Edmunde Wilson, for 10 dole of beer	10. 3. 0
Edmund Wilson, for 15 tonnes of beer	14.10. 0
Ditto, for 10 ton 1 pipe of beer	10. 3. 0
John Garner, for 10 dole of Gaskoine wine	80. 0. 0
(also bought sweet wine, Reynishe wine and Rochell wine)	

The Spicerye and Chandrye	£. s. d.	Wages, Liveries, and Alms	£. s. d.
Thomas Steevens, for 256 pounds of wax	10 10 0	The Wages of the Household Servants, and for their liveries	434 11 8½
Ditto, for 30 dozen of candles	3 5 0	Amongst which are 13 velvet liveries for the gentlemen,	
Ditto, for 72 dozen of ditto	5 8 0	at 40s. each	26 0 0
Ditto, for 50 dozen of ditto	3 18 0	The liveies for the Yeomen	
The Kechyn and Larder		amount to	78 18 0
Amounts to	597 4 11½	The Chambre and Robes_	
Fish is the most considerable article under this head.			
Lamprey pies are mentioned		Velvet is from 20s. to 30s. per yard.	

The Acatrye.

Thomas Shepy, for 120 muttons	30 0 0
William West, for 80 muttons	20 0 0
Henry Trafford, for 2 hogges of bacon	1 0 0
Thomas Burchall, for 60 oxen	160 0 0
To ditto, for 56 muttons	12 3 6
To ditto, for 20 ditto	4 0 0
To ditto, for 32 veales	8 0 0
For 12lb. of lard	0 12 0
For 66 muttons	13 4 0
For 100 ditto	20 0 0

The Pultrye

Amounted to	311 5 4½

But the particular prices are not mentioned.

The Squillerie.

Richard Bryce for 23 loads of coals	6 6 6
Ditto, for 22 ditto	6 1 0
Ditto, for 23 ditto	6 5 10
Ditto, for 30 ditto	7 12 0

The Saucerye

Amounts to	21 8 2

The Wood-yard

Amounts to	87 11 10

The Stable.

Paid William Chambers for 12 bushels of oats	0 6 0
Paid Humphrey Broke, for one gelding	5 13 4
Paid William Ciney, for two geldings	12 9 6

Two French hoods	2 8 9
Half a yard and 2 nails of velvet for partlets	0.18.9
Paid to Edward Allen, for a bible	1 0 0
Paid Thomas Crowche, gold-smithe, the 7th of January, for 74 oz. 4 dwts. of gilt plate, at 8s. 8d. the oz. brought for New Yere's Gifts	32 3 10
Paid to dyverse Noblemen's servants, which brought New Yere's Gifts January 4	4 6 8
Paid to the King's Majesty's dromer and phiphe 20s.; Mr. Haywoode 30s.; and to Sebastian, towards the charge of the children, with the carriage of the plaire's garments, £4. 19s.	7 9 0
Paid to sondrie persons at St. James's, her Grace being there.	9 15 0
A Frenchman that gave a boke to her Grace	0 10 0
Paid to Beamonde, the King's servante, for his boies that plaied before her Grace	0 10 0
Paid in rewarde to sondrie persons the 10th of August, *viz.* to Former, that plaied on the lute, 30s.; to Mr. Ashefielde's servant, with two prise oxen and ten muttons, 20s. more; the harper, 30s.; to him that made her Grace a table of walnut tree, 44s. 9d.; and to Mr. Cocker's servant which brought her Grace a sturgeon, 6s. 8d. In all	11 11 5
Paid to my Lord Russell's minstrells,	20s.

Remote from the Court, it was hard for the Princess to judge which way the wind was blowing. But she had realised from her earliest years the importance of diplomacy where her brother was concerned, and had, it seems, heard rumours about his health. Towards the end of his reign she wrote to him from Hatfield,

TO THE KINGES MOST EXCELLENT MAJESTIE.

Like as a shipman in stormy waither plukes down the

Elizabeth I, The Ermine Portrait, by Nicholas Hilliard, 1585.
(Hatfield House)

The Royal Lion, from a set of Queen's Beasts carved for Elizabeth I's
visit to Sandwich in 1573. (The Guildhall, Sandwich)

Elizabeth I: the Ditchley Portrait, by Marcus Gheeraerts the Younger, c.1592.
(National Portrait Gallery)

The Great Hall of the Old Palace of Hatfield, where Elizabeth held her first Privy Council meeting.

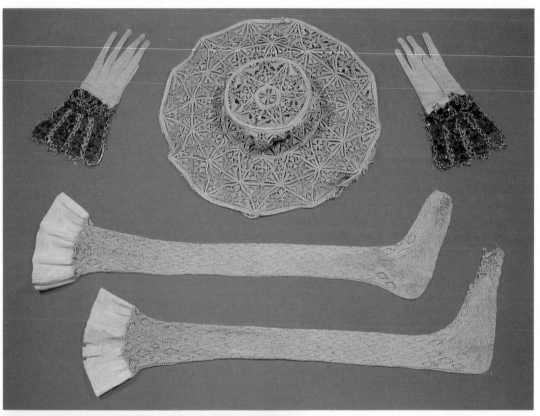

Garden-hat, gloves and silk stockings, said to have been worn by Elizabeth I. (Hatfield House)

Elizabeth I. The Rainbow Portrait of c.1600, attributed to Isaac Oliver. (Hatfield House)

sailes tarrijnge for better winde, so did I, most noble Kinge, in my unfortunate chance a thursday pluk downe the hie sailes of my joy and comforte, and do trust one day that as troublesome waves have repulsed me backwarde, so a gentil winde will bring me forwarde to my haven. Two chief occasions moved me muche, and grived me gretly, the one, for that I douted you Majesties helth, the other, because for all my tarrijnge I wente without that I came for; of the first I am relieved in a parte, bothe that I inderstode of your helthe, and also that your Majesties loginge is far from my Lorde Marques chamber: of my other grief I am not eased; but the best is that whatsoever other folkes wil suspect. I intende not to feare your grace's goodwil, wiche as I knowe that I never disarved to faint, so I trust stll stike by me. For if your grace's advis that I should retourne (whos will is a commandmente) had not bine, I would not have made the halfe of my way, the ende of my journey, And thus as one desirous to here of your Majesties helthe, thogth unfortunat to se it, I shal pray god for to preserve you.

From Hatfielde, this present Saterday.

Your Majesties humble Sister to commandment,

Elizabeth.

Between the lines one reads the nervousness of the situation. After Edward's death and the accession of Mary, there followed the most difficult and stormy period for Elizabeth, when her very life was in danger. It must have been a tremendous relief when eventually she was allowed to return to Hatfield. Under the genial control of Sir Thomas Pope, the household permitted itself a little merrymaking — even at the risk of offending the Queen. At Shrovetide 1556, Pope commissioned a masque to entertain the Princess. It was staged in the Great Hall. Under the magnificent timber roof a castle of cloth of gold was set up, its battlements decorated with pomegranates and heraldic shields. Music was performed by twelve minstrels 'antickly disguised'; then entered forty-six ladies and gentlemen dressed in crimson satin embroidered with gold and fringed with pearls. From the golden castle emerged six knights to joust in front of the Princess. Then in the evening there was a banquet of seventy dishes, followed by a dessert of thirty spiced confections and subtleties. On the following day there was a play, *Holofernes*. All this was done at Sir Thomas Pope's expense. However, the Queen was not pleased when she heard of these frivolities, and she ordered them to cease. She might not have disapproved so much had she been present too, but she did not think them fitting just for the Princess. Elizabeth was not allowed fully to indulge her taste for pageantry until she became Queen herself.

It was at Hatfield that she heard the news. A deputation of lords came to announce it, headed by the Earl of Pembroke, Lord Clinton (who was Lord Admiral), and the Earl of Arundel (who was Lord Chamberlain). To these three were added Sir Thomas Parry, Sir William Cecil, Sir Ambrose Cave, Sir Ralph Sadleir and Sir Richard Sackville. They constituted Elizabeth's first Privy Council, which met there and then in the Great Hall. Sir Thomas Parry was appointed Comptroller of her Household, Sir Edward Rogers became Vice-Chamberlain and Captain of the Guard, and (most important of all) Sir William Cecil her Principal Secretary. Shrewdly she included in her first full council thirteen men who had been members of Mary's Privy Council; but Sir Thomas Pope, who had treated her so generously, was not one of them, perhaps because he would not change from the old religion. Perhaps, too, because now she was Queen, Elizabeth wanted to make a clear break from the life she had led as a princess. This, together with the fact that even at four times its present size, Hatfield was never a particularly large palace, may also be the reason why, as Queen, she used it only for the briefest of visits.

The story of Hatfield continues with the Cecil family. William Cecil was the most trusted adviser Elizabeth ever had, and he entertained her lavishly at his mansion, Theobalds. Of his two sons, Thomas and Robert, he had a greater liking for the latter who was the son of his second marriage. While Thomas inherited his title and Burghley House, it was Robert he groomed to follow him in high office, as Secretary of State, first under Elizabeth and, after her death, under James I.

Robert Cecil (c.1563-1612) was not physically prepossessing; he had a misshapen back and was no more than five foot three inches tall; but of the sharpness of his intellect there was no doubt. He rose in royal favour and under James I was created Viscount Cranborne (1604), and in the following year Earl of Salisbury. Meanwhile, on the death of his father in 1598, he had inherited Theobalds; and it was at this mansion that he entertained the King and his court. In 1606 there were two kings there, when James came for four days with his brother-in-law Christian IV of Denmark. Robert Cecil had set up an artificial oak tree with taffeta leaves, and the company was regaled with a masque of Solomon and the Queen of Sheba. The masque ended in drunkenness and disorder; but disastrous though the entertainment may have been,

James had no fault to find with its setting. He had come to Theobalds first in May 1603, on his journey south from Scotland into the England he had never seen until it became his kingdom. He was amazed. He was used to castles built for defence, not pleasure-palaces. If a mere subject could have so fine a mansion, what would the royal residences be like? Friendly and unassuming Hatfield was one which did not quite come up to his hopes. Consequently he made a deal with Robert Cecil, and in May 1607 exchanged it for Theobalds. The King also added some other property, to even the balance and to enable his Secretary of State to rebuild.

The building of the Hatfield House we know today was begun in the following year. Robert Cecil's project was ambitious, magnificent, expensive; he wanted a house fine enough to entertain the King there. Eight million bricks went into the building of it. The house is shaped like a flattened 'U', with its principal rooms on the first floor; the two wings were designed to hold the King's and Queen's chambers, and the main block between to provide a series of regal state-rooms. The family were expected to occupy the floor below. Although Inigo Jones is known to have been there in 1609 and may have designed the colonnade on the south front, the principal designer was Robert Lyminge, who was also responsible for Blickling Hall in Norfolk. The gardens were laid out by John Tradescant who figures on one of the newel posts at the top of the Grand Staircase. A vineyard was created and stocked with 30,000 vines given by the French ambassador. Five hundred mulberry trees were also planted; Cecil knew of James's interest in establishing a silk-industry in his new kingdom. At the same time he commissioned Maximilian Colt, the King's Master Sculptor, to carve his own tomb and set it up in Hatfield Church — a prophetic gesture, for within three years he was dead. His stiff little effigy lies over his cadaver, supported by four opulent virtues. The house was scarcely completed. He had only lived there a few months, and the grand royal state visits he had hoped for were never made.

Hatfield House still contains a number of objects and paintings connected with Elizabeth I. There is a pair of yellow silk stockings — it is said that once she had felt silk on her legs she was determined never to wear anything else — and a garden-hat. Whether it was authentically Elizabeth's or not, the intricate flat-crowned hat has great charm. There is also a pair of gloves with extremely long fingers, just as the Queen had.

By the Grand Staircase hangs a large picture of a grey horse, painted in 1594, which is reputedly the stallion that Elizabeth rode when she went to review her troops at Tilbury in 1588. There is also a painting of a feast at Bermondsey, by Joris Hofnagel. This depicts rustic celebrations in a leafy village, which are graced by black-clad members of the nobility, one of whom may possibly be Elizabeth herself.

There are two exceptionally fine portraits of the Queen at Hatfield, both of them allegorical.[1] The earlier is attributed to Nicholas Hilliard (better known as a miniature-painter) and dates from 1585. Elizabeth is shown wearing a jewel-encrusted gown, a diaphanous veil about her shoulders, and a lace ruff of incredible delicacy. On this perches her head, pale, fey and inscrutable, crowned with a diadem and a frizz of fair hair. On her left forearm clambers an ermine wearing a gold collar shaped like a crown, and by it lies the sword of state. (The white ermine was a symbol of purity, the crown-like collar and the sword signify majesty.)

The Rainbow portrait of the Queen is even more impressive. Although the names of John de Critz and Marcus Gheeraerts have been put forward, it is now generally attributed to Isaac Oliver (1565?-1617). Conceived in a more volumetric way than the two-dimensional patterning of the Ermine portrait, it shows the Queen wearing a dress sprigged with wild flowers, and over it a mantle of orange satin. The mantle is patterned with a design of eyes, ears and mouths, signifying the fame of the wearer. Pearls, always a symbol of virginity, edge her high head-dress and are knotted round her neck, and she wears a huge wing-like gauze collar. On her left sleeve is embroidered a serpent (wisdom), and in her right hand she holds a rainbow, the symbol of peace — especially peace following a period of storms. Above it is the inscription 'Non sine sole Iris' — 'no rainbow without the sun'. Elizabeth is equated with the all-powerful sun, bringing peace to her realm and a new golden age.

Elizabeth's pedigree is also to be seen at Hatfield. A colourful and contemporary document executed on a long parchment roll and illuminated with countless coats-of-arms, it attempts to trace the Queen's ancestry back to Adam. She never did do things by halves.

[1]For a detailed analysis, see Frances Yates, Astraea.

Kenilworth Castle.

KENILWORTH CASTLE

Robert Dudley was what the Elizabethans termed a lusty man. Among his peers there were few who had a good word to say for him. He was, they had to admit, good-looking, 'singular well-featured, and all his youth well-favoured, and of a sweet aspect', Sir Robert Naunton described him. He was lively, athletic, a nimble dancer, fine horseman, good talker, and noble in his bearing. Yet he was labelled gypsy, monster, poisoner, terrestrial Lucifer, 'by many thought to do nothing by chance, nor much by affection'.[1] To what extent this criticism was well founded, and to what based on envy, it is hard to judge. He emerges as a man of great personal charm, and undeniably amorous. As far as the Queen was concerned, he must have had some sort of magic aura; for she forgave him much (even his marriages), and for about thirty years he remained her most intimate friend.

[1] *Reliquae Wottoniae.*

It is said that he was born on the very same day as Elizabeth and was her exact contemporary. Like her, and at the same time, he was imprisoned in the Tower. For the Dudleys were an ill-starred family. Robert's father, John, Duke of Northumberland, had been Protector and virtual ruler of England during the latter part of the reign of Edward VI; but his ambition over-reached itself when he claimed the crown for Lady Jane Grey whom he had pushed into marriage with his elder son, Guildford. In consequence John Dudley was executed, and so later were Guildford and Lady Jane Grey. Robert, too, had been under sentence of death, but he fared better, and was set free in 1554.

Queen Elizabeth made Robert Dudley her Master of the Horse, a Privy Councillor and Knight of the Garter. Her intimacy with him was first noticed in about 1559, and many people believed that it was only a matter of time before she married him. But Dudley already had a wife; he had married Amy Robsart in 1550. She was never encouraged to come to Court — but that was no uncommon thing, many courtiers' wives resided quietly in the country — and she was based at Cumnor Court near Oxford. It was rumoured that she was terminally ill, and the Queen was only waiting for her to die before she married Robert. She certainly seems to have been in a state of extreme depression, and on 8 September 1560, having sent all her servants off to the fair at Abingdon, she was found dead at the bottom of the stairs with her neck broken. Did she fall or was she pushed? Or rather, was she poisoned? These were the rumours that began to circulate. Dudley's name, and even the Queen's, were bandied about in connection with Amy Robsart's death. The English ambassador in Brussels reported the current gossip there, 'What religion is this, that a subject shall kill his wife, and the prince not only bear withal but marry him?'

While Elizabeth was convinced of Lord Robert's innocence (and there is no evidence that she herself was implicated), she took notice of what people said. Thus the death of his wife, rather than facilitating a marriage with her favourite, made it virtually impossible if she was to retain her status in European politics.

However, Robert Dudley continued in favour with the Queen. She created him Earl of Leicester in 1564 (tickling the back of his neck as she did so), and had, in the previous year, presented him with Kenilworth Castle.

The ancient fortress of Kenilworth originated in the early twelfth century. It was part of the manor of Stoneleigh, which Henry I gave to his chamberlain, Geoffrey de Clinton. The latter founded both a priory and a fine defensive castle. Kenilworth was a superb site, standing on a natural mound with a lake to the south and west side. The priory became an abbey and the monks were allowed to fish in the lake on Thursdays. This provided them with food for Fridays when they were not allowed to eat meat. The castle remained in the de Clinton family for two generations, then reverted to the Crown in exchange for property in Buckinghamshire.

Early in the thirteenth century the original small lake was extended into the great Mere —over 200 hundred acres (81 hectares) of water, stretching half a mile along the valley and encircling three-quarters of the castle's perimeter. Two great dams holding back the mere to the south east and north east, became the main routes to the stronghold. There were also ponds at a lower level to the east.

In King John's reign the structure of the castle was also extended, including the wall around the outer court. According to the terms of Magna Carta, Kenilworth was one of the castles he was supposed to hand back to the barons, but he somehow avoided doing it, and it was still in royal hands at the time of Henry III. Henry III's sister, Eleanor, married Simon de Montfort, and the King gave them Kenilworth as a present. He later had cause to regret this, for it became a stronghold of baronial opposition. Simon de Montfort was killed at the Battle of Evesham, but in 1266 his son, also called Simon, held it for almost nine months against the royal forces. He was greatly aided by the lake system, and it was only on account of disease and lack of food that the garrison eventually capitulated. By Christmas the castle was once more in the King's hands, and he gave it to his second son, Edmund, Earl of Lancaster. It was at Kenilworth that the unhappy Edward II was compelled to sign his abdication before being despatched to a very unpleasant end at Berkeley Castle.

In 1359, John of Gaunt (or Ghent) married into the powerful Lancaster family, and thereby acquired Kenilworth. Here he spent a good deal of his time. He rebuilt much including what must have been a magnificent Great Hall, measuring 89 by 45 feet (27 x 14 metres) (the widest single-span medieval hall apart from Westminster). In 1379 forty oak trees were cut up to repair the chamber floor so that it should be fit for dancing on at Christmas. Kenilworth was changing from being a defensive stronghold to a place of delight. So it continued under John of Gaunt's son, Henry IV, and his grandson, Henry V. He further refined it by making a pavilion, or pleasance, at the far end of the Mere. Finally Henry VIII added a timber-framed east wing to the inner court.

Thus, by the time Kenilworth came into the hands of the

Dudley family, it had already shaken off its gloomy medieval past and acquired some tradition as a palace of pleasure.

John Dudley, Duke of Northumberland held it briefly before his son did. The site of the abbey was granted to him at the time of the Dissolution of the Monasteries, and he acquired the castle in 1553. The same year he was executed. For ten years Kenilworth was once again in royal hands, and then Elizabeth gave it to Robert.

The Earl of Leicester's finances were largely supported by taxes on sweet wines, currants, oils, velvets and barrel-staves. These brought him in a very substantial income and made it possible for him to plan on a lavish scale. The Queen first visited him at Kenilworth in 1565; afterwards he set about modernising and extending the castle so that it should be suitable for entertaining her on the lavish scale he had in mind. In all he spent some £60,000 on it. In 1570 he destroyed the village of Blackwell, giving the villagers 200 acres (81 hectares) elsewhere. He stocked the woodlands with red as well as fallow deer. He put tall Tudor windows into the old Norman keep (a difficult task in walls fifteen feet (4.5 metres) thick), bay-windows along either side of the John of Gaunt state suite, rebuilt the keep forebuilding, erected a turreted gatehouse and a new stable-block. Then, in about 1571, he set up the Leicester Buildings; a tall block of hard stone, but rather slender construction, it projected beyond the walls of the inner court and was designed to accommodate distinguished visitors. 'Every room so spacious,' Laneham described it at the time of the Queen's visit in 1575, 'so well belighted and so high-roofed within; so seemly to sight by due proportion without; a day time on every side so glittering by glasses; a nights, by continual brightness of candle, fire and torchlight transparent through the lightsome windows.'

Meanwhile, new pleasure-gardens were laid out on the north side, ornamented with 'obelisks, spheres and white bears all of stone' (the bear with the ragged staff being Leicester's insignia). A terrace was constructed along the castle wall, and on the north side, an aviary full of exotic birds, many of them songbirds. Beyond, a garden terrace or platform commanded a view over the lake.

When the Earl of Leicester entertained the Queen so extravagantly in 1575 (see page 74), at a cost of about a thousand pounds a day, he did it in the hope of satisfying his highest ambition, that of marriage with the Queen. At the same time, he was disregarding the fact that he had contracted a secret marriage two years earlier with a beautiful young widow, Lady Douglas Sheffield. Afterwards he declared that the ceremony performed with just one witness and only four days before the birth of his son, was invalid. Valid or not, the Queen was furious at this secret marriage, and Leicester was temporarily out of favour.

The 1575 festivities having failed in their principal purpose, three years later Leicester married — bigamously, some would say — Lettice Knollys, Countess of Essex. In order to achieve this, it was rumoured that he had attempted to poison Lady Sheffield (with the result that her hair fell out), and had indeed poisoned Lettice Knollys's husband. Yet despite these amorous and possibly murderous intrigues, which set him at odds with everyone else, Leicester's influence with the Queen continued, and she entrusted him with military command. In 1585 he went on the expedition to the Low Countries (where his valorous nephew, Sir Philip Sidney, died at Zutphen). Then in the Armada year of 1588, he was appointed commander of all the forces amassed at Tilbury. But he scarcely lived long enough after that to realize that the 'invincible' fleet from Spain had in fact been defeated. He succumbed to a sudden illness and died on 4 September at Cornbury in Oxfordshire. Rumour had it that he had swallowed poison intended for his wife; but rumour was always rife where Leicester was concerned.

The debts he left were enormous. His son by his last marriage only lived to the age of four; so Leicester had attempted to leave the larger part of his legacy to Sir Robert Dudley, the son of his union with Lady Sheffield. But Dudley could not prove his legitimacy, and both castle and earldom went instead to Robert Sidney (Sir Philip's brother).

The Queen's reaction to her favourite's death is interesting. Publicly she was concerned with retrieving the debts he had incurred (chiefly on her account); privately she wept, and ever after kept in a drawer a miniature of him wrapped in paper on which she had written 'My Lord's picture'.

As for Kenilworth Castle, it was slighted (rendered indefensible) by the Roundheads at the time of the Civil War — this process included draining the Mere — then, after the Restoration, was for some time in the hands of the earls of Clarendon. Given to the town council in 1937, it is today in the guardianship of the Secretary of State for the Environment, and managed by the English Heritage.

Meanwhile its fame underwent a revival in the nineteenth century. In Warwick Castle is an enormous sideboard carved for the Great Exhibition of 1851; it illustrates, in extraordinary detail, the events and characters of the 1575 visit. But the renewed interest in Kenilworth was due, above all, to Sir Walter Scott's novel of that name. It is a historical romance which, in order to tell a good story — as it certainly does — juggles amazingly with chronological fact. For example, in the novel Amy Robsart travels secretly to Kenilworth for the 1575 festivities — fifteen years after her death! Nevertheless, Scott had consulted the original sources, and his description, for instance, of the preparations for the Queen's coming to the castle, is both convincing and evocative:[2]

'The Queen's purveyors had been abroad, sweeping the farms and villages of those articles usually exacted during a royal Progress, and for which the owners were afterwards to obtain a tardy payment from the Board of Green Cloth. The Earl of Leicester's household officers had been scouring the country for the same purpose; and many of his friends and allies, both near and remote, took this opportunity of ingratiating themselves, by sending large quantities of provisions and delicacies of all kinds, with game in huge numbers, and whole tuns of the best liquors, foreign and domestic. Thus the high-roads were filled with droves of bullocks, sheep, calves, and hogs, and choked with loaded wains, whose axle-trees cracked under their burdens of wine-casks and hogsheads of ale, and huge hampers of grocery goods, and slaughtered game, and salted provisions, and sacks of flour. Perpetual stoppages took place as these wains became entangled; and their rude drivers, swearing and brawling till their wild passions were fully raised, began to debate precedence with their waggon-whips and quarter-staves, which occasional riots were usually quieted by a purveyor, deputy-marshal's-man, or some other person in authority, breaking the heads of both parties.

Here were, besides, players and mummers, jugglers and show-men, of every description, traversing in joyous bands the paths which led to the Palace of Princely Pleasure; for so the travelling minstrels had termed Kenilworth in the songs which already had come forth in anticipation of the revels which were there expected. In the midst of this motley show, mendicants were exhibiting their real or pretended miseries, forming a strange, though common, contrast betwixt the vanities and the sorrows of human existence. All these floated along with the immense tide of population, whom mere curiosity had drawn together; and where the mechanic, in his leathern apron, elbowed the dink and dainty dame, his city mistress; where clowns, with hob-nailed shoes, were treading on the kibes of substantial burghers and gentlemen of worship; and

[2] Sir Walter Scott, *Kenilworth*, Chapter XXV.

where Joan of the dairy, with robust pace, and red sturdy arms, rowed her way onward, amongst those prim and pretty moppets, whose sires were knights and squires.

The throng and confusion was, however, of a gay and cheerful character. All came forth to see and to enjoy, and all laughed at the trifling inconveniences which at another time might have chafed their temper. Excepting the occasional brawls which we have mentioned among that irritable race the carmen, the mingled sounds which arose from the multitude were those of light-hearted mirth, and tiptoe jollity. The musicians preluded on their instruments — the minstrels hummed their songs — the licensed jester whooped betwixt mirth and madness, as he brandished his bauble—the morrice-dancers jangled their bells — the rustics halloo'd and whistled — men laughed loud, and maidens giggled shrill; while many a broad jest flew like a shuttle-cock from one party, to be caught in the air and returned from the opposite side of the road by another, at which it was aimed.'

The Earl of Leicester's New Year's Gifts to the Queen

The presents the Earl gave Elizabeth each year were of incomparable magnificence, and, as far as can be ascertained, were as follows:[3]

In 1571-2

'one armlet or skakell of golde, all over fairely garnished with rubyes and dyamondes, haveing in the closing thearof a clocke, and in the fore parte of the same a fayre lozengie dyamonde without a foyle, hanging thearat a rounde juell fully garnished with dyamondes, and perle pendant; weying 11 oz. qu [a] dim', and farthing golde weight; in a case of purple vellate all over embrauderid with Venice golde, and lyned with greene vellat."— In 1572-3, "one riche carkenet or collor of golde, haveing in it two emeraldes, 4 rubyes, and fully garnished with small rubyes and dyamondes." — In 1573-4, "a fanne of white fethers, sett in a handell of golde; the one side thearof garnished with two very fayre emeraldes, especially one, and fully garnished with dyamondes and rubyes; and the backe syde and handle of lyke golde, garnished with dyamondes and rubyes; and on each syde a white beare and twoe perles hanging, a lyon ramping with a white moseled beare at his foote." — In 1574-5, a doublett of white satten, garnished with goldsmith's worke, and sett with 18 very fayre payre of claspes of goldsmith's worke enamuled, every paire of them set with fyve diamondes and eight rubyes, one diamonde in every paire bigger than the rest, one of the smaller dyamondes lacking, with a fayre pasmayne lace of damaske golde and damaske silver." — In 1575-6, "a juell, being a crosse of golde, conteyning 6 very fayre emeraldes, whearof two bigger than the rest, the one of the biggest being cracked, and 3 large perles pendaunte." — In 1576-7, "a coller of golde, contayning 13 peeces, whearin are 13 greate emeraldes, and 13 peeces of golde, with 13 troches of perles, in every troche, and in every peece 4 small rubyes." — In 1577-8, "a carcanett of golde enamuled, 9 peeces whearof are garnished with sparcks of dyamondes and rubyes, and every of them a pendante of golde enamuled, and garnished with smale sparcks of rubyes, and an ophall in the middes. Ten other peeces of golde lykewise enamuled, and every of them

[3] From Nichols's *Progresses.*

garnished with very smale dyamonds; two large raged pearles sett with a rose of sparcks of rubyes, and every of the two lesser pearls pendant, and a pendant of golde, and in every peece a lozengye dyamonde and a smale rubye, and in the middes a large pendant of golde garnished with meane rubyes, an ophall, and a meane perle pendant. And six dosen of buttons likewise enamuled, and every button of golde garnished with smale sparcks of rubyes, in every of them a large ragedd pearle." — In the Progress of 1578 the Earl gave the Queen, "oone faire cup of cristall fationed like a slipper, garnished with golde, and a cover of golde, enamaeled, with white faulcone in the toppe, weighing $30\frac{1}{4}$ ounces." — In 1578-9, "a very faire juel of golde, being a clocke fully furnished with small diamondes and rubyes: abowte the same are six bigger diamondes pointed, and a pendaunte of golde, diamonds, and rubyes, very smale; and upon eche side a losengye diamonde, and an apple of golde enamuled greene and russet." — In 1579-80, "two bodkyns of golde; in the topp of the one is a very fayre table dyamonde, garnished aboute with smale rubyes; and in the toppe of the other is a very fayre rubye garnished aboute with smale diamondes, and a capp of black velvet, with a broweke of golde, garnished with 18 diamondes, and a bande abowte it, with 14 buttons of golde, garnished with dyamonds, being raged staves and true-love knotts, garnished with rubyes and dyamondes, and 36 smale buttons, being true-knotts and raged staves." — In 1580-1, "a cheyne of golde, made lyke a payre of beades, contayning 8 long peeces, fully garnished with small diamondes, and fower score and one smaller peeces, fullie garnished with like diamondes; and hanging thereat a rounde clocke fullie garnished with dyamondes, and an appendante of diamondes hanging thearat."—In 1581-2, "a litle boke of golde, enamuled, garnished and furnished with smale diamondes and rubyes, bothe claspes, and all hanging at a chayne of golde, *viz.* 6 peces of golde enamuled, two of them garnished with raged staves of smale sparcks of diamondes, and 4 of them in eche, 2 smale diamonds and two smale sparcks of rubyes, 16 lesser peeces of gold, in every of them a smale diamonde, and also 24 peeces of gold, in every of them 4 perles, with a ring of gold to hang it by."—In 1582-3, "a faire juell of golde, being a carkenet, contayning 20 peeces, being letters and a sipher in the midest, all garnished with smale dyamonds, and betwene every letter 2 perles, and every letter having a smale diamond pendant; and at thesipher a pendant garnished with smale dyamonds, and 3 smale rock rubyes in 3 of the said peeces." — In 1583-4, "a faire juell of golde, being a chaine, contayning 24 knotts lyke bonser knotts, 12 matreues knotts, and 12 lytle seenkfoyles, all garnished with smale dyamonds on thone side, and a key of golde hanging at it, garnished on thone side with like diamondes." — In 1584-5, "a sable skynne, the hedd and four feete of gold, fully garnished with dyamonds and rubyes of sundry sorts." — In 1585-6, "one fold of perle, contayning 101 juells thearat hanging, with one greate table diamonde in the midest, 2 rubyes on eche side; the residue of the juell garnished with 14 smale diamonds on thone side of the same juell, the other side inamuled with a peare pearle; all together with the lace 2 oz. q [a]. dim'." — In 1586-7[1], "a purse of golde, enamuled, and garnished with smale diamondes, rubies, and ophalls of sundry bignesses, and a blewe saphire in the topp, with 2 strings, having pendants of perles of sundry bignesses hanging at a smale chaine of golde; and one bracelet of golde, contayning 6 peeces, 4 peeces like crosses, 2 peeces like half crosses, fully furnished with diamondes, rubyes, and perles of sundry bignesses, on thone side, with a rowe of perles and smale rubyes on eche side of the said bracelet enamuled."

In exchange she gave him a quantity of gold plate.

---

[1] This is the last time the Earl of Leicester's name appears among the New-year's Gifts. He died in 1588.

BURGHLEY HOUSE AND THEOBALDS

'God send us both long to enjoy her for whom we both
mean to exceed our purses in these.'

(Sir William Cecil, writing to Sir Christopher Hatton
about his own house, Theobalds, and Hatton's Holdenby.)

How could she ever have managed without him? In referring to Sir
William Cecil as her 'spirit', Elizabeth was implying that she could
not. Yet he was very different in character from her. To her
occasional impetuosity his grave counsel acted as a counter-balance.

William Cecil's forebears belonged to the squirearchy rather
than the aristocracy. His grandfather, David, had been a Yeoman
of the Guard. Though he originated from Wales, he bought
property near Stamford, on the Lincolnshire-Cambridgeshire
border, thus establishing the first link between the family and that
part of the country. He prospered sufficiently to become Mayor
and Member of Parliament. His son Richard, William's father, was
at the Field of the Cloth of Gold, and then served under Henry
VIII as a groom of the Privy Chamber. He added to the existing
family property and bought some land at the Dissolution of the
Monasteries; from this germ was to grow the magnificent Burghley
House.

William was born about 1520, the elder son of Richard's first
marriage. He was employed as a Court page before going to
Grantham Grammar School. At the age of fourteen (not at that
time considered exceptionally young) he went up to Cambridge
and studied at St John's College. Then he became a law student at
Gray's Inn. This was the only time in his life when he showed any
wildness, in contrast to the grave and contemplative statesman he
was to become. He became engaged to his first wife, Mary Cheke,
and married her in 1541. From this marriage derived his elder son,
Thomas.

Mary died in 1543, and two years later William married again.
His new wife, Mildred Cooke, was far better connected than his
first (her father had been Governor to Prince Edward), and far
more intellectual. She was to give birth to his son, Robert, and his
daughters, Elizabeth and Anne. Her memorable portrait, probably
by Hans Eworth, is at Hatfield House.

William Cecil rose in royal favour, first under Henry VIII, and
even more in the reign of Edward VI, when he became Master of
Requests to the young King's elder uncle, the Duke of Somerset.

Burghley House, the West Front.

Having accompanied the Duke on his campaign in Scotland, Cecil was rewarded by being promoted to Personal Secretary. But Somerset proved a dangerous patron; he was ousted by the Duke of Northumberland and executed in 1552. His fall inevitably affected his adherents, and for a while Cecil was imprisoned in the Tower. But two years after his release he was knighted, and by this time he was working for the Duke of Northumberland. However, Northumberland was the instigator in the movement for the succession of Lady Jane Grey after the death of King Edward, who was now desperately ill. He drew up a document diverting the sovereignty from Mary to Jane; but Cecil — so aware of the danger of the situation that he went about fully armed — avoided putting his name to it. He only gave it his support when, as he understood, the dying King ordered him to do so. But as soon as it was clear that the cause of Lady Jane Grey had failed, he wrote promising his allegiance to Mary Tudor.

William Cecil, Lord Burghley, riding on a mule. (Bodleian Library)

The times demanded flexibility, and Cecil could bend with the best of them. There was something of the Vicar of Bray about him. Staunchly Anglican as he had been in Edward's time, nevertheless in Mary's reign he attended mass; under Elizabeth he was, in fact, more inclined towards severe Protestantism than the Queen herself. But at this early stage he felt it wiser to keep a low profile and remove himself from the centre of Court and political life. And this was the time (1555) that he began to build Burghley House, starting with the east range.

119

'I like what is done,' commented Sir Ralph Sadler, having visited Cecil's mansion on his way to Scotland in August 1559, 'and the order of the rest as your man showed it cannot but be fair. God send you enough money to end it with; other lack I see none.'

Cecil was always careful about money. 'Live not in the country without corn and cattle about thee,' he later advised his son, 'for he that putteth his hand to the purse for every expense of household is like him that putteth water into a sieve.' And with his ever-increasing rise to power and prosperity during the reign of Elizabeth (she created him Lord Burghley in 1571), he never lacked funds.

Cecil's first building seems to have incorporated the monastic remains bought by his father. By 1564-65 the south side was finished. Then there was a ten-year pause while he concentrated on the building of Theobalds; but in 1575-77 there was a further spate of building at Burghley and the west front with its turreted gatehouse was completed. The final phase was the building of the north front, and the whole mansion was finished in 1587, thirty-two years after work first began.

Burghley House is built of tough local stone from Barnack. While planning it, Cecil consulted recent stylistic authorities from France (Philibert de l'Orme's *Nouvelles Inventions pour bien bastir*, and du Cerceau's *Livre d'Architecture*), also he ordered some ready-made decorative masonry from Antwerp; but there is no evidence that he employed an architect, and every evidence that the general design was his own.

Cecil's eclecticism, combined with the fact that building was spread over more than three decades, may account for its incoherence of style. The size and magnificence of Burghley is entirely captivating; it is full of excitement and romance. Yet when one comes to analyse it, it is an extraordinary conglomeration. Basically it is a courtyard house with projecting towers at the corners, and on the west front a tall gate-house set between them: a concept derived from a medieval castle, and with its octagonal turrets not unlike the Tudor appearance of Hampton Court. At the same time, there is French influence in the emphatic string-courses which seem to tie the building together like bands around a barrel. Then there are high English windows, Flemish-derived cresting along the roof-line, chimneys grouped in fours and masquerading as fragments of classical temples, and finally a most amazing obelisk crowning the clock-tower — dated 1585 and supported, almost clambered upon, by huge heraldic beasts.

The Cecil family prospered, and from 1680 onwards the rooms

The Old Kitchen, Burghley House.

were transformed into the baroque style by the fifth Earl of Exeter; so the interior of Burghley, as it now stands, contains little that its builder would have recognized. There is the vaulted kitchen, the Great Hall with its double hammerbeam roof, and a staircase dating from 1560 — and apart from movable objects, that is virtually all. There is a bedroom referred to as Queen Elizabeth's bedroom; it was formerly part of a Long Gallery, the interior is much altered and the bed belongs to a somewhat later age. However, amongst Burghley's wonderfully rich collection of paintings there are some fine sixteenth-century portraits, including a head and shoulders of the Queen herself, painted by Marcus Gheeraerts, probably as true a likeness as we possess of how she looked in her later years.

Burghley was indeed a mansion flamboyant enough to entertain the Queen. Although there is little doubt that she came, there is not much evidence concerning her visits to the house. She had intended one on her way to Oxford in 1566; but unfortunately

121

Cecil's younger daughter Anne[4] (she was his favourite and he nicknamed her 'Tannakin') was ill with smallpox. So to avoid infection the Queen was entertained at the Grey Friary in Stamford, which also belonged to Cecil.

Cecil had a London house, on the north side of the Strand. He needed it, being so much at the heart of affairs. It was a brick house, with turrets at each corner, and it was usually known as Cecil House. But the building he principally used for entertaining the Queen was his great mansion, Theobalds. He wrote of it enthusiastically in his diary:

'To speak of the beauty of this most stately house as it deserveth, for curious buildings, delightful walkes and pleasant conceites within and without, and other things very glorios and elegant to be seene, would challenge a great portion of this little treatise.... I leave it, as indeed it is, a Princely Seate.'

In the first place Theobalds was intended for his younger son, Robert. Cecil made no secret of his preference for his younger son rather than Thomas, the child of his first marriage. Cecil acquired the land, at Cheshunt, just outside Waltham, together with a small moated house in June 1563, and the building rose relatively quickly. By September 1571 it was ready for him to entertain the Queen there. He gave her some verses and a portrait of the house, which at that time consisted of two large courtyards, the Base Court and the Inner Court. (The house is, of course, no longer in existence.)

There survives a list of rooms and how they were used to accommodate the royal party; this is dated 27 May 1583. The Base Court was used for the lesser fry. The Queen herself was allocated (in the Inner Court) the Great Hall, the Gallery on the south side, a bed chamber in a turret, and two rooms, normally dining-rooms, became her Withdrawing Chamber and Privy Chamber. In her train were many nobles, ladies, gentlemen and servants: among them the Earl of Leicester, the Earl of Warwick, Lord Howard,

---

[4] The unhappiness of his daughters brought great grief to Cecil. The elder, Elizabeth, born in 1564 at his London house and a god-daughter of the Queen, married Lord Wentworth but died only two years later. The younger, Anne, was married to the dissolute Edward de Vere, Earl of Oxford, when she was only sixteen. As well as being a drunkard, he was reputed to be an atheist and a homosexual. Thus Anne's married life was most unhappy. She died at the age of thirty-three and was buried in Westminster Abbey.

Lord Hunsdon, Lady Stafford, Sir Christopher Hatton, all with their own servants; also Raleigh and Greville, Blanche Parry the Mistress of the Wardrobe, the Queen's cooks, the Gentlemen Ushers, the Squires of the Body, the grooms of the Privy Chamber — a whole army of people to be accommodated. Lord and Lady Burghley had to move out of their usual apartments and make do with lesser rooms at the west end of the Inner Court. Normally the housekeeping bill at Theobalds was £80 a week. When the Queen came, it could soar to many times that amount — £2,000-£3,000 a visit, Cecil estimated.

The Queen's visits became so frequent (she paid thirteen in all) and so large-scale (sometimes bringing foreign ambassadors among her guests) that Cecil decided to build a third great courtyard. This was Fountain Court, and as we know from the plan made of Theobalds by John Thorpe in 1611, it corresponded in size to the Inner Court. The Fountain Court seems to have been built between 1584 and 1588, and to have included, on the south side, a Great Hall about sixty feet (18 metres) long and thirty feet (9 metres) wide overlooking the pleasure-gardens. Along the south front was a loggia, according to the Duke of Wurtemberg who visited the house in 1592, which was 'well painted with the Kings and Queens of England, and the pedigree of Lord Burghley, with paintings of many castles and battels.'

In this setting Cecil entertained the Queen with 'rich shews, pleasant devices, and all manner of sports'[5] and he had made delightful gardens, with white marble fountains and long walks bordered with elm and ash trees. There was a two-tiered semi-circular summer-house; in the lower half were statues of twelve Roman emperors set around a stone table, and above were lead cisterns supplied with running water so that fish could be kept in them. During the Queen's visit in 1593-94 Cecil, now an old man, appeared in the guise of a hermit, presented the Queen with bell, book and candle, and requested that on account of his age and infirmity he should be retired from her service and his son, Robert, should take his place. But she was reluctant to let him go, and this did not happen for another two years.

Sir William died on 4 August 1598, at Cecil House. Though his funeral was in Westminster Abbey, he was buried at St Martin's Church in Stamford. His richly carved and painted tomb — like his architecture, a blend of the classical, medieval and Flemish —contains a figure of him in full armour. This is surprising, for he

[5] Peck's *Desiderata Curiosa.*

was a peace-loving man and declared that whoever takes up soldiering for his profession 'can hardly be an honest man or a good Christian', and 'A reign gaineth more by one year's peace than ten year's war.' Cecil was diplomatic, shrewd, moderate, secret, a pious Protestant, ambitious for his family and faithful in the service of his Queen. She knew his value. 'No prince in Europe', she said, 'hath such a counsellor as I have in mine.'

Longleat, view of the house from Heaven's Gate.

LONGLEAT

'Divers men being bent on building, and having a delectable view in spending of their goods by that trade, doo dailie imagine new devizes of their owne to guide their workmen withhall.'

(William Harrison)

Architecture is a comparatively modern profession. In the sixteenth century it was not uncommon for even a great mansion to be by its owner. Such a man was Sir John Thynne, and such a house was Longleat.

The Thynnes began as a French family from Poitiers, who were called Botteville. They came over to England in the time of King John, and settled first in Shropshire. The reputed origin of the name Thynne is as follows. There were two members of the family

125

called John, one of whom lived in a large house or 'inn'. To distinguish himself from the other, the latter became known as John O' the Inn — this was afterwards contracted to John Thynne.

The John Thynne who was to build Longleat bought the site in 1541. He was in his youth a protégé of Edward Seymour, Duke of Somerset. In his heyday the Duke was the most powerful man in England, being Protector of the realm during most of the reign of Edward VI, which made him the most useful patron a man could have. He knighted Thynne at the Battle of Pinkie in 1547, and no doubt bestowed on him many more material benefits as well. In the following year Thynne augmented these by marrying an heiress, the daughter of the Lord Mayor of London, Richard Gresham. But with the downfall of Somerset the year after that, he found himself imprisoned, like his former patron, in the Tower. The Duke was executed in 1552. Thynne remained imprisoned for two years, and was only released on payment of a heavy fine of £6,000. He went straight back to Wiltshire and thereafter (apart from being a member of Parliament) kept well away from state affairs.

The name Longleat derives from the waterway or 'leat' which runs to the south west of the house. Like so many Elizabethan mansions, it had its origins in a monastic foundation. To begin with, by the late thirteenth century, there was a minor Augustinian priory. In the late fifteenth century this was taken over by the monks of Hinton Charterhouse (Carthusians); then at the Dissolution of the Monasteries it came into royal hands. Thynne bought the property for the modest sum of £53.

What he had obtained — apart from the estate — was a shabby little cluster of monastic buildings, probably grouped round a central court; they included chapel and cloisters. These he set about converting to domestic use ready for his marriage in 1548. Containing about twenty-seven smallish rooms, it can only have been a fairly modest dwelling, a quarter of the size of the present house. The adaptations he made seem to have included altering the windows, removing the buttresses, adding a tower to the front, and putting a mezzanine floor in the chapel. On his release from prison, however, Thynne set about a thorough rebuilding. This second Longleat grew slowly over a period of fourteen years, and was a far more ambitious project incorporating a new wing and a much larger Great Hall. A Long Gallery and other rooms were added to the east and north, and on the exterior crenellated towers and a row of gables. The old ecclesiastical character of the building seems to have been eliminated. The house was barely completed when, on 21 April 1567, fire broke out, raged for four hours and gutted many of the rooms. Thynne went to live at Corsley for the next five years. His steward wrote to him a month after the fire, reporting on the state of the house: 'The west side of Longleate hous ys almost taken down to the corbell.'

Nothing daunted, Thynne began building a third Longleat. For this purpose he assembled a highly skilled group of craftsmen. His right-hand man on the previous house had been the Englishman, William Spicer; a contract survives specifying that it was built 'according to a platt [plan] thereof made and signed by the said Sir John Thynne and William Spicer'. Spicer also worked for his employer as a bailiff and rent-collector. But there seems to have been some disagreement and in 1563 Spicer left abruptly, taking some of the rent-money with him. Later he worked for the Earl of Leicester at Kenilworth, and finally reached the top of his profession by becoming Surveyor of the Royal Works in London.

Thynne then took into his employ two Frenchmen, Adrian Gaunt (a joiner) and Alan Maynard (a sculptor). These two may have done much to introduce a classical element into the design of the third Longleat. Gaunt was paid a total of £4 15s. for making a wooden model showing how the completed building was to look. The first instalment was paid in December 1567.

In 1568 the young Robert Smythson joined the team.[1] He was to become the most notable of them all; the first and only Elizabethan one could properly term an architect.

Clearly, though, he was not the designer of Longleat. That was more likely to have been Sir John Thynne himself. Described as 'an ingenious man and a traveller', he was very much aware of continental architecture, particularly French. In addition he had no doubt taken careful note of Somerset House, his former patron's house in the Strand.

One of the most remarkable things about Longleat is its plan. Contemporaries must have thought so too and a late sixteenth-century drawing of it survives at Hatfield. It shows a rectangular double-courtyard house, its outward symmetry concealing the intricacy of the interior. The whole structure was covered with countless gabled roofs. The roofs still exist, although not easily visible behind the cresting and balustrades. The exterior of the third version of Longleat finally disappeared behind the elegant classical façades of the fourth (begun in 1572). Outwardly the mansion was transformed. In its final Elizabethan form it was wrapped round with classical façades incorporating orders

---

[1] For a fascinating and detailed study of his work, see Mark Girouard's *Robert Smythson and the Elizabethan Country House* (Yale, 1983).

correctly placed — Doric below, then Ionic, and finally Corinthian at the top. With its generous outward-looking windows, the house had a serene look, and such qualities of unity and harmony that instinctively one labels it Renaissance.

On closer inspection, however, all is not quite as it seems, and there are one or two interesting quirks. The chimneys necessary in a British climate were made to masquerade as coupled Doric columns; little staircases giving access to the roof were enclosed in turrets or 'types', while larger turrets served as 'banketting houses'. These provided an intimate setting where guests could consume sweetmeats and wine and admire the view over the Wiltshire countryside.

The cost of all this was considerable, but building was Thynne's one extravagance. In fact his craftsmen were not overpaid. Smythson and Maynard, the principal masons, were contracted to work at 16d. and 14d. a day; but Thynne undercut them by putting them on piece-work instead and employing other less skilled men at lower rates. However, the programme was enormous; when Sir John died, the cost of his building at Longleat was calculated at £8,016 13s. 8¼d.

People had begun to wonder where he got his money from, and Thynne was asked to appear before the Privy Council to account for his wealth. He answered them calmly that the fortune he had gained from his marriage had been augmented by his industrious and frugal way of life. 'For the rest, my Lords,' he said, 'you have a good mistress our gracious Queen; and I had a good master, the Duke of Somerset.'

From these enquiries alone it is clear that Thynne was not working away in obscurity. Enormous interest was aroused in what appeared at the time a quite revolutionary building. Of neighbouring critics his steward reported, 'Some were pleased and some were grieved'; but Longleat rapidly achieved far more than local renown. Plans of it were sent to Sir William Cecil; Lord Hertford asked for advice on designing a 'garden house', and Thynne's workmen were much in demand elsewhere. His carpenter was required to help constuct the roof of the hall of the Middle Temple, his 'connynge plaisterer' was invited to work for Sir William Cavendish at Chatsworth (once he had finished at Longleat), and Robert Smythson was recognized as an up-and-coming man and was offered commissions for other great projects, such as Wollaton.

What had prompted Sir John Thynne to dig so deeply into his pockets and create so magnificent a house? Unlike Hatton's

Holdenby or Cecil's Theobalds, it was not primarily to entertain the Queen. Rather it was to satisfy his own personal interests and ambitions. While he does not seem to have been a particularly lovable man (he treated his workmen shabbily on occasion), he was single-minded in pursuing the main preoccupation of his life — building. He worked at it slowly and deliberately, and not the smallest detail escaped his attention.

The Queen's curiosity was aroused; she wanted to see for herself the fabulous house in Wiltshire. But Sir John was reluctant. 'I thought it good to let you know', Sir Henry Seymour wrote to him, 'how of late Her Majesty had speech concerning you, that you seem unwilling to receive her this yeare at your house, making excuses of sickness and other letts [hindrances] thereby to divert her from the country.' The owner was a perfectionist and perhaps felt that all was not entirely ready. However, in the end she did make a visit. This was in 1574 on her way back from Bristol, and she was most impressed by the house. Afterwards Lord Hertford reported to Sir John, 'Thanks be to God, Her Majesty is well returned with good health and great liking her entertainment in ye West parts, and namely [particularly] at your house, which twice sithence to myself, and last Sunday to my Lady's grace, she greatly commended.'

The Longleat we see today is in some respects altered from the house Elizabeth admired in 1574. Sir John Thynne, its initiator, died in 1580, and the building was continued by his son, another Sir John. To him is accredited the raising of the top (Corinthian) storey of the façade, and also certain of the chimneys and turrets. Some of the panelling and the screen in the Great Hall also date from his time. The Great Hall with its fine fireplace with caryatids, stone-flagged floor and bold hammerbeam roof, is one of the few rooms inside Longleat that still retain their Elizabethan character, for between 1806 and 1820 much was altered by Sir Jeffrey Wyatville for Thomas Thynne, second Marquis of Bath. Wyatville also completed the North Front, matching the design of the other façades, and set up the stable block. Later in the century (1870s and 1880s) the fourth Marquis, who had been on the Grand Tour, had the interior remodelled in the Italian fashion by the firm of J.D. Grace, replacing the work of old Sir John's 'connynnge plaisterer' with ornately gilded ceilings incorporating some of the pictures he had bought on his travels. Meanwhile, on the outside, baroque statues had been set up on the roof in 1685, where they blend in very well and make an attractive embellishment alongside the Elizabethan cresting. The gardens, which would have been of the formal geometric type characteristic of sixteenth-century taste, were altered in the late seventeenth century and then transformed in 1757-62 by 'Capability' Brown. A cluster of small gabled buildings to the west, probably part of the old monastery, were done away with, and the grounds were landscaped with avenues of trees and wide stretches of greensward. These though alien to the character of the building, yet provide a gentle and unobtrusive setting to this most classical of Elizabethan mansions.

'A very fair, neat, and elegant house' William Camden described it, in his *Britannia* of 1586.

Knole, exterior. The main structure here seems to have been built by Henry VIII to house his retinue, and is likely to have been used for a similar purpose by Elizabeth during her visit in 1573.

KNOLE

'It has the deep inward gaiety of some very old woman who has always been beautiful.'

(Victoria Sackville-West, *Knole and the Sackvilles*)

It is remarkable how so vast a house can yet be intimate. The name signifies a mound or knoll, and describes its commanding position. It lies to the east and a little above the town of Sevenoaks; beyond park to the south there is a steep descent to the Weald — now mostly farmland, but at least until Saxon times dense forest inhabited by wild boar. Knole Park has been enclosed since 1456. Though at times parts have been ploughed, and the whole has provided a profitable warren for rabbit-catching, almost all its many acres are now grass, bracken and beech trees. Deer roam them at will.

Thus Knole has a natural setting, and built as it is of Kentish ragstone, blends gently with it. It is enormous; it has sometimes been called a 'calendar' house, for it is said to contain three

131

hundred and sixty-five rooms, fifty-two staircases and seven courtyards. With its tranquil sequence of courtyards it is like a very large college; at the same time it had, in its heyday, the character of a whole town. Water was supplied by a well in Water Court, and then from reservoirs under Stone Court — the latter were fed by rainwater pipes. The drainpipes are dated 1605 and bear the initials of Thomas Dorset. As well as kitchens, there were numerous workshops — brewhouse, smithy, dairy, saddle-maker's, slaughterhouse and chandlery; it could be virtually self-sufficient. Despite this, and its dominant position, Knole is not in any way assertive; only an aerial view will reveal the extent of the buildings — there are seven acres (3 hectares) of roof. Courtyard opens into courtyard and horizontals predominate, only punctuated by not very high towers and rows of leopard-crowned gables.

The oldest part is on the north-east side, where the masonry is, in places, ten or twelve feet (3 or 4 metres) thick. There is a tradition that there was a Roman building on the site, though little evidence survives. The first documentary reference is in the Lambeth Palace papers, where it states that in 1281 it belonged to William and Roger de Knole. After that it belonged to the Lords Say and Sele, but it is hard to discover how Knole appeared in those days — perhaps more like a castle — and which parts of the present house date from them. This is because the usual practice at Knole has been not to demolish old walls but to add on to them.

On 4 July 1450, James Fiennes, Baron Say and Sele and the King's Lieutenant for Kent, was set upon in the Jack Cade Rebellion and decapitated. His son, William, caught up in the Wars of the Roses, decided to sell the family property. So in 1456 the house was bought by Thomas Bourchier, Archbishop of Canterbury; he paid £266 13s. 4d. for the whole estate. Bourchier was descended from the powerful Bohun family, Earls of Hereford, and he bought Knole as a private individual. He was a cardinal and Lord Chancellor, an influential and wealthy man. Before his death he gave Knole to the see of Canterbury. The archbishops already had a manor-house at Otford, only three miles away — Otford had been a favourite haunt of Becket's and was to be rebuilt and extended into a palace by Warham. But Bourchier preferred Knole; he lived there for thirty years and died there in 1486.

It is from his time that most of the structure of the house derives. The Great Hall, for instance (although internally much altered), dates from about 1460, as does the Brown Gallery. Accounts for

1467 and 1468 refer to a new tower; the tower between Stone Court and Green Court still bears his name. The colonnade may also date from this time. In the accounts for 1468-69 Knole is referred to as a 'great house'. What is difficult to determine is whether it was already a great house when Bourchier took it over, or whether he was responsible for almost the entire building — which would make it the largest fifteenth-century private house in the country. In any case there was constant expenditure, as the accounts for 1468 demonstrate: 'Repairs at Knole. One labourer for six days work in the great chamber and the new seler, 2s. [This probably means 'solar' rather than celler, and is likely to refer to the room now called the Ballroom.] Making of 700 lathes to the new tower, 14d. One labourer $4\frac{1}{2}$ days in the old kitchen, 4d.', and the sum of 113s. 2d. was paid for repairing the slaughterhouse.

Bourchier was succeeded as Archbishop by Cardinal Morton, and he made further additions to Knole; but it is uncertain which parts are his and which are Bourchier's — this applies both to the chapel and to the oriel window above the gatehouse between Green Court and Stone Court. Morton died at Knole in 1500 and was succeeded by Dean and Warham. It is not known whether either of these contributed anything to the building — Warham at least seems to have concentrated his attention on Otford. He was followed by Cranmer, and it was during his time that Knole became royal property. Cranmer did his best to retain it, but eventually had to give way. His secretary Ralph Norice left the following account of the transaction:

'My Lord, minded to have retained Knole unto himself, said that it was too small a house for his Majesty. Marry, said the King, I had rather have it than this house, meaning Otford; for it standeth on a better soil. This house standeth low, and is rheumatick, like unto Croydon, where I could never be without sickness. And as for Knole, it standeth on a sound, perfect and wholesome ground; and if I should make abode here, as I do surely mind to do now and then, I will live at Knole and most of my house shall live at Otford. And so by this means both those houses were delivered into the King's hands.'

Henry VIII will have kept a considerable household at Knole whenever he used it, and its proximity to the Boleyns' home at Hever Castle may have been an added attraction for a while. It is thought that the three sides of the first or Green Court (excluding range the which includes Bourchier's Tower) were built to accommodate some of his suite. The buildings to the left of this are still called the King's Stables. From this time also dates a bell in Bourchier's Tower cast by Jan de Steghe, a Fleming, in 1540, and inscribed to St George.

Knole continued as Crown property until the reign of Elizabeth I, though from time to time it was let out, and at one stage (1561-66) was the house of the Earl of Leicester. Again it is difficult to tell how much interest he took in it, but the name Leicester Gallery still survives. In June 1566 the Queen decided to make it over to Thomas Sackville (1536-1608); he was a second cousin of hers on the Boleyn side.

Thomas Sackville was the only son of Sir Richard Sackville, Chancellor of the Exchequer and so wealthy a man that he was nicknamed Fill-Sack; his seat was at Buckhurst. As a young man Thomas excelled as a writer. Some of his work appears a little stilted now, but he wrote some very fine poetry, and together with Thomas Norton was the author of *Ferrex and Porrex* (later called *Gorboduc*), the first blank-verse tragedy to be written in English. It was probably in this context that Thomas, as a young man, first came to the Queen's notice, for the play was performed in front of her in 1560-61. He travelled in France and Italy and spent a good deal of his father's money. The year after he had been given Knole he was knighted and created Lord Buckhurst. Thereafter he sobered down, abandoned literature (unfortunately) and devoted himself to public affairs. He became one of the Queen's most trusted statesmen and diplomate. In 1586 he was given the difficult assignment of announcing her death warrant to Mary Queen of Scots. He rose in office and in 1604 James I created him Earl of Dorset; four years later he died, dramatically but fittingly, at the Council table.

Although the house had been given to him nearly forty years earlier, it was let to tenants, and Thomas Sackville was able to live there only for the last six years of his life. However, he spent vast sums of money on it — at one stage £40,000 in ten months — and almost totally transformed the interior. He may possibly have had John Thorpe as his surveyor. The names of some of his craftsmen are recorded. Cornelius Cuer was a master-mason; he was paid £26 10s. in 1607 for stones for the magnificent tall chimney-piece in the ballroom, and it is possible he carved it as well. Richard Dungan, who was also the King's plasterer, produced some splendid geometrical ceilings. William Portinton, relying heavily on Flemish pattern-books, probably carved the flamboyant oak

Knole, the Painted Staircase. On the newel posts and on the walls opposite appears the leopard badge of the Queen's trusted counsellor, Sir Thomas Sackville.

screen in the Great Hall, while to Paul Isaacson is attributed the allegorical and *trompe-l'oeil* painting on the Great Staircase. Isaacson was also responsible for painting the Cartoon Gallery, for which he was paid £100. It is thought that he is identical with the Paul Jackson who painted a hall screen at Greenwich Palace for Queen Elizabeth in 1594.

The famous collection of furniture at Knole includes some early seventeenth-century X-framed chairs; most other items are later in date, and there are several royal pieces obtained when a later Sackville, as Lord Chamberlain, was allowed to acquire out-moded furniture from such palaces as Whitehall and Hampton Court. The house has continued to be lived in by the Sackvilles to this day, although it is now owned and administered by the National Trust. Its story is very much the story of the family. Fire damaged part of the house in 1623, including the Venetian Ambassador's Room, and this resulted in some rebuilding. But the general character of Knole has remained unchanged; the pervading styles are still Tudor and Jacobean. It is a rambling house, the rooms not over-large or over-light; it is a place to be explored.

Elizabeth I visited it in 1573, and stayed there for five days before going on to Birlingham and Sir Thomas Gresham's house at Mayfield. Beyond the bare fact that her visit was of this duration (and Knole is referred to, not very accurately, as her own house —belonging to Thomas Sackville, it was occupied at the time by John Lennard of Chevening), nothing seems to be known about it. In default of hard fact, one turns to literature. Virginia Woolf's *Orlando*,[1] a fantastic biography spanning nearly five centuries and based on Victoria Sackville-West and her forebears at Knole, contains this description of the Queen's arrival:

'After an hour or so — the sun was rapidly sinking, the white clouds had turned red, the hills were violet, the woods purple, the valleys black — a trumpet sounded. Orlando leapt to his feet. The shrill sound came from the valley. It came from a dark spot down there; a spot compact and mapped out; a maze; a town, yet girt about with walls; it came from the heart of his own great house in the valley, which, dark before, even as he looked and the single trumpet duplicated and re-duplicated itself with other shriller sounds, lost its darkness and became pierced with lights. Some were small hurrying lights, as if servants dashed along corridors to answer summonses; others were high and lustrous lights, as if they burnt in empty banqueting-halls made ready to receive guests who had not come; and others dipped and wavered and sank and rose, as if held in the hands of troops of serving-men, bending, kneeling, rising, receiving, guarding, and escorting with all dignity indoors a great Princess alighting from her chariot. Coaches turned and wheeled in the courtyard. Horses tossed their plumes. The Queen had come.

...Orlando, overcome with shyness, darted off and reached the banqueting-hall only just in time to sink upon his knees and, hanging his head in confusion, to offer a bowl of rose water to the Queen herself.

Such was his shyness that he saw no more of her than her ringed hand in water; but it was enough. It was a memorable hand; a thin hand with long fingers always curling as if round orb or sceptre; a nervous, crabbed, sickly hand; a command-

[1] The manuscript of *Orlando* is still at Knole.

ing hand too; a hand that had only to raise itself for a head to fall; a hand, he guessed, attached to an old body that smelt like a cupboard in which furs are kept in camphor; which body was yet caparisoned in all sorts of brocades and gems; and held itself very upright though perhaps in pain from sciatica; and never flinched though strung together by a thousand fears; and the Queen's eyes were light yellow.'

Penshurst Place, the South Front.

PENSHURST PLACE

Thou art not, Penshurst, built to envious shoe
Of touch or marble, nor can boast a row
Of polished pillars, or a roof of gold
Thou hast no lantern whereof tales are told...
Thou joyest in better marks, of soil, of air,
Of wood, of water; therein art thou fair.

Ben Jonson (1573-1637), *To Penshurst*

Penshurst in Kent is surely one of the loveliest houses in England, and one of the least ostentatious. Even at the time critics were beginning to find there was something not quite satisfying about the fashionable trends in Elizabethan architecture; being so linear, so patterned, so two-dimensional, it lacked substance. It was like cut paper-work', William Harrison remarked in his *Description of England*. It had a transitory look, as if it had been raised in a day, and in a day might disappear. No such charge could be levelled against Penshurst. There the building was of gradual growth, spanning centuries. No formal scheme has been imposed on it. Its successive owners have added to it according to their own tastes and requirements, and the result is an irregular ground-plan, hardly anywhere more than one room deep. Consequently it is outward-looking; and in this resembles the characters of those who built and lived in it.

The house is made of warm sandstone, and it lies among the pleasant watermeadows about four miles south west of Tonbridge. Throughout the Middle Ages there had been a manor house at Penshurst. The first owner whose name has come down to us was Sir Stephen de Penchester; he was Constable of Dover Castle and Warden of the Cinque Ports. Since he had no son, after his death in 1299 the estate passed to the husband of his daughter, Alice, and then to his grandsons, Thomas and Stephen de Columbers. It was from them that Sir John de Pulteney bought the property in about 1338. Sir John was a prosperous wool-merchant, four times Mayor of London. He founded a Carmelite friary in Coventry, a chantry in St Paul's Cathedral and a college for a master, thirteen priests and four choristers in St Lawrence's Church in the City. (The church was afterwards named St Lawrence Poultenay or Pountney after him.) Renowned not only for his piety but for the splendour of his table, he was much in favour with Edward III who knighted him and borrowed large sums of money from him.

Writing nearly three centuries later, Sir Francis Bacon remarked, '... you cannot have a perfect palace, except you have two several sides; a side for the banquet... and a side for the household; the one for feasts and triumphs, and the other for dwelling.' This was exactly the balance fourteenth-century Penshurst achieved. The heart of the house was the Barons' Hall. Ranged on one side with the solar, or withdrawing room, with the crypt underneath; on the other the domestic offices, pantry and buttery, and between them a passage leading to where the kitchen was. The overall plan of the medieval house makes a flattened 'H'.

Entering by the Screens Passage from the south door, one walks straight into the fourteenth century, for the superb Barons' Hall survives almost unaltered. Cool, lofty and spacious, it is surmounted by a magnificent chestnut roof. Great arched braces of timber curve to support purlins and collar-beams; above them crown-posts rise to the apex. At the base of each arch is a life-size carved wooden figure — men and women, ten of them in all, and like the roof dating from the fourteenth century. The company would have sat at trestle tables, similar to the fifteenth-century ones still in the hall today, and were warmed by an open hearth, above which there used to be a louvre to let out some of the smoke. At the end nearest the solar a low dais accommodated the host and principal guests, while above was a slit window with a view down into the hall. The room continued to be used in this way until at least the sixteenth century, when a panelled screen and minstrels' gallery were added at the further end. It is extraordinary to think that in the reign of Elizabeth the way of life continued here just as in the Middle Ages.

Sir John de Pulteney seems to have died in the Black Death in 1349, leaving his wife, Margaret, and a son, William, who was only nine years old. Since William died without issue the estate went to Margaret's second husband, Sir Nicholas de Lovayne. They had a son Nicholas and a daughter Margaret. Nicholas married another Margaret, eldest daughter of the Earl of Oxford, but they had no children. Margaret de Pulteney then married a third time, to Sir John Devereux, and he inherited Penshurst. This was in the reign of Richard II, who knighted him, made him Steward of the Royal Household, and in 1392 gave him a licence to crenellate Penshurst, where he built a defensive system of curtain-walls and towers. When he died in 1394, Penshurst reverted to his wife, Margaret, and at her death it went to her daughter (Margaret, sister of Nicholas de Lovayne). She married twice, first to Richard Chamberlayne of Northamptonshire, and secondly to John

Penshurst Place, the Barons' Hall.

Seyntclere of Ightham in Kent. When both she and Sir John died at almost the same time (1408), the estate went to their young son, another John Seyntclere. He, however, sold it to John, Duke of Bedford, third son of Henry IV. The Duke was made regent of France during the minority of Henry IV. He waged war successfully in France and his nephew was crowned king of that country in 1431. The Duke died four years later and was buried in Rouen.

Meanwhile he had made additions to Sir John Pulteney's Penshurst, and built a new wing beyond the upper end of the hall. The gables bear his badges of falcon and ibex.

Since the Duke of Bedford had no children, the estate was passed on to his brother, Humphrey, Duke of Gloucester ('Good Duke Humphrey', fourth son of Henry IV). He was an educated and forceful man; he founded the Divinity Schools at Oxford and his collection of books formed the nucleus of the Bodleian Library.[1] He acted as regent in England during the minority of Henry VI; he opposed his nephew's marriage to Margaret of Anjou, thus making an enemy of her. She had him arrested (1447) and a few days later he was found dead in bed. Duke Humphrey

---

[1] A book by John Capgrave in the Library of Oriel College, Oxford, bears the inscription 'This book belongs to me, Humphrey, Duke of Gloucester, the gift of brother John Capgrave, who presented it to me at my Manor of Penshurst, New Year's Day, 1438'. The original is in French.

also being childless, the propery went to Henry VI, who passed it on to Humphrey Stafford, Duke of Buckingham. He died at the Battle of Northampton in 1460, and after that it went to his grandson Henry. Henry joined with Richard, Duke of Gloucester against the boy-king Edward V, and was instrumental in putting Richard on the throne. But in supporting the cause of the Earl of Richmond (later Henry VII) he fared less well; he was taken prisoner and beheaded at Salisbury in 1483. His eldest son Edward became Duke of Buckingham and inherited Penshurst; in 1519 he feasted Henry VIII in the Barons' Hall. But over-ambition was his downfall — he said he expected to be the heir to the throne if Henry should die childless — and he was likewise beheaded (at the Tower, 17 May 1521).

At Penshurst, the so-called Buckingham Building lies on the left side of the south front; but it is thought that this second period of building, far more defensive than Pulteney's, is more likely to date from the dukes of Bedford and Gloucester.

After the execution of the Duke of Buckingham, Penshurst and the other estates became Crown property. Edward VI gave it away to Sir Ralph Fane. He was a supporter of the Duke of Somerset, and like him was executed (26 February 1552). Then the King granted it to Sir William Sidney and his heirs.

It is with the Sidneys that Penshurst is most strongly associated. The earliest known Sidney was John de Sydenie who owned property in Chiddingfold on the Surrey-Sussex border in about 1280. William Sidney of Kingsham in Sussex was MP for the county in the Parliaments of 1429 and 1433. The Sir William who was granted Penshurst had held a post in the household of Henry VIII. Then he made a name for himself in military service, fighting under Ferdinand of Aragon against the Moors, then in sea battles, and at Flodden Field. He was at the meeting of Henry VIII and François I of France at the Field of the Cloth of Gold. He died at Penshurst less than two years after he had been given it.

On the porch of the gatehouse Sir William's son, Henry, put up a tablet commemorating the grant of Penshurst by Edward VI to his 'trustye and wellbeloved servant'.

Henry was Sir William's heir, and there were also four daughters, one of whom, Frances, founded Sidney Sussex College, Cambridge. Sir Henry was brought up alongside young Edward VI and became one of his Gentlemen of the Bedchamber. It was in his arms that the King died. By all accounts he grew into an estimable man. Holinshed said this of him, 'for his comeliness of person, gallantness, and liveliness of spirit, virtue, quality, beauty and good composition of body, he was the only ... paragon of the Court'. Knighted as a young man, he was sent on ambassadorial duties in France and Scotland. In 1551 he married Lady Mary Dudley. He was fortunate not to be implicated in that family's plot to place Lady Jane Grey on the throne, on account of which his wife's father and brother, Guildford, were executed, as well as her sister-in-law, Lady Jane. On the death of Edward VI he made a timely retirement to his newly inherited Penshurst. He did, however, add the Dudleys' badge of the Bear and Ragged Staff to the Sidney insignia of the Porcupine, and these are much in evidence at Penshurst.

Sir Henry's eldest son, Philip — whose fame was to outshine his father's — was born at Penshurst on 30 November 1554, and a tree was planted there in commemoration. The child was named after the King of Spain, whom his father escorted to England to be married to Mary Tudor. Despite having married a Dudley, Sir Henry was fairly well in favour with the Queen, and continued to be respected by Elizabeth who made him Lord President of the Marches of Wales.

Meanwhile more children had been born — Margaret in 1556 (who died only two years later, and was buried at Penshurst), Elizabeth in 1560 (named after the Queen who was her godmother, she died in Ireland at the age of seventeen and was buried in Dublin Cathedral), Mary in 1561, born in Wales (she was to become the celebrated Countess of Pembroke), Ambrosia (who died at Ludlow Castle in 1574), then in 1563, Robert (later Earl of Leicester), and finally in 1569, Thomas (died in 1595).

Sir Henry's official duties took him from Wales to Ireland then back to Ludlow Castle, which became a second home for the Sidney family. In 1562 he was obliged to leave them in order to go as ambassador, first to France and then to Scotland (he carefully noted his expenses: £240 9s. 5d. for the French trip, £132 6s. 8d. for the Scottish). He was rewarded by being made a Knight of the Garter. Queen Elizabeth obviously had a good opinion of him, but he was never one of the Court circle she liked to keep close at hand. She sent him as Lord Deputy to Ireland, to suppress rebellion in Tyrone and Tyrconnel. He was shipwrecked on the way and lost many possessions, including his wife's clothes and jewels. Sir Henry did his best in Ireland, at some cost to his health as well as to his purse. The Queen, however, recalled him in 1567 and summoned him to Hampton Court. When five years earlier she had been critically ill there with smallpox, Henry's wife, Mary, had helped to nurse her, and in doing so had caught the disease herself.

Sir Philip Sidney. (National Portrait Gallery)

He was appalled when he saw the change in his wife's appearance: 'I left her a full fair lady, in mine eye at least, the fairest; and when I returned I found her as foul a lady as a small-pox could make her.'

Philip, meanwhile, had been sent to school at Shrewsbury; from there he went to Christ Church, Oxford (1568), but left the university in 1571 because of the terrrible plague in the city (see page 67). He was only sixteen years old. He travelled abroad for three years and studied languages. He was back in London in June 1575, and at Kenilworth for the festivities later that summer (see page 74). It was there that he probably met Penelope Devereux whom he celebrated in verse as 'Stella'.

Sir Henry enjoyed a temporary respite at Penshurst when he was recalled from Ireland in 1567 but, much against his will, he was sent back. Briefly he was replaced and returned to his duties in Wales; then despite his poor health was once again posted to Ireland. Philip was there too, with the Earl of Essex. When the Earl died there, Philip returned and was sent on an embassy to Austria. Meanwhile his sister Mary had been married to the Earl of Pembroke; when he came back, Philip visited them at Wilton. Both were writers and there seems to have been a genuine sympathy between them.

The graceful and accomplished young Philip was much in favour with the Queen, and spoke up on behalf of his father when she criticized him. But he himself was then banished from the Court because he opposed the idea of Elizabeth marrying the Duc d'Anjou. However, he mollified her with presents, and she gave him the portrait of her which is still at Penshurst. In January 1583 he was knighted, and in September married Frances Walsingham. The Queen was godmother to their daughter who was naturally christened Elizabeth. Philip took a great interest in the New World, and made plans to join Sir Francis Drake on a secret expedition, but the Queen got to hear of it and would not let him go. She had other plans for him. She had decided to help the Protestant Low Countries against Roman Catholic Spain, and in November 1585 she appointed him Governor of Flushing. He left to take up his post the same month.

Sir Henry Sidney, broken and impoverished in the Queen's service, died at Penshurst in May 1586. So much of his time had been spent in Wales and Ireland that he had had little opportunity to relax at Penshurst. Yet he added much to the house, especially to the north and west[2].

[2] Much of the west front was restored by L.B.Rebecca for Sir John Shelley Sidney in the early nineteenth century.

Along the north front there survives from his time the President's Tower at the west end and the King's Tower in the centre. The President's Tower bears the inscription:

'Sir Henrie Sydney Knight of the
Most Noble order of the Garter,
Lorde President of Wales, and the
Marches of the same. One of the
Quenes Maiesties most honorable
Privye Counsell and Late Lorde
Deputie Generall of the Realme
Of Ireland, Anno Domini 1579.'

Lady Mary Sidney did not long survive her husband and died on 9 August the same year; she too was buried at Penshurst. Philip, who had inherited the estates, was in the Netherlands. He had captured the town of Axel and was encamped outside Zutphen. The Battle of Zutphen was joined in order to prevent supplies reaching the town. At the first charge Philip's horse was shot dead under him; at the third and last charge he was wounded in the thigh. His chivalry on this occasion has become a legend. Thirsty from loss of blood, he called for water; but as he was about to drink it, he saw a dying soldier and handed the bottle to him with the words: 'Thy necessity is yet greater than mine.'

The wound turned gangrenous and within a month he died. Seldom has a young man of thirty-two been more widely and sincerely mourned. Perhaps even more after his death than in his life, Sir Philip Sidney came to be regarded as the embodiment of everything the perfect gentleman and courtier should be.[3] 'Her majestie hathe lost a rare servaunt and her realme a worthy membre' wrote Sir Francis Walsingham to the Earl of Shrewsbury (27 October 1586).[4] Seven hundred mourners attended his funeral at St Paul's. At Penshurst is preserved the helmet, with the Sidney porcupine badge, which was carried in front of his coffin.

The estate was inherited by his brother Robert who was not quite twenty-three. Like Philip, he had been educated at Shrewsbury, like him, too, he had a talent for languages and also it seems, from a recently identified notebook, for poetry, but as a young man he longed above all for a soldier's life, 'good warres' to

---

[3] Baldassare Castiglione's *Book of the Courtier*, which sets out this ideal, had already been translated into English by Thomas Hoby (1561).

[4] The letter may be seen at Longleat.

fight in, as he expressed it. In 1584 he married an heiress, Barbara Gamage; although if she had known in time, the Queen would have prevented it. In 1585 he set out with his uncle, the Earl of Leicester, to join Philip in the Low Countries; he was with him at Zutphen, and when he died. Three years later he was made Governor of Flushing, a post he held for twenty-eight years.

On the death of the Earl of Leicester (1588) Sir Robert inherited his estates in addition. Leicester's sword may still be seen at Penshurst. When in the following year Leicester's brother, Ambrose Dudley, Earl of Warwick, died, Robert became his heir as well. Eventually he was to become Viscount Lisle, Chamberlain to Queen Anne of Denmark, Knight of the Garter and Earl of Leicester.

His wife, Barbara, had given birth to a large family; the six eldest appear with her in a charming group portrait at Penshurst. The only son to survive, Robert, was to inherit when his father died. He and his descendents continued to participate in state affairs, to be renowned for their courage or distinguished for their writing, and so the line continues unbroken to this day.

Clearly Sir Robert and Lady Barbara had a great affection for Penshurst. He built the Long Gallery, the stables and the brick walls around the garden. Varied and delightful, the Long Gallery extends along the west wing, and its mullioned windows command views across the gardens and the park.

'My Lady takes great pleasure in this place' his steward Rowland Whyte reported to Sir Robert, 'and surely I never saw a sweeter. All things finely prospering about it.'

Penshurst is still a place to take pleasure in, a quiet pleasure deriving largely from the sense of continuity, the unspoilt, unaffected mellowness. One finds oneself agreeing with Ben Jonson,

> 'Now, Penshurst, they that will proportion thee
> With other edifices when they see
> Those proud, ambitious heaps and nothing else,
> May say, their lords have built, but thy lord dwells.'

HARDWICK HALL

'You shall have sometimes fair houses so full of glass, that one cannot tell where to become to be out of the sun or the cold.'

(Francis Bacon, *Essays, 'Of Building'*)

The best preserved, the most authentic in its detail, of all Elizabethan mansions, is the magnificent Hardwick Hall in Derbyshire. The name immediately calls to mind the old jingle, 'Hardwick Hall, more glass than wall'; and the brave display of tall mullioned windows is indeed the house's most obvious feature.

It was only in Tudor times that glass came much into use for domestic purposes. In the Middle Ages it had been largely confined to church-building. William Harrison, in his *Description of England,* written towards the end of the sixteenth century, commented,

'Of old time our country houses, instead of glass, did use much lattice, and that made either of wicker or fine rifts of oak in checker-wise. I read also that some of the better sort did make panels of horn instead of glass. But as horn in windows is now quite laid down in every place, so lattices are also grown in less use, because glass is come to be so plentiful. Only the clearest glass is most esteemed and each one that may will have it for his building'.

The change had come about not only because of the ready availability of glass, but because there was no longer any need to build for defence. Hardwick Hall stands superbly on the crest of a hill, overlooking a craggy landscape and visible from miles away. It is surmounted by six great towers, each crowned with 'ES', the initials of Elizabeth Shrewsbury (Bess of Hardwick), like an extravagant form of battlement. But there is nothing warlike about the building; the Hardwicks had been established yeomen farmers in the area for generations, and when Bess built the house her right to the property was undisputed.

With its vast expanse of glass, Hardwick must always have been a chilly house in winter. And with the principal state rooms situated on the top floor, remote from the kitchen, it cannot have been the most convenient of mansions. 'Houses are built to live in, and not to look on', Bacon's essay 'Of Building' begins, 'therefore let use be preferred before uniformity, except where both may be

Hardwick Hall, South-west view.

had.' But what Hardwick lacks in convenience, it amply makes up for in drama.

It is above all the expression of one woman, the Countess of Shrewsbury, and therefore her life is of relevance when considering the house. Sometime between 1520 and 1525, from origins of gentry rather than aristocracy, Bess was born plain Elizabeth Hardwick. She was one of a fairly large family, one boy and four girls; and provided with only a small dowry (£26 13s. 4d.) she had little but her wits and her looks to set herself up in the world. So, at the age of about twelve she was placed in the household of Lady Zouche in London. Bess could already read and write — not a universal accomplishment among those of her background — but she was practical rather than scholarly, and would have welcomed the opportunity to refine all those skills she would already have begun to learn, in baking, brewing, spinning, weaving, embroidery, the making of butter and cheese and the growing and use of herbs, which would equip her to understand household management at

149

all levels and, ultimately, it was hoped, to be a mistress of her own domain. This sort of genteel apprenticeship did much to facilitate the climbing of class barriers; Bess may have become one of the *nouveaux riches,* but she never seemed at a loss how to behave. The system was also favoured because it increased the likelihood of making a 'good marriage'. In Lady Zouche's home she met a young man called Robert Barlow — he was only fourteen and she was some years older. He was of a more prosperous family than Bess, but of a much less robust constitution. She was solicitous in looking after him while he was ill (which seems to have been most of the time), and with the approval of both families they were married. But only a few months later he died, and she found herself a youthful widow with an inheritance of £66 a year.

It seems possible that at this stage she joined the household of the Marchioness of Dorset, mother of Lady Jane Grey. But it is certain that in 1547 she married, very advantageously, Sir William Cavendish. He had been a member of the Royal Commission at the Dissolution of the Monasteries, and was at least fifteen years older than her. By him she had eight children, three sons and five daughters, of whom all except two daughters survived infancy. Despite the difference in their ages, this seems to have been a genuinely happy marriage. Bess rejoiced in being mistress of her own household, and rejoiced too, no doubt, when the couple decided to quit town life and spend most of their time in Derbyshire. In 1549 they acquired Chatsworth, and set about first repairing it, and then rebuilding it. Then, in 1557, Sir William was suddenly taken ill while he was in London on business; Bess rushed to his bedside, but despite all her careful nursing, he died.

Heartbroken she may have been, but she had six children to support, and within two years she married again, this time to a widowed courtier from the West Country, Sir William St Loe. He had held the post of butler of the Royal Household, and it was during this marriage, shortly after the accession of Elizabeth I, that Bess first came to Court. This was a mixed blessing, for she was held to be implicated in the affairs of Lady Catherine Grey (who, now pregnant, had married the Earl of Hertford without the Queen's knowledge or approval), and she was imprisoned for seven months in the Tower. Sir William, who was much older than Bess, died in 1564-6 and she inherited much of his property.

Her fourth marriage was the grandest, and the longest-lasting, although not the happiest. In 1568 she married George Talbot, the extremely rich sixth Earl of Shrewsbury. This was a match of which the Queen thoroughly approved, and the matter of Catherine

' Bess of Hardwick ', Elizabeth Countess of Shrewsbury. (Hardwick Hall)

Grey was forgotten. "I have been glad to see my lady St Loe"
Elizabeth said "but now more desirous to see my lady Shrewsbury.
I hope my lady hath known my good opinion of her...There is no
lady in the land that I better love and like."

The Earl of Shrewsbury was also well thought of by the Queen,
who, in 1569, accorded him the doubtful privilege of being
custodian of Mary Queen of Scots, and this was his task until 1584,
at a cost, he said, of £1,000 a year. Although to begin with Bess was
on reasonably good terms with Mary (they shared a liking for

151

Arbella Stewart, aged 23 months. (Hardwick Hall)

embroidery), this was not so later. Her husband's custodianship meant that the family was constantly split up. Allegedly without the Earl's knowledge, Bess's daughter Elizabeth married in 1574 Charles Stewart, brother of Lord Darnley, the murdered husband of Mary Queen of Scots. Why Bess should have been so rash as to encourage this match is unclear. The immediate consequence was that both she and Lady Lennox (Charles's mother) were imprisoned in the Tower. However Bess was released in time to be present at the birth of the couple's daughter, Arbella, in the following year. Charles Stewart died not long after, and Elizabeth when her little girl was only six, so Arbella was brought up by her grandmother at Hardwick. She became the central pivot for Bess's hopes and aspirations.

There then followed a good deal of mud-slinging between Bess and Mary Queen of Scots (Bess declared that Mary was having an affair with the Earl) with, inevitably, the breakdown of her marriage. They separated finally in 1584.

Hardwick had belonged to Bess's brother, James, but in 1581 he died incarcerated in the Fleet Prison for debt. Two years later Bess bought it for the sum of £9,500 from the Lord Chancellor and Auditor acting on behalf of his creditors, so there was no disputing her right to it. The ownership of Chatsworth was another matter, as the Earl of Shrewsbury was also laying claim to it. Finally it was entailed to Bess's eldest son, Henry Cavendish; so Bess concentrated on the rebuilding of Hardwick (the now-ruined mansion known as the Old Hall), and it was arranged that after her death Hardwick should go to her second son, William. Before the Old Hall was completed, Lord Shrewsbury died, and Bess, already an extremely wealthy woman, and now richer by half as much again, started to plan the construction of the New Hall.

Her motives in this were almost certainly tied up with her ambitions for Arbella Stewart. Arbella was, after all, a direct descendant of Henry VIII's elder sister, Margaret; and especially after the execution of Mary Queen of Scots (her aunt), it seemed she might well be next in line for the throne. Assuming, that is, that her cousin James's claim was discounted on the grounds that he was a Scotsman who had never yet set foot in England, let alone been born there. Queen Elizabeth seems at times to have favoured Arbella, and she certainly kept a very close eye on how she was brought up. At Hardwick Arbella was given an education fit for a queen, similar to that Elizabeth I had received from Roger Ascham and William Grindal. For this the Queen allowed the sum of £200 a year. Bess tried to persuade her to increase this to £600, but did not succeed and had to bear any additional cost herself. Arbella was far more scholarly than her grandmother and found this academic instruction entirely congenial; but what she did increasingly resent was the way her grandmother kept her virtually a prisoner.[1]

As for Bess, she was fondly awaiting the day when either the Queen would visit her at Hardwick and openly acknowledge Arbella as her heir, or, perhaps even better, the Queen would die and a deputation of lords would arrive and acclaim Arbella as the new sovereign. When Bess wrote to the Queen she referred to her grand-daughter as 'my jewel Arbelle'. What she was trying to do at Hardwick was not only to realise her own ideas of the perfect house but to construct for this jewel a suitable setting.

Rather than demolish the Old Hall, Bess started to build the New alongside it. She and Arbella lived in the old while the work was going on. The Old Hall was impressive enough with its gabled central façade, flanked by a tower six storeys high, while across the middle of the house was a lofty Great Hall. Unlike the New Hall, it was an asymmetrical building. Now in ruins, it is looked after by the Department of the Environment; but through the gaping windows one can still discern the fine plasterwork in the two reception rooms, the Hill Great Chamber and the Forest Great Chamber. It is a desolate and romantic place; the floors are gone, and birds fly in and out of the empty fireplaces.

In the construction of her New Hall, Bess mainly used building materials from local sources, often from her own estates. She had her own stone and her own timber. The lead came from mines left to her by her first husband, lime from Skegby and Crich, and the glass, which is such a feature at Hardwick, from Wingfield. The master-mason was John Rodes, who had also worked at Wollaton, and he was assisted by his brother, Christopher. We know from the accounts that he was paid 4d. a foot for windows, 6d. a foot for cornices, and $1\frac{1}{2}$d. a foot for plain ashlar.

The building of the New Hall took nine years in all, though she moved in two years before it was completed. While Bess was doubtless watching closely every process involved, as well as checking the cost, the overall design is most likely to be credited to Robert Smythson. This attribution is based not only on stylistic

---

[1] It is strange that no serious plans — apart from being betrothed as a toddler to the Earl of Leicester's son, who died shortly after — were made for Arbella's marriage. Eventually she rebelled against her grandmother's regime and was disinherited. On the death of Queen Elizabeth she went to Court. She made a secret marriage with William Seymour in 1610, and after a series of adventures and misadventures died in the Tower of London, distraught and emaciated, in 1615.

grounds (he had already been responsible for Wollaton, which Hardwick New Hall somewhat resembles), but on an entry in the Hardwick account book for the week ending 27 March 1597 which states,

'Geven to Mr Smythson the surveyour XXs
and to his Sonne Xs'

The ground-plan of the house is basically a long rectangle with square turrets jutting out, two at the front, two at the back, and one on each side. The turrets rise a storey higher than the main block, and it is this which gives the house its uniquely assertive and dramatic look. Their bold verticals contrast with the horizontal lines of the rather low loggias which border the east and west fronts. Quite a modest doorway leads into the hall, which runs from front to back, across the main axis of the building.

In medieval castles and early Tudor mansions the Great Hall had been the heart of the house, and the scene of feasting, celebration and entertainment. At the New Hall of Hardwick it had a rather different function. It was an entrance hall — hence the formality of the fine stone screen and the overmantel decorated with the Hardwick arms held up by capering stags entwined with eglantine — and it was also a servants' hall flanked by pantry, buttery and serving-room. Kitchen and chapel are also at this level, and the Hall houses many of the fine embroideries for which Hardwick is also renowned.

Stone staircases, wide and simple, yet subtle in their gradations, lead to the rooms above. Apart from the turrets, Hardwick Hall consists of three principal floors, but the most formal and lavish of the state-rooms rise to the height of two storeys. As one explores the interior of Hardwick, the general impression is one of gradual crescendo towards the top of the house. The staircase leads upwards to ever more magnificent apartments, from the tranquil Withdrawing Room on the south side, the Low Great Chamber (or Diningroom) on the north — with its stern admonishment over the fireplace, 'The Conclusion of All Thinges to feare God and keepe His Commaundementes'— to the glories of the Long Gallery and the High Great Chamber above.

The Long Gallery extends for 166 feet (51 metres), is from 22 to 40 feet (7-12 metres) wide and 26 feet (8 metres) high. It is adorned by two fine chimney-pieces and a set of thirteen tapestries illustrating the story of Gideon. These were bought by Bess in 1592, along with two other sets, from the nephew of Sir

Christopher Hatton who had died the previous year, deeply in debt, largely on account of his lavish entertainment of the Queen. The Long Gallery also houses most of Bess's picture collection — all portraits of royalty, family or friends.

The High Great Chamber is ornamented with a remarkable plasterwork frieze, almost certainly by Abraham Smith, a local craftsman from Ashford. Bess was so delighted with his work that as well as his wages she rewarded him with a wedding present of 40 shillings. She had good reason to be pleased. Smith's frieze depicts a forest, with hunting scenes, animals (lions, elephants and camels as well as the native deer), and the Court of Diana, no doubt as a compliment to the Queen. Lively and lyrical, the frieze is picked out in colour. Below are tapestries, sixteenth-century from Brussels, illustrating the story of Ulysses — it seems the room was planned to hold them. Among the furnishings is the Eglantine Table, of delicate inlaid work illustrating Tudor pastimes (music, card-games, chess, writing), with the coats-of-arms of the Cavendish and Hardwick families. The motto in the centre, supported by two stags, reads,

'The redolent smele of Aeglentyne
We stagges exault to the deveyne'

The eglantine or wild rose was a symbol of chastity and hence a reference to the virgin Queen; the stags represent the Hardwick family.

The High Great Chamber was sometimes known as the Presence Chamber, but no queen ever graced it. Not even Mary Queen of Scots; although there is a room known as the Scots room, containing one or two things which genuinely relate to her, she never set foot in Hardwick Hall, in fact she was executed four years before the new building was started. Nor did Elizabeth I, despite all the references to her in the decoration of the house; her progresses never extended so far north. And for all that the Long Gallery had been prepared as a setting for the fulfilment of Bess's hopes for her grand-daughter, no deputation of nobles ever arrived to proclaim Arbella queen, only Lord Brounker to inform her of Elizabeth's displeasure and to investigate her dealings with the Earl of Hertford.

Bess, now eighty-three, was furious and bitterly disappointed. She wrote to the dying Queen, apologising for Arbella's 'vain doings' and asking for her to be removed from her care. An attempt to rescue Arbella was made by her uncle, Henry

Cavendish, together with forty armed men, but Bess kept her firmly indoors.

As for Hardwick, even though the chief purpose for which it was built came to nothing, the house remains as the supreme expression of one of the most dynamic women of her time. We see it now very much as Bess knew it, with many of the furnishings listed in her inventory still in place — more than any other house, an evocation of the vigour, drama and intricacy of the Elizabethan age.

WOLLATON HALL

'Each one desireth to set his house aloft on the hill, to be seen afar off, and cast forth its beames of stately and curious workmanship into every quarter of the country.'

(William Harrison, *Description of England*)

Many great houses have evolved slowly, being built to fulfil the tastes and requirements of generation after generation. A few, however, and Wollaton is one of them, have been conceived as works of art, and were commissioned by one man at one particular time. They have been designed all of a piece, often not so much for everyday habitation, as to dazzle the onlooker with their splendour. They are the rich man's equivalent of a traditional front parlour with its ornaments and curtains facing outwards — a place not so much for living in as for impressing the neighbours.

In the Middle Ages Wollaton was a separate village; now it is a suburb three miles from the centre of Nottingham. The Elizabethan mansion stands on a hill, though there was an earlier Wollaton Hall on lower ground by the church. It belonged to the Morteyn family. In 1314 Roger de Morteyn gave 80 acres (32 hectares) of woodland to Richard Willoughby. Five years later Richard married into the Morteyn family and thereby consolidated the estate. Wollaton continued in the hands of the

Wollaton Hall, exterior

Willoughby family from that date until 1925, when it was acquired by the local authority who use it as a natural history museum.

The Willoughby family were originally wool-merchants, but increasingly their prosperity was based on coal. One of the sixteenth-century Willoughbys (Sir Hugh) broke the family mould and became a navigator and explorer; he led an expedition in 1553 to try and find a north-east passage to India and China, but near Nova Zembla his ship was caught in the ice and he and his men all froze to death.

The Francis Willoughby who built the present Wollaton Hall inherited the estate in 1558. Although a coal-magnate and an entrepreneur in various industrial enterprises, he was no *nouveau-riche*. As well as being able to trace his family back to the Middle Ages, he was a cultured man, educated at Cambridge, and possessing an extensive library. Yet something — perhaps a sense of balance, perhaps a sense of humour — was missing from his personality. He was gloomy and suspicious, and consoled himself by commissioning a building of quite outrageous extravagance.

Wollaton Hall was begun about 1580, took eight years to complete, and cost Sir Francis about £8,000. The exterior has hardly altered to this day. It is built of stone from Ancaster, which was paid for in kind with buckets of coal.

Willoughby's 'surveyor' was Robert Smythson, and while he may have consulted with his patron and no doubt made use of his library, his was the overall design for the house. He had already worked for Sir John Thynne at Longleat, and made some name for himself; but at Wollaton he appears to have been given virtually a free hand — something quite exceptional in Elizabethan architecture.

The mansion is roughly square in plan, with elaborate corner pavilions. The original idea was that the grounds should be laid out in an equally symmetrical way, the house being placed centrally in a chequerboard of gardens. The Great Hall at Wollaton is positioned in the middle of the house, and is lit by clerestory windows. At one end Smythson designed a stone screen. Above, the roof appears to be hammerbeam, but this is decoration, not structure. The Hall was originally flanked by great chambers to the north and south and a long gallery to the east. The staircases were a feature of the house, but there were hardly any corridors. Ranges of huge windows are punctuated with classical pilasters, and the pavilions are covered with strapwork motifs culled from Flemish pattern-books. But the most extravagant feature of the house is the Prospect Chamber, perched like a mad conservatory on top of the

Great Hall. One wonders if it was ever used: it could be reached only from the roof and there was no means of heating it. In the design of the windows there is a hint of Gothic tracery, an archaism as deliberate as that of Spenser's *'Faerie Queene'*.

Wollaton is admittedly a wild mixture of styles. To some extent Smythson will have drawn on his knowledge of other great houses; but one imagines that also he must have combed Willoughby's library in a search for decorative motifs of every possible nature. Yet allowing that Wollaton is a show-piece, such exuberance had its place in the taste of the time. It is, as John Buxton expressed it, 'an interpretation of a medieval castle in terms of Elizabethan chivalry'. Sir Francis hoped, no doubt, that the Queen would come. She never did, and it took generations of Willoughbys and a great deal of coal to recoup the family fortunes. Most of them regarded it as a bit of a white elephant, and would have found a bitter truth in the words of Francis Bacon, 'Leave the goodly fabrics of houses, for beauty only, to enchanted palaces of the poets, who build them with small cost.'

KIRBY HALL and HOLDENBY
Houses of Sir Christopher Hatton

'The Queen did fish for men's souls' Sir Christopher Hatton was in the habit of observing, 'and had so sweet a bait that no-one could escape her network.' He omitted to say that if there was one fish who was well and truly caught it was himself. Nearly all her other admirers married sooner or later; Sir Christopher remained single. According to contemporaries, he had danced his way into her favour; Elizabeth was susceptible to young men with an elegant turn of leg. And he meanwhile came to regard her with something like idolatory.

This found expression above all in his building. Kirby Hall and Holdenby both date from much the same time. Their primary function was to entertain guests, in the case of Holdenby specifically to entertain Elizabeth. Once they were no longer required for this purpose, it was inevitable that sooner or later decay and demolition should set in. Today Kirby Hall is mainly a ruin, albeit well preserved, and of the magnificent Elizabethan Holdenby little survives but two archways and some pleasant gardens. The gardens at Kirby Hall are now being laid out in the seventeenth century style, and stocked with plants of the period.

Kirby Hall

Sir Christopher Hatton, builder of Kirkby Hall and Holdenby. (National Portrait Gallery)

Kirby Hall was begun in 1570 for Sir Humphrey Stafford. Stafford died in 1575; the estate was bought by Sir Christopher Hatton and the house completed for him. Its designer is unknown, which is tantalizing for it is an extraordinarily interesting piece of architecture. It is constructed of Weldon stone, and the mason is likely to have been Thomas Thorpe, father of the better known John Thorpe[1], and it was John, as a little boy, who laid the

[1] Surveyor and author of a book on *Les plus fameux bâtiments* of England.

foundation. The site is a remote one in Northamptonshire, two miles north of Corby; it stands alone, in a rather empty landscape.

It is none the less impressive for that. Whereas much Elizabethan architecture aspires to the vertical, Kirby is spread about and seldom more than one or two storeys high. Yet it was deliberately and precisely planned. The south range held the principal reception rooms, including the Great Hall, and being single-storey, it was possible to give it optimum dramatic treatment, with enormously high grid-pattern windows between giant classical pilasters. Lest the horizontal nature of the building should prove monotonous, there are gateways half as tall again, and here the giant orders have been replaced by three layers of detailing, the top one concealing gable and chimneys. On either side of the north courtyard was a series of rooms two storeys high; these have much smaller windows, and were sets of lodgings purpose-built to receive guests. Between these on the north side is an arcaded loggia with a gallery over it. To the west Sir Christopher Hatton added a great staircase, and to the south (unusually for this date) two semi-circular bays of windows. It must have been a delightful house to stay in, especially in the summer — each important guest being given a suite of rooms, independent yet communal, and the whole building admitting light and sun at every point.

Sir Thomas Heneage wrote to Sir Christopher about a visit to it, and in his reply the latter referred to his other house. He said he would leave his 'other shrine, I mean Holdenby, still unseen until that holy saint may sit in it, to whom it is dedicated.' The holy saint was, of course, Elizabeth.

Sir Christopher had been born at Holdenby, which lies seven miles north west of Northampton. The building of his great mansion, once the largest in England, was begun in about 1577; it was completed in 1583, the date on the two surviving archways. These led to the Base or Green Court. Even more than with Kirby Hall, it requires an effort of mind to imagine what it must have been like to live or stay in it.

Hatton seems to have been rather nervous about this ambitious enterprise, and referred to Lord Burghley for advice: 'for as the same is done hitherto in direct observation of your house and plans of Theobalds, so I earnestly pray your Lordship that by your good corrections at this time, it may appear as like to the same as it hath ever been meant to be.' He need not have worried; Burghley gave it his gracious approval (indeed he may have been a little jealous at the young favourite's house outdoing his own in size). He wrote to

163

him in 1579,

> 'I found great magnificence in the front or front pieces of the house, and so every part answerable to other, to allure liking. I found no one thing of greater grace than your stately ascent from your hall to your great chamber; and your chamber answerable with largeness and lightsomeness, that truly a Momus could find no fault. I visited all your rooms, high and low, and only the contention of mine eyes made me forget the infirmity of my legs.'

Holdenby was a double courtyard house with rectangular pavilions at each corner and intersection. The main block was 350 feet (107 metres) long and 225 feet (69 metres) wide; there were three storeys with mullioned windows and pilasters between. In the central range between the two courtyards was an arcaded loggia with a tower rising above it. By the edge of the garden and detached from the main part of the building was a banqueting-house or lodge. Even here things were planned on a large scale; we know from John Thorpe's drawing that it was three storeys high, quite a fair-sized house in its own right.

The mansion was planned with two great series of state rooms, one overlooking the garden for the Queen, and an opposite one, including a Great Chamber, for Sir Christopher. The sad thing was that the Queen never came, and in building Holdenby her faithful courtier bankrupted himself. Though she ultimately rewarded him by making him Lord Chancellor (1587), in money matters she was unbending. He died on 20 November 1591, it was said of a broken heart because the Queen would not forgive him any part of his debts. He owed her £56,000.

Loseley Park, the North Front.

LOSELEY PARK

'Invidiae claudor, pateo sed semper amico' ('I am shut to envy, but always open to a friend')

(Inscription over inner entrance door, Loseley Park)

Of all Elizabethan houses, Loseley Park is one of the most welcoming and friendly. 'Shut to envy', there is nothing pretentious about it, and the visitor is never overawed. Perhaps its friendliness is partly due to the fact that it is still in the hands of the More-Molyneux family whose ancestor built it in the sixteenth century. It is hard to determine why, but this invests it with a special atmosphere, as if one had been invited into somebody's home.

Loseley Park lies between Guildford and Godalming in Surrey. The manor, including an old house on a site near the present one, was bought in 1508 by Sir Christopher More, Sheriff of Surrey and Sussex, who came to acquire this interesting office of Remembrancer to Henry VIII. His son, William More, inherited

165

the property in 1549, and in the period 1562-68 built the present house at a cost of £1,640 19s. 7d. It is thought that he designed it himself; it has indeed the feel of a house planned to suit its owner, rather than impress outsiders. Queen Elizabeth had a good opinion of William More; when he was knighted in her presence in 1576 she commented that he well deserved the honour. For some time she entrusted him with the custody of Henry Wriothesley, Earl of Southampton[1], who was suspected of papacy and conspiring for Mary Queen of Scots. She herself stayed at Loseley Park on three occasions.

Even in the sixteenth century the building would have never looked startlingly new, for the greenish Bargate stone of which it was principally made was already centuries old; it came from the ruined Waverley Abbey near Farnham. To this were added quoins and mullions of white clunch from Guildford; contrasting with the darkish stone, they give the façade an irregular grid-like pattern. Projecting square bays lend variety to the profile, and are finished with right-angled gables.

Sir William died in 1600, and it was about this time that an additional wing was erected on the north-west side. This included a chapel, a gallery and riding-school, but was totally demolished in about 1830. Sir William's successor was Sir George More, 'a man', his son-in-law wrote, 'but little of stature, but of great abilities. By nature very passionate, yet in his wisdom he conquered that passion so much that you would think him to be of a mild disposition.' One occasion when he failed to conquer his passions was over the matter of the marriage of his seventeen year old daughter Ann who made a runaway match with the poet and divine John Donne. He had Donne deprived of his office as secretary to a nobleman at Court and incarcerated in the Fleet Prison. 'John Donne, Ann Donne, undone', the poet commented succinctly.

Sir George entertained James I at Loseley Park on two occasions, and there is a magnificent carpet in the King's Room, patterned with the Crown, the Rose of England and the Thistle of Scotland.

Much Tudor furnishing survives inside the house. In the Great Hall may be found painted panels with the initials of Henry VIII and Katherine Parr, also carved panels with series of arches simulated in low relief; these came from Nonsuch Palace, as did the marble table. In the drawing room is a magnificent fireplace made to a design by Holbein and carved — most unusually — out of

[1] His son, another Henry, was Shakespeare's patron.

Knole: the house from the air.
(Reader's Digest photograph)

Barbara Gamage, Lady Sidney, with six of her children. Attributed to Marcus Gheeraerts the Elder.
(Penshurst Place)

Loseley Park, the Great Hall.

Montacute House: gazebo and border.

chalk. By it are two Elizabethan maid-of-honour chairs, said to have been worked by Queen Elizabeth (though she hated sewing). The ceiling is decorated with the family badges of moorhen and cockatrice, and there is a fine German cabinet of pearwood inlaid with other woods. Portraits in the house include one of Edward VI in 1549, Anne Boleyn, Sir Thomas More (to whom the family was connected by marriage), James I and his Queen, a full-length portrait of Mary Queen of Scots in black, and the builder of the house, Sir William More, with a skull as a *memento mori* — this last by Lucas de Heere.

Some of the furnishings refer directly to Queen Elizabeth's visit to Loseley. Over the mantlepiece in the library are carved in wood her coat-of-arms, initials, and the date 1570; and there is a symbolic flower-painting done on glass, inscribed 'Rosa Electa', the chosen rose — Elizabeth herself.

The Queen had expressed a wish to visit Loseley in August 1576, although Sir Anthony Wingfield told her it was too small. She does appear to have been in Guildford seven years earlier, on 3 and 12 August 1569, the year after the house was completed, so she certainly would have known about it, and very likely stayed there. In 1577 there was plague about, and most of the summer she spent at Greenwich; however, she did stay two nights at Loseley. She enjoyed her visit so much that she decided to come again in 1583, for four or five days in August. Sir Christopher Hatton, as her Vice-Chamberlain, wrote to Sir William More asking him to make the house 'clean and sweet', put straw down on the drive, and remove some of his family and servants to make way for the Queen's retinue. It cannot have been easy to entertain her in a house which, however charming, is of modest size.

The More family motto (to be found in the drawing room) means when translated 'The mulberry tree dying slowly, the fruit about to die quickly'. The Latin word for mulberry is *morus,* so it is a pun on their name. Mulberry trees are known for their longevity, although the fruit does indeed decay swiftly; the idea is that the family survives, even though individual members perish. On one of her visits Elizabeth planted a mulberry tree in the garden. During the Second World War it fell to the ground, yet did not die, and it, even surviving the hurricane of October 1987, is still alive today; and there are four young Mores in the new generation.

MELFORD HALL

A man of solid worth, who had risen to eminence in the time of Mary Tudor, might still command respect in the reign of her sister, Elizabeth. Such a man was William Cordell.

He was before all things a lawyer, and he was made Speaker of the House of Commons. In 1556-7 he had given Queen Mary a New Year's gift of two porringers, worth £7; in exchange he received a silver-gilt cup with cover, weighing 13¾ ounces (376 grammes), and in the following November he was made Master of the Rolls. He retained that office under Queen Elizabeth, holding it right up to his death as an old man in 1581.

Little is known about his early life. He became owner of the Melford estate in 1554. It lies just to the side of the delightful Suffolk village of Long Melford; a village which in the later Middle Ages enjoyed great prosperity on account of the wool trade — a fact perpetuated in the great length and magnificence of its church. Cordell was clearly a well-respected figure locally as well as in London, and known for his charitable work; in Long Melford he endowed almshouses to shelter twelve poor old men.

On the site of his Melford Hall there had been a medieval manor-house belonging to the abbots of St Edmunds. It is thought that a good deal of this was incorporated by Sir William when he was rebuilding, and the cellars were probably the ground floor of the earlier house. Sir William Cordell's house must have been built sometime between his acquisition of the property and the visit of Elizabeth in 1578.

Apart from the porch and facings of stone, the building materials he chose could hardly have been more local. He used brick, a warm mellow red brick, the clay for which he may well have obtained by enlarging the medieval pond system. The house was originally planned round all four sides of a courtyard (we know this from John Thorpe's plan of about 1606, in the Sir John Soane's Museum); the gatehouse wing was removed later, so the shape is now a squared-off 'U'. The building rises to just two storeys (discounting the gabled roof), and its plain and horizontal nature is relieved only by tall chimneys and equally tall octagonal turrets. There are six of these and they are topped with onion-shaped cupolas. The character of Melford Hall is reminiscent of the palaces of Henry VII and VIII: Richmond, Nonsuch, and the Tudor part of Hampton Court. For its date, therefore, it is a conservative building. The only exception is the stone porch which sits rather oddly in the centre of all this brick and is in the Italianate

Melford Hall, the exterior.

manner, possibly based on Serlio's designs; it bears the builder's initials but no date. His cockatrice badge appears on the rainwater heads. The windows were designed with a central mullion and one transome, but were altered to sashes by Sir Cordell Firebrace in about 1740. Much of the interior was remodelled also in the eighteenth century, whether by him or by the Hyde Parker family, so most of the rooms are Georgian. In 1942, fire necessitated much reconstruction of the north wing. The house is now in the hands of the National Trust.

By the wall on the west side of the garden is the rare survival of a charming Tudor pavilion. Built of brick like the house, it has two floors and rises to pointed gables and pinnacles. The interior was altered in the eighteenth century and later a furnace put in on the ground floor. It has been suggested that it was intended as a guard-house; but each floor having its own fireplace, may have been used for a different purpose — possibly a guardroom below and an intimate banqueting house above.

Inside the house the portaits include one of its builder, Sir William Cordell. Also from his period there are two 'Nonsuch' chests, two Elizabethan court cupboards, several panels of sixteenth century glass (placed there by the ninth baronet at a later date), and a survey commissioned by Sir William in 1580 and

Melford Hall, the Garden Pavilion

Thank You for purchasing Foot-Joy Golf Shoes!

Like many high quality products, Foot-Joy shoes will benefit from a little regular maintenance. By looking after Foot-Joy shoes in the ways outlined below, the comfort and performance of the shoe is preserved and the life of the shoe extended.

- Allow Foot-Joy golf shoes to dry naturally after becoming wet. Never "force dry" them near a fire or radiator as excessive heat will draw the natural oils from the leather causing it to become hard and brittle.

- To preserve the shape at all times, but especially during drying, we recommend the use of shoe trees.

- Remove mud and grass after every round and protect the leather with a good quality shoe polish.

- To Classics and Classics-Lites, apply Leather Sole Treatment by Mars Oil to the sole and welt areas.

- Always use a shoe horn to help your foot into the shoe. This will preserve the support in the heel and ankle areas.

- Replacement spikes should be fitted when the spikes are worn down to approximately half of their original length.

The Foot-Joy Warranty Scheme

The shoes you have purchased are made from the finest materials and designed for comfort and durability. They are guaranteed against failure due to manufacturing defects for a period of 1 year of reasonable wear from the date of purchase. There is, however, no waterproof guarantee given or implied with this model.

In the event of a claim under this warranty please return the shoes to the place of purchase together with this card where the retailer will compensate you for the potential loss of use resulting from the failure. Please note that this warranty does not cover failure due to misuse, neglect, wilful damage or excessive wear and the compensation payable shall not in any event exceed the purchase price of the shoes. This warranty is offered without prejudice to your statutory rights.

Model Purchased --- Date ----------------

Retailers Signature -- Club ----------------

carried out by Israel Amyce. By the staircase is a stained glass portrait of Elizabeth, said to be wearing the dress she wore at the thanksgiving service in St Paul's after the defeat of the Spanish Armada.

When Queen Elizabeth arrived in Suffolk in 1578, it seems it was at short notice; there was a hurried buying-up of all the silks and velvets that could be found. Two hundred young men were quickly decked out in white velvet, and a hundred, more senior, attired discreetly in black. Sir William feasted her lavishly, and 'did lighte such a candle to the rest of the shire', according to Thomas Churchyard's report, that many 'were glad bountifully and franckly to follow the same example.'

Parham Park, the South Front.

PARHAM PARK

Charming, unpretentious, H-shaped, Parham Park lies in the shelter of the South Downs, four miles from Pulborough in West Sussex. It is built of grey stone and, with its four acres of walled garden, it is set among smooth lawns and ancient oaks. The park is stocked with fallow deer, as it has been since at least the early seventeenth century, and probably well before that, and the house is tranquil, friendly and intimate.

The manor of Parham was given to Robert Palmer, a mercer from London, at the time of the Dissolution of the Monasteries. His son, William, married Eleanor Verney, a god-daughter of Queen Elizabeth, and their son Thomas as a little boy laid the foundation-stone of a larger house on the site, incorporating the old one. This was in 1577, and this is essentially the Parham that we see today.

There is a legend, though not documented, that the Queen visited the house in 1593, and dined there on her way from Sutton Place to Cowdray. It is difficult to prove the truth of this, for few details appear to survive of what she did that summer; most of it she seems to have spent at Windsor.

Thomas Palmer sold the estate in 1601 to Thomas Bysshop of Henfield. The Bysshop family, eleven generations of them, kept Parham for over three hundred years. Then in 1922 the seventeenth Baroness Zouche of Haryngworth sold it to the Hon. Clive Pearson, second son of the first Viscount Cowdray. His eldest daughter, Veronica Tritton, still lives at Parham.

The house retains much of its Elizabethan character. Admittedly some of the windows have been converted to sashes, but the original tall mullioned ones are still there in the Great Hall, and bathe the room with light. An extremely tactful and imaginative restoration of the house took place in the time of Clive Pearson. He revealed hidden internal windows between the Great Hall and the Great Chamber, and he employed Esmond Burton to do plaster-work very much in the Tudor tradition, and Oliver Messel to cover the ceiling of the Long Gallery with a tracery of painted branches.

One of the chief delights of Parham is its wealth of furnishings, paintings and embroideries. The Great Hall has its original panelling and carved oak screen, Tudor benches and chest. There is a portrait (said to be of Queen Elizabeth) of a lady in late sixteenth-century dress with stiff elongated bodice and leg-of-mutton sleeves embroidered with mulberry leaves and silk-worms. There is a portrait of Edward VI by Guillim Stretes, and paintings of many of the Queen's friends and advisers: William Cecil, Lord

Parham Park, the Great Chamber. The four-poster bed has 16th century hangings.

Burghley, three brothers of the Dudley family — Robert, Earl of Leicester, Ambrose, Earl of Warwick, and Lord Henry Dudley —and Robert Devereux, Earl of Essex. There too is the Queen's god-daughter, Eleanor Verney (whose son laid the foundation-stone of the house), the poet Henry Howard, Earl of Surrey, and a fascinating equestrian portrait of young Henry, Prince of Wales (James I's elder son) — this has recently been cleaned, revealing a figure of Old Father Time; it used to be attributed to Isaac Oliver, but is now thought to be by Robert Peake.

The embroideries at Parham are exceptionally fine, surpassed only by those at Hardwick; they include Elizabethan work such as the needlework picture of Adam and Eve in the West Room, and the hangings on the superb four-poster bed in the Great Chamber. There is a tradition that some of the latter were done by Mary Queen of Scots; the coverlet bears the initial 'M' and the three *fleur-de-lis* of France.

Equally evocative is the narwhal's tusk in the Great Hall, with its painted wooden case. It was thought to be a unicorn's horn and to possess magic properties.

MONTACUTE HOUSE

Building Montacute was, in a sense, an act of faith. The usual pattern was that first a person made a name for himself, and then put up a splended mansion to impress his neighbours and entertain his peers or his sovereign. With Sir Edward Phelips it was rather the other way round. And when he reached the stage of entertaining royalty, it was James I at Wanstead and not Elizabeth at Montacute.

His grandfather, Richard Phelips, had been a person of some rank; he was Surveyor General to Henry Grey, Marquis of Dorset and Earl of Suffolk. Grey was the father of the unfortunate Lady Jane. Phelips was exonerated from any implication in the plot to put her on the throne; however, the association was, naturally, not to his advantage, and after that the family lived quietly in the West Country. So when Edward Phelips built Montacute he was fairly obscure, though ambitious. He was trained as a lawyer, and became a Member of Parliament (mainly for rotten boroughs); and it was not until James I's reign that he became Speaker of the House (he held that office at the time of the trial of Guy Fawkes), and later Master of the Rolls. He died in 1614.

Montacute lies four miles to the west of Yeovil; the name signifies *'mons acutus'* or 'steep hill', which there is nearby. The land on which the house was erected was part of the manor of Hide in the parish of Montacute. It was not a monastic site; the Cluniac priory, by then dispossessed, lay at the other end of the village.

Edward Phelips began building his extremely impressive house in about 1588 (the Armada year), and it was probably completed in 1601, the date over the east doorway. The material chosen was stone from Ham Hill, a yellowish stone which mellows to a warm ochre colour.

As with most Elizabethan houses, it is difficult to ascribe the design to any one man. Phelips's master-mason was William Arnold, a craftsman of excellent repute locally; he also worked at Wadham College, Oxford, and later at Cranborne, Dorset, for Lord Robert Cecil. Probably he and his employer collaborated at Montacute. It is interesting that of all the buildings with which Arnold's name is associated, Montacute is the earliest.

The house is a wide 'H' shape, and the principal entrance was originally on the east front, so this was the façade which was given the most dramatic treatment. It is nearly 200 feet (61 metres) wide, and rises in three storeys of mullioned windows, some of them projecting as bays. Above the cornice along the roof line Flemish-

Montacute House, North-east view

type curved gables alternate with balustrading and obelisks. Set in the gables are niches holding statues of the Nine Worthies.[1] Below, six columns are spaced along the terrace, and from the terrace six shallow steps lead down into the forecourt garden. One of the most delightful and unusual features at Montacute is the way this forecourt is integrated with the house. It is surrounded with a balustrade, echoing the one on the roof, and once again there are obelisks; but there are also decorative stone lanterns mid-way along the north and south sides, and the most charming pavilions at the corners. The pavilions are architectural embellishments, not intended to be functional. Apparently two storeys high, but designed with no floor in between, their ground-plan is a square

[1] The Nine Worthies: said to be 'three Jews, three Paynims (pagans) and three Christian men'. They are usually listed as Hector of Troy, Alexander the Great, and Julius Caesar; Joshua, David, and Judas Maccabeus; Arthur, Charlemagne, and Godfrey of Bouillon. In Shakespeare's *Love's Labour's Lost,* Pompey and Hercules are included.

interlaced with a quatrefoil. They have wittily curving ogival roofs, tipped with skeletal stone spheres which echo the design of the lanterns.

Montacute stayed in the hands of the Phelips family for three hundred years. In 1786-8 another Edward Phelips altered the main entrance to the west side. Six miles away a house called Clifton Maybank was about to be demolished; from this Phelips acquired the porch, made of the same Ham stone as the rest of Montacute but about fifty years earlier in date. It blends in remarkably well with the Elizabethan house. Behind it he added corridors to make the interior more convenient.

The corridors run along the middle bar of the 'H', alongside the old arrangement of rooms: screens-passage in the middle, Dining-room to the left and Great Hall to the right.

The rooms at Montacute are spacious and light, most of them little changed since the house was built. There is fine stained glass, largely heraldic, in the Great Hall, Parlour and Library. The Library has an internal porch, a useful windproofing device in a house with projecting wings and enormous windows. There is an elaborate stone screen in the Great Hall, some dominant fireplaces, and a very lively plasterwork frieze showing a husband being hen-pecked at home and then subjected to a skimmity ride[2] by his neighbours.

The Long Gallery on the second floor is said to measure 172 feet (38 metres), which makes it one of the longest of this period extant.

The fortunes of the Phelips family declined; for a while the house was let to tenants, including Lord Curzon between 1915 and 1925. In 1931 it was taken over by the National Trust. At this time is was almost entirely empty. It is by no means so today, and the wealth of furniture, tapestries and pictures look so appropriate and at home that it is hard to remember that they have not been there for generations. In the Long Gallery is now installed, on loan from the National Portrait Gallery, an exceptionally wide and representative collection of Tudor and Jacobean portraiture, which is itself enhanced by being placed in such a lovely setting.

Although it was built chiefly for ostentation, embodying Sir Edward Phelips's desire to re-establish his family's status, and although much of its decoration was culled from Flemish pattern-books, Montacute is neither forbidding nor vulgar. The warm colour of the stonework and the lightness of the rooms make it

[2] Skimmity or skimington ride: the victim, or his effigy, is dragged through the village on a hurdle or pole, and subjected to derision. See Thomas Hardy's *The Mayor of Casterbridge*.

seem welcoming, and the little corner pavilions in the forecourt are sheer poetry.

Had she seen it, Queen Elizabeth would surely have approved.

Appendix I

EXPENSES OF THE QUEEN'S TABLE, 1576

EXPENCE OF THE QUEEN'S TABLE[1].

The Queenes Majestys Dyett, A⁰ 18 REGINÆ ELIZABETHÆ, A.D. 1576.

A Declaration made as well of the Ordinary Dyett of the Queenes Majesty's book, signed with her own hand; as also of the Extraordinary whiche hathe been dailye servid unto her Majestie in sondrie Offices, as followethe:

The Queenes Majesty's Booke, signed with her hand.

The Queenes Majesty's dyett as she hath bene daylye servid.

BREAKFAST

			s.	d.				s.	d.
Cheate and mancheate	—		0	6	Cheate and mancheate	8		0	8
Ale and beare	—	—	0	3½	Ale and bere	6 g.		010½	
Wine	— — 1	pt	0	7	Wine	— — 1 p.		0	7

Flesh for pottage.   **Flesh for pottes.**

		s.	d.			s.	d.
Mutton for the pott	3 st.	1	6	Mutton for the pott	4 st.	2	0
Longe bones	— 2	0	6	Long bones	— 4	1	0
Ise bones	— 2	0	2	Ise bones	—3	0	3
Chines of beafe	— 1	1	4	Chines of beef	— 1	1	4
Short bones	— 2	0	4	Chines of mutton	2	2	0
				Short bones	— 1	0	2
Chines of beafe	—1	1	4	Chines of veal	3	0	6
Connyes	—2	0	8	Chickens for grewell	2	0	7
Butter	— —6 dish	0	6	Veale	— — 2 s.	2	0
				Chines of beafe	1	16	0
				Butter	— 2 lb.	0	8

Summa, 8*s.* 6½*d.*   Summa, 13*s.* 11½*d.*

Surchardge, 5*s.*5*d.*

[1]From the Harleian MSS. No.609

DAILY EXPENCES OF THE QUEEN'S TABLE, 1576

Sunday Supper the 19th of November, anno ut supra.

The Queenes Majesty's booke

1st Course.

		s.	d.
Cheate and mancheate	6	0	6
Bere and ale	— 4 g.	0	7
Wine	— — 3 p.	1	9
Fleshe for the potte,			
Mutton boylde	2 s.	1	0
Mutton rost	— 2 s	1	0
Capon gr.	— 2	4	0
Herons	— 2	5	0
Connyes	— 3	1	0
Chickins bake	1 s.	2	0

2d Course.

			s.	d.
Lambe or kydde dim̃			0	10
Cocks or godwitts	7		3	6
Partridges	— 4		3	4
Pejons or plovers	9		3	9
Larks	2 doz.		1	0
Tarte	— — 1 s.		1	4
Butter	— 16 dishes		1	4
Eggs	— — 1 qa		0	10

Summa, 32s. 9d.

The Queenes Majesty's daylie service.

1st Course

		s.	d.
Cheate and mancheate	14	0	8
Bere and ale	— 7 g.	0	10½
Wine	— — 1s 2 p.	3	6
Sallets	)		
	)		
Mutton boylde	2 s	1	0
Chickins boylde	4	1	2
Larks boylde	18	0	9
Partridges	— 2	1	1
Slised beafe	— 1 s.	1	8
Mutton rost	— 3 s.	1	6
Capon gr.	— 2	4	0
Chickins	— 9	2	7½
Teales	10	2	6
Tonges	2	1	0
Udders	2	0	8
Cocks	— 7	3	6
Chickin pies	— 1	2	0
Doucetts	— 1 s.	1	4

2d Course.

		s.	d.
Feasants	— 2	5	0
Partridges	— 3	2	6
Snites	— 9	2	3
Plovers	— 9	3	9
Larks	— 2 doz.	1	0
Connyes	— 6	2	0
Bitters	— 2	5	0
Great birdes	— 9	0	9
Larks bake	— 2 doz.	2	0
Tarte	— — 1	1	4
Butter	— 14lb.	4	8
Eggs	— — 3 qtrs.	2	6

Summa, 63s. 2d.

Surchardge, 30s.5d.

Surchardge for one wnole day, 71s.5½d.

DAILY EXPENCES OF THE QUEEN'S TABLE, 1576.

Mondaye Dynner the 20th of November, anno ut supra.

The Queenes Majesty's booke.				The Queenes Majesty's daylie service.			
			s. d.				*s. d.*
Cheate and mancheate	5 loves		0 6	Cheate and mancheate	8		0 8
Bere and ale	— 4 g.		0 7	Bere and ale	— 7 g.		0 10½
Wine	— — 3 p.		1 9	Wine	— — 1 s. 2 p.		3 6
1st Course				**1st Course**			
Fleshe for the pott,				Capon gr. boylde	1		2 0
Beafe	— — 2 s.		4 0	Cocks boylde	3		1 6
Mutton	— 3 s.		1 6	Larks b.	— 12		0 6
Veale	— — 1 qrtr.		2 6	Chickins b.	— 4		1 2
Signet	— 1		3 4	Mutton b.	— 2 s.		1 0
Capon gr.	— 2		4 0	Salt brewes	— 1 br.		0 8
Connyes	— 3		1 0	Beafe	— — 1 crop		6 8
				Beafe	— dim̃		
Friants	— 1 s.		2 0	surloyne			1 8
Custerde	— 1		1 4	Veale rost	— 3 s.		3 0
Fritter	— 1 s.		0 8	Capon gr.	— 2		4 0
				Cocks	— — 7		3 6
				Plover	— 9		3 9
2d Course				Snites	— 9		2 3
Lambe or kidde	dim̃.		0 10	Connye pies	— 2		2 6
Herons or feas	2		5 0	Custerde	— 1		1 4
Cocks or goodwitts	7		3 6				
Chickin	— 7		2 0½	**2d Course**			
Pejons	— 9		0 10	Pullets gr.	— 2		0
Larks	— — 2 doz.		1 0	Teales	— — 7		1 9
Tarte	— — 1		1 4	Partridges	— 3		2 6
Fritter	— 1 s.		0 8	Feasants	— 2		5 0
Butter	16 dishes		1 4	Chickins	— 9		2 0
Eggs	— — 1 qrtr		0 10	Connyes	— 6		2 0
				Larks bake	2 doz		2 0
				Tarte	— — 1		1 4
				Butter	— 14lb.		4 8
				Eggs	— — 3 qrtr		2 6
				Pannado.			
Summa, 45*s.* 5½*d.*				Capon gr.	— — 1		2 0
				Previe Kichen.			
				Cheate	— 12)		
				Mancheate	— 18)		1 6

Summa, 70*s.* 7*d.*

Surchardge, 30*s.* 1½*d.*

Appendix II

Costs of Entertainment at Lichfield, 1575

The Queen's removal from Kenilworth was to *Lichfield,* where she continued eight days; and enjoyed a grand musical treat by attending divine service in that noble Cathedral. Within that period also she seems to have made excursions into the neighbourhood.

The following curious document was communicated by Mr. Sharp of Coventry:

Accompte of Symon Byddull and John Wakelet, Baylieffs and Justic's of Peace within the Cyttye of Lich', from St James Apostle, 1575 to 1576.

Charges when the Queene's Matie was at the Cytte of Lich', A° 1575

(July 27 to Aug 3.)

	£.	s.	d.
Imp'mis, to the Queenes most excellent Matie in golde	40	0	0
It'm, for charges for viij dayes, when the Queene's Matie was here, as appeareth by p'tyculers in the booke, to the some of —	7	10	6
It'm, paid to Thomas Harvye, for poles for the scaffold —	0	1	0
It'm, to olde Bate, for goinge to Mr Sprott — — —	0	0	2
————Wm Hollcroft, for kepynge Madde Richard ———— when her Ma^{tie}was here — — — —	0	5	0
It'm, to Gregorye Ballard's Maid for brynginge checkyns	0	0	3
It'm, to the Pavyoures, for pavynge about the M'ket crosse — — —	0	2	0
It'm, bestowed upon the Harbengers at Widdowe Hills	0	0	8
It'm, for payntynge the M'kett Crosse — — —	0	19	0
It'm, to Gostalowe, for takynge downe the skaffold	0	1	0
It'm, to the Queene's Ma^{ties}Harbengers — — —	0	10	0
It'm, to the Clerke of the M'kett	2	0	0

	£.	s.	d.
It'm, to the Fotemen — — —	3	0	0
It'm, to the Messengers of the Chamber — — —	1	0	0
It'm, to the Trumppettors — — — —	2	0	0

183

It'm, to the Trumpettors, at the tyme of p'clamc'on,
made by the Clerke of the M^r ket — — —   0 10 0
It'm, to the Knyght M'shall's men — — —   0 13 4
——————— Yeomen of the bottells — — —   0 13 4
It'm, to Robes — — —   0 2 0
——————— the Queene's Porter's — — —   0 10 0
——————— Keeper of Mr Raffe Boo's tent — — —   0 2 6
——————— Blacke Gards — — —   1 0 0
——————— them of the P'vye backhowse — — —   0 3 4
It'm, to the Slawghter men — — —   0 3 4
It'm, to the Queene's Coachemen — — —   0 10 0
——————— Post maister — — —   1 0 0
——————— Sergiant of Armes — — —   3 0 0
——————— Harrolde of Armes — — —   (*sic.*)
——————— Yoman that caryed the sworde — — —   0 10 0
——————— Yoman that caryed the mace — — —   0 10 0
——————— Yoman that surveyed the wayes for ye Queene   0 6 8
————— Mr Cartwright, that shuld have made the Orac'on —   5 0 0
————— the Ringers of Saynt Marye's Churche — — —   1 4 0
It'm, for ij dayes laborynge at Longbridge, to cast downe
the waye for the Queene's Maties comynge — — —   0 7 4
It'm, for mendyng the dyche in akeryard — — —   0 0 6
It'm, to Gregorye Ballard, for going wth l'res
to Kyllyngworthe — — —   0 3 4
——————— Kelynge, for payntynge and mendyng
——————— the geylehall   0 3 10
——————— Rob'rt Dale, for salt fysshe — — —   0 6 0
——————— Wyddowe Hill, for ij dos' waxe torches, and one
——————— lyncke — — —   1 4 0
——————— Nycholas Smyth, for victualls — — —   1 17 1
——————— James Oliver, for beare — — —   0 12 0
——————— vi men, to go wth the Queene's treasure to
——————— Rydgeley[1] — — —   0 1 0

Other Extracts from the "Charges Extraordinary" of the year,
appearing to be connected with the Queen's Visit, are as follow :

             £. s. d.

It'm, to Thomas Ylseleye, for goinge to Kyllyngworthe,
with our Charter — — —   0 10 0
——————— Kyllam Hawks, for a horse hyre to Kyllyngworthe 0 1 0

[1]Rugeley, to which place the Queen's 'Treasure' was carried, is a market town in the
direct road between Lichfield and Stafford.

—————— to my Lorde of Warwyk's Players[2] — — —   0 8 8
—————— Kyllam Hawkes, for a horse hyre to Worcester —   0 1 6
It'm, given to the Queene's Bearward in reward — — —   0 3 4

[2] In 1574 the Queen granted a Licence to James Burbage, John Perkyn, John Lanham, and two others, servants to the Earl of Lycester, to exhibit all kinds of Stage-plays, during pleasure, in any part of England.

Appendix III

EXTRACTS FROM THE HOUSEHOLD BOOK OF LORD NORTH 1575

A brieff Collecc'on & Declaracon of all suche provision as was spent at ye howse of ye Right Honourable the Lord North off Kertlinge, at ye Q Mat^{ies} comyng thither on Monday y^e of Sept. to supp^r & tarying there untill Wednesday aft^r dynn^r next following (being in the xxth yeare off her Mat^{ies} reigne) also a brieff Note of the gifts, rewards, and oth^r charges y^t grewe upon ye same[1].

		£. s. d.
Manchett 1200) (wch was made of — —		
Cheatbread 3600) cast (xvij^n q^{tr} dí dí by wheate) — —		17 11 3
White bread and cheat bread bought xxiij dooss		23 0
Hoggesheads of beare	lxxiiij	32 7 6
Tonnes of ale	ij	4 14 0
Hoggesh' of claret wyne	vj	27 0 0
Hoggesh of white wyne	i	4 10 0
Rundlets of sack cont: 20 gall^s	i	53 4
Hoggesh' of vinegar	i	33 4
Steares and oxen	xi dí	46 0 0
Muttons	lxvij	26 16 0
Veales	xvij dí	11 13 4
Lambes	vij	35 0
Pigges	xxxiiij	34 0
Geese	xxxij	32 0
Capons	xxx doos & iij	27 4 6
Turkies	vi	20 0
Swannes	xxxij	10 13 4
Mallards and yong ducks	xxij doos & ix	6 16 6
Cranes	i	0 13 4
Hearnshewes	xxviij	4 13 4
Bitters	$^{xx}_v$ x	18 6 8
Shovellers	xii	3 0 0
Chickins	$^{xx}_{iiij}$ xix doos dí	19 18 0
Pigeons	cv^{xx} xvij doos	11 17 0
Pewytts	viij doos, x	5 17 8
Godwytts	lxviij	17 0 0
Gulls	xviij	5 10 0
Dottrells	viij doos, iij	5 8 0
Snypes	viij	0 4 0

[1] Extracted from "The Booke of the Howshold Charges and other Paiments laid out by the L. North and his commandement: beginning the first day of January 1575, and the 18 yere of" Queen Elizabeth. Communicated by the late William Stevenson, Esq. of Norwich, F.S.A. in a Letter to Thomas Amyot, Esq. F.S.A. and first printed in the Archæologia, vol. XIX. pp. 283 and seq.

		£.	s.	d.
Knotts	xxix	29		0
Plovers	xxviij	30		0
Stynts	v	0	5	0
Redshanks	xviij	0	18	0
Yerw helps	ij	0	2	0
Partiches	xxii	0	11	0
Pheasants	i	0	4	0
Quailes	xxvij doos, ij	13	11	8
Curlewes	ij	0	13	4
Connyes	viij doos	4	16	0
Staggs	iiij made into 48 pasties			
Bucks	xvi made into 128 pasties			
Gammonds of bacon	viij	30		0
Larde	xiij lbs.	0	8	8
Neats tongs, feet & udd^{rs}	xi^{xx}.i	53		4
Butter	iiijC xxx lb.	6	7	6
Eggs	ijMvC. xxij	3	3	0
Sturgeons	iij caggs	46		8
Craye fyshes	viij doos	13		4
Turbutts	viij	0	53	4
Oysters	a cartload & 2 horseloads	5	0	0
Anchoves	1 barrell	0	10	0
Pykes	ij	20		0
Carpes	ij	0	6	8
Tenchies	iiij	0	6	0
Pearchies	xii	0	12	0
Redd herring	iijC	0	7	6
Holland cheeses	vj	20		0
M^rche panes	x	5	0	0
Ypocras	vj gall'	30		0

	£.	s.	d.
Gyftes and rewards to ye Quenes Maties Officers and Servants	48	0	0
Rewards to Noble mens Servants, Gent.Servants, and others	41	0	0
Paym^{ts} to sundrie p'sons labouring and taking paynes about this busyness	7	0	7
Charge of ye bancketting howse, ye new kychens, & trymîng upp chambers & oth^r rowmes	32	2	4
Baskets, hamps, jacks, casks & oth^r necess^s	11	0	0
Carriage of provisionsh ye hale, and oth^r things	3	13	8
Ryding charges & furniture of horses	3	19	11
Wax lights and toorchies	4	7	0

	£.	s.	d.
Suger	16	4	0
Grocerie ware, banketting stuff, salletts, rootes and hearbes	39	0	21
Keping off wyldefowle		20	0
Hyering of pewt[r] vessell		20	0

	£.	s.	d.
Keping & scowring of pewt[r] vessell		26	8
The losse of pewt[r] vessell [1]			
Charcoales bought & spent		3 0	3
P[d] to y[e] cookes of London [2]	21	0	0
Making a standing for y[e] Q. in the parke		25	0
Candles spent v[xx] lb.		25	0
Wheat flower and Rye meale spent in y[e] pastrie		3 0	0
Thincrease of expences (above the ordin'ie charge) by the space of a fortenight before and after her Ma[ties] comyng	20	0	0
Fforen charges about this busynes		4 0	0
Laburers wages after y[e] Q departure		22	2
The jewell given to y[e] Quenes M[tie]	120	0	0

R North.   Tot'lis — £762 4s 2d

My Lord charges following the Co[r]te after her Ma[ties] departure from Kertlinge untill his L. returne thither again the xxvi[th] off Septem[r] 1578.

	£.	s.	d.
Horsemeate and stable charge	3	0	4
Boordwages	4	13	0
My L. dyett	0	11	10
Apparell		46	8
Rewards for buck[3], &c.		25	0

---

[1] The amount of this Item which is here omitted, will be found under the date of October 1 following, viz. xlv lb. at 8d. le. lb. - 32s.2d.

[2] This is a very curious charge at that period.

[3] Buck venison was eaten in summer, and that of Doe in Winter. It was frequently rendered by tenure, and the reception of this Doe and Buck was, till Queen Elizabeth's days, solemnly performed at the steps of the Quire by the Canons of the Cathedral, attired in their sacred vestments, and wearing garlands of flowers on their heads; and the horns of the Buck, carried on the top of a spear, in procession, round about the body of the Church with a great noise of horn-blowers.

R. NORTH.   S'm — £11 16s 10d.

Provision bought at Sturbridge ffayer & the houshold charges in my
Lords absence (following the Co^rte as appearith above) untill his L.
returne to Kertlinge the xxvj^th off Sept. 1578.

	£.	s.	d.
Codds bought CCC dí	8	15	0
Soape bought 2 firkins		28	0
Salte bought	3	13	4
Lynnen clothe p^d for		37	0
Ordyn'ie at Kirtlinge		28	4

R. NORTH.   S'm £17 1s 8d

Appendix IV

NEW YEAR'S GIFTS TO THE QUEEN, 1577-78

Anno Regni Regine Elizabethe vicesimo, 1577-8
New-yer's Guifts guiven to her MAJESTIE *at her Honor of Hampton Corte, by these Persons whose Names do hereafter ensue, the first day of January, the Yere aforesaid.*

By the Lady *Margaret Leneox*, a casting bottell of agathe,
garneshed with golde, and sparcks of rubyes, and a woman
  holding in her hand a scrowle written with this word,
ABUNDANCIA. per oz.
Delivered to the Lady *Howard.*

£. s. d.

By the Lady *Mary Gray*, 2 peir of swete gloves, with
fower dosen buttons of golde, in every one a sede perle.
Delivered to Mrs. *Eliz. Knowlls.*

By the Lady *Margret* Countess of Darby, a petticote of
white satten, reysed and edged with a brode
  embrawdery of divers colloures.
Delivered to *Rauf Hoope*, Yoman of
the Roobes. By Sir *Nicholas Bacon*, Knight,
Lorde Keeper of the Greate Seale of
Inglande, in golde   13 6 8

By the Lorde *Burligh*, Lorde Treausorour of
Inglande, in gold   20 0 0
By the Lorde Marques of *Winchester*, in golde   20 0 0
  Delivered to *Henry Sakford*, Grome of the
  Previe Chamber.

ERLES AND VICOMTS.

By therle of *Leycetor*, Master of the Horses, a carcanet of golde enn£. s. d.
amuled, nyne peces whereof are garneshed with sparks of diamonds and
rubyes, and every one of them a pendant of golde ennamuled, garneshed
with small sparks of rubyes and ophall in the mydds; and tenne other
peeces of golde lykewyse ennamuled, every of them garneshed with

verey small diamonds; two large ragged perles set in a rose of sparks of rubyes, and every of the two lesser perles pendant, and a pendant of golde, in every of them a small diamond lozenged, and a small rubye, and in the myddes a large pendant of golde garneshed with meane rubyes, an ophall, and a meane perle pendant, and six dosen of buttons of golde lykewyse ennamuled, every button garneshed with small sparks of rubyes, in every of them a large ragged perle.

Delivered to the said Lady *Howarde.*

By therle of *Arondell,* in golde	30	0	0
By therle of *Sussex,* Lord Chamberleyn, in golde	20	0	0
By therle of *Lincoln,* High Admirall of Ingland, in golde	10	0	0
By therle of *Bedford,* in golde	20	0	0
By therle of *Shrewesbury,* in golde	20	0	0
By therle of *Darby,* in golde	20	0	0
By therle of *Huntingdon,* in golde	10	0	0
Delivered to *Henry Sakford.*			

By therle of *Warwick,* a gowne with hanging sleeves of black vellat alov' with small wyer of golde lyke scallop shelles set with spangills, embrawdred with a garde with sondry byrds and flowers enbossed with golde, silver and silke, set with seede perle.

Delivered to *Rauf Hoope.*

By therle of Rutlande, in golde	10	0	0
By therle of *Penbroke,* in golde	20	0	0
By therle of *Northumberlande,* in golde	10	0	0
By therle of *Southampton,* in golde	20	0	0
Delivered to *Henry Sakford.*			

By therle of *Hertford,* a juell, being a ship of mother-of-perle, garneshed with rubys, and 3 small diamonds.

By therle of *Ormonde,* a fayer juell of golde, being a phenix, the winges fully garneshed with rubyes and small diamonds, and at the fete thre feyer diamonds and two smaller; in the top a branche garneshed with six small diamonds, thre small rubyes, and 3 very meane perle, and in the bottome thre perles pendant.

Delivered to the said Lady Howarde.			
By the Vicounte *Mountague,* in golde	10	0	0
Delivered to *Henry Sakford.*			

DUCHESSES, MARQUISSES, AND COUNTISSES.

By the Duches of Suffolke, a feyer cushyn of purple vellat, very feyerly embrawdred of the story of Truth

set with garnetts and sede perle, the backsyde
purple satten frynged, and tassells of Venice golde and
sylke.
Delivered to *Richard Tod,* Keeper of the Warderobe.

£. s. d.

By the Duches of *Somerset* in golde
Delivered to *Henry Sakford.*

13 6 8

By the Marques of *Northampton* a kyrtill of white satten
embrawdred with purles of golde like clowdes, and leyed
rownde abought with a bone lace of Venice golde.
 Delivered to *Rauf Hoope.*

By the Lady Marques of *Winchester,* Dowager, in
golde
 Delivered to *Henry Sakford.*

10 0 0

By the Lady Marques of *Winchester,* a smock of
cameryck wrought with tawny sylke and black, the ruffe
and collor edged with a bone lace of silver.
Delivered to Mrs *Skydmore.*

By the Countes of *Sussex,* in golde
Delivered to *Henry Sakford.*

10 0 0

By the Countes of *Lincoln,* a dublet with
double sleves, assh collour, upon tyncell leyed with
pasmane lace of gold and silver, lyned with yellowe
sarceonet.
 By the Countes of *Warwyck,* a fore parte and a peir of
sleves of white satten, embrawdred with branches and
trees of damaske golde, two gards of black vellat, upon the
fore parte embrawdred with golde, silver, and sylke, set
with sede perle, and lyned with tawney sarceonet.
 By the Countes of *Shrewesbury,* a gowne of white satten
leyed on with pasmane of golde, the vernewyse, lyned with
strawe collored sarceonet.
 Delivered to *Rauf Hoope.*

By the Countes of *Huntingdon,* in golde
 Delivered to *Henry Sakford.*

8 0 0

By the Countess of Oxford a dublet of white satten alov'
enbrawdred with flowers of golde, and lyned with strawe
collored sarceonet.
 Delivered to *Rauf Hoope.*

By the Countes of *Essex,* ruffs of lawnde white worke, edged
with sede perle, and a yelo here, and another like black.
 Delivered here to Mrs. *Eliz. Knowlls,* and the ruffs to Mrs.
  Jane Bresells.

By the Countess of *Penbroke,* Dowager, in golde   12 0 0
    Delivered to *Henry Sakford.*

By the Countes of *Penbroke* a dublet of lawne embrowdred al over with golde, silver, and sylke of divers collors, and lyned with yelow taphata.

By the Countes of *Bedford,* a dublet and fore parte of murry satten embrowdred with flowers of golde, silver, and sylke, and lyned with orenge tawny taphata.
    Delivered to *Rauf Hoope.*

By the Countes of *Northumberlande,* in golde   10 0 0
By the Countes of *Southampton,* in golde   10 0 0
By the Countes of *Rutlande,* in golde   10 0 0

    Delivered to *Henry Sakford.*
By the Contes of Kent, a remnant of white satten prented cont' 19 yds. di.
    Delivered to *Rauf Hoope.*

By the Countes of *Kent,* Dowager, a fan flowers of sylke of sundry collors, the handill of an inbrawdry worke set with small sede perle.
Delivered to Mrs. *Eliz. Knowlls.*

By the Countes of *Cumberlande,* a fore parte of lawnde cut-worke wrought with blacke and white unmade.
    Delivered to Mrs.*Skydmore.*

VICECOUNTESS

By the Vicountess *Mountague,* in golde   10 0 0

BUSSHOPPS

By tharchebusshop of *Yorke*[1], in golde   30 0 0
By the Busshop of *Ely*[2], in golde   30 0 0
By the Busshop of *Durham*[3], in golde   30 0 0
By the Busshop of *London*[4], in golde   20 0 0
By the Busshop of *Winchester*[5], in golde   20 0 0
By the Busshop of *Salisbury*[6], in golde   20 0 0

[1] Edwyn Sandys, Bp. of Worcester, 1559; of London 1570; Abp. of York 1566—1588.
[2] Richard Cox, Bp. of Ely 1559—1581.
[3] Richard Barnes, Bp. of Carlisle 1570; of Durham 1577—1587.
[4] John Aylmer, Bp. of London 1576—1594.
[5] Robert Horne, Bp. of Winchester 1560—1579.
[6] Edmund Gheast, Bp. of Rochester 1559; of Salisbury 1571—1578.

By the Busshop of *Lincoln*[7], in golde	20	0	0
By the Busshop of *Norwiche*[8], in golde	20	0	0
By the Busshop of *Worcetor*[9], in golde	20	0	0
By the Busshop of *Lichfelde and Coventrie*[10], in golde	13	6	8
By the Busshop of *Hereford*[11], in golde	10	0	0
By the Busshop of *St. David*[12], in golde	10	0	0
By the Busshop of *Carlille*[13], in golde	10	0	0
By the Busshop of *Exetour*[14], in golde	10	0	0
By the Busshop of *Bathe*[15], in golde	10	0	0
By the Busshop of *Peterborowe*[16], in golde	10	0	0
By the Busshop of *Glocetour*[17], in golde	10	0	0
By the Busshop of *Chichester*[18], in golde	10	0	0

Delivered to *Henry Sakford*.

By the Lady *Drury* a fore parte and a peir of sleves of white satten set with spangills, and lyned with tawney sarceonet.
Delivered to *Rauf Hoope*.

By the Lady *Hennage*, a juell, being a dolphyn of mother of perle, garnished with small sparks of rubyes and ophall.
Delivered to the said Lady *Howard*.

By the Lady *Walsingham*, two pillowbiers of cameryck, wrought with sylke of divers collors, cut.
By the Lady *Willowbye*, Sir Francis Willowbye's wyf, a lynyng for a collor, and a peir of sleves networke, floreshed with silver and golde.
Delivered to Mrs. *Skydmore*.

By the Lady *Ratclif*, five creppins of lawne, garneshed with golde and silver purle; two swete baggs of sylke; and a night coyf of white cutworke, floreshed with silver and set with spangills; and five to the pykes, beinge quilles.
The crepyns delivered to Mrs. *Blanche*; Th'rest to Mrs. *Skydmor*.

[7] Thomas Cowper, Bp. of Lincoln 1570; of Winchester 1584—1595.
[8] Edmund Freake, Bp. of Rochester 1571; of Norwich 1575; of Worcester 1584—1593.
[9] John Whitgift, Bp. of Worcester 1577—1584.
[10] Thomas Bentham, Bp. of Lichfield and Coventry 1559—1578.
[11] John Scorey, Bp. of Rochester 1551; of Chichester 1551; deprived by Queen Mary in 1553; and in 1559 made Bp. of Hereford by Queen Elizabeth; died in 1585.
[12] Richard Davies, Bp. of St. Asaph 1559; of St. Davids 1561—1582.
[13] John May, Bp. of Carlisle 1577—1598.
[14] Wm. Bainbridge, Bp. of Exeter 1570—1759.
[15] Gilbert Berkeley, Bp. of Bath and Wells 1559—1581.
[16] John Piers, Bp. of Peterborough 1576; of Salisbury 1578.
[17] Richard Cheyney, Bp. of Gloucester 1561—1581.
[18] Richard Curteys, Bp. of Chichester 1570—1585.

By the Lady *Frogmorton* a kyrtill of yelow satten, al over with Venice silver, with roses of twists of silver, lyned with sarceonet.
Delivered to *Rauf Hoope.*

By the Lady *Arondell,* a ring of golde with one small diamonde with small sparks of diamonds and rubys abowte it.
Delivered to the said Lady *Howard.*

By the Lady *Wylfords,* a fore parte of lawne cutworke, white.

By the Lady *Marvyn,* two parteletts of networke, thone floreshed with golde, thother with silver.
Delivered to Mrs. *Skydmor.*

By the Lady *Crofts,* a feyer cushyn embrawdered with silke of sundry collors, with thistory of Icorus, lyned with changeably taphata, and iiii buttons with tassells of silke of sondry collors.
Delivered to *Richard Tod.*

By the Lady *Sowche,* Sir John Sowche's wyf, a smock of camerick, the sleves and parte of the boddy wrought with black silke and golde, the ruffs and collors edged with a bone lace of golde.
Delivered to Mrs. *Skydmor.*

KNIGHTS.

By Sir *Fraunces Knowlls,* Knight, Treasurer of the Householde, £. s. d. in golde   10 0 0
By Sir *James Crofts,* Knight, Comptroller of the Householde, in golde   10 0 0
Delivered to *Henry Sakford.*

By Sir *Christofer Hatton,* Knight, Vice Chamberleyn and Capitaine of the Garde, a feyer juell of golde, being a crosse of diamonds fully garneshed with small diamonds, and a feyer perle pendant; the Queen's picture on the back side; and more, a juell of golde, wherein is a dog leding a man over a bridge, the boddy fully garneshed with small diamonds and rubys, and thre small perles pendant; the back side certayne verces written.
Delivered to the said Lady *Howard.*

By Sir *Rauf Sadlier*[1] Knight, Chancellor of the Duchy of Lancaster in golde   15 0 0
Delivered to *Henry Sakford.*

[1] Sir Ralph Sadler died in the 80th year of his age, anno Domini 1587, and was buried in the chancel of Standon church, Herts.

By Sir Frauncis Walsingham, Knight, Principall Secretary, a gowne of blewe satten, with rewes of golde, and two small pasmane laces of Venice golde, faced with powdred armyns.
    Delivered to *Rauf Hoope.*

By *Thomas Wylson,* Esquir, Secretary, a cup of agathe garneshed with golde, and set with stone.
    Delivered in charge to the Master of the Juel House.

By Sir *Walter Myldemey,* Knight, Chancellor of thexchequer, in golde	10	0	0
By Sir *William Cordell,* Master of the Rolls, in golde	10	0	0
By Sir *Christopher Haydon,* Knight, in golde	10	0	0
By Sir *William Damsell,* Knight, receyvor of the courte of wards, in golde	10	0	0
By Sir *Henry Crumwell,* Knight, in golde	10	0	0
By Sir *Thomas Gresham,* Knight in golde	10	0	0
By Sir *Owen Hopton,* Lieutenant of the Tower, in golde	10	0	0
By Sir *John Thyn,* in golde	5	0	0

    Delivered to *Henry Sakford.*

By Sir *Gawen Carewe,* a smock of camerick, wrought with black silke in the collor and sleves, the square and ruffs wrought with Venice golde, and edged with a small bone lace of Venice golde.
    Delivered to Mrs. *Skydmor.*

By Sir *Gilbert Dethick,* alias Garter Principal King at Armes, a booke of the states in King William Conqueror's tyme.
    Delivered to Mrs. *Blanche.*

THE QUEEN AT GREENWICH, 1598-99

The Queen's Court at Greenwich, in 1598, is thus described by Hentzner:

"We arrived next at the Royal Palace of Greenwich, reported to have been originally built by Humphrey Duke of Gloucester, and to have received very magnificent additions from Henry VII. It was here Elizabeth, the present Queen, was born, and here she generally resides, particularly in Summer, for the delightfulness of its situation. We were admitted, by an order Mr. Rogers procured from the Lord Chamberlain, into the Presence Chamber, hung with rich tapestry, and the floor, after the English fashion, strewed with hay[1], through which the Queen commonly passes in her way to Chapel: at the door stood a Gentleman dressed in velvet, with a gold chain, whose office was to introduce to the Queen any person of distinction that came to wait on her : it was Sunday, when there is usually the greatest attendance of Nobility. In the same Hall were the Archbishop of Canterbury, the Bishop of London, a great number of Counsellors of State, Officers of the Crown, and Gentlemen, who waited the Queen's coming out; which she did from her own apartment when it was time to go to prayers, attended in the following manner: first went Gentlemen, Barons, Earls, Knights of the Garter, all richly dressed and bare-headed; next came the Chancellor bearing the seals in a red-silk purse, between two: one of which carried the Royal scepter, the other the sword of state, in a red scabbard, studded with golden fleurs de lis, the point upwards: next came the Queen, in the sixty-fifth[2] year of her age, as we were told, very majestic; her face oblong, fair, but wrinkled, her eyes small, yet black and pleasant; her nose a little hooked; her lips narrow and her teeth black (a defect the English seem subject to, from their too great use of sugar); she had in her ears two pearls, with very rich drops; she wore false hair, and that red; upon her head she had a small crown, reported to be made of some of the gold of the celebrated Lunebourg Table[3]. Her bosom was uncovered, as all the English Ladies have it till they marry; and

[1] He probably means rushes.

[2] This fixes the period of Hentzner's Visit to the year 1598. She was born Sept. 7 1533.

[3] At this distance of time, it is difficult to say what this was.

she had on a necklace of exceeding fine jewels; her hands were small, her fingers long, and her stature neither tall nor low; her air was stately, her manner of speaking mild and obliging. That day she was dressed in white silk, bordered with pearls of the size of beans, and over it a mantle of black silk, shot with silver threads; her train was very long, the end of it borne by a Marchioness; instead of a chain, she had an oblong collar of gold and jewels. As she went along in all this state and magnificence, she spoke very graciously, first to one, then to another, whether foreign ministers, or those who attended for different reasons, in English, French and Italian; for besides being well skilled in Greek, Latin and the languages I have mentioned, she is mistress of Spanish, Scotch and Dutch: whoever speaks to her, it is kneeling[1]; now and then she raises some with her hand. While we were there, W. Slawata, a Bohemian Baron, had letters to present to her; and she, after pulling off her glove gave him her right hand to kiss, sparkling with rings and jewels, a mark of particular favour; whereever she turned her face, as she was going along, everybody fell down on their knees. The Ladies of the Court followed next to her, very handsome and well-shaped, and for the most part dressed in white; she was guarded on each side by the Gentlemen Pensioners, fifty in number, with gilt battle-axes. In the anti-chapel next the Hall, where we were, petitions were presented to her, and she received them most graciously, which occasioned the acclamation of "Long live Queen Elizabeth". She answered it with "I thank you my good people." In the Chapel was excellent music; as soon as it and the service was over, which scarce exceeded half an hour, the Queen returned in the same state and order, and prepared to go to dinner. But while she was still at prayers, we saw her table set out the following solemnity[2]: a Gentleman entered the room bearing a rod, and along with him another who had a table cloth, which, after they had both kneeled three times with the utmost veneration, he spread upon the table, and after kneeling again, they both retired.

[1] Her father had been treated with the same deference. It is mentioned by Fox, in his Acts and Monuments, that when the Lord Chancellor went to apprehend Queen Catharine Parr, he spoke to the King on his knees. King James I. suffered his courtiers to omit it. Bacon's Papers, vol.II. p.516.

[2] "The excess of respectful ceremonial used at decking her Majesty's table, though not in her presence, and the kind of adoration and genuflection paid to her person, approach to Eastern homage. When we oberve such worship offered to an old woman, with bare neck, black teeth, and false red hair, it makes one smile; but makes one reflect what masculine sense was couched under those weaknesses, and which could command such awe from a nation like England!" WALPOLE

Then came two others, one with the rod again, the other with a salt-seller, a plate, and bread; when they had kneeled, as the others had done, and placed what was brought upon the table, they too retired with the same ceremonies performed by the first. At last came an unmarried Lady (we were told she was a Countess) and along with her a married one, bearing a tasting-knife; the former was dressed in white silk, who, when she had prostrated herself three times in the most graceful manner, approached the table, and rubbed the plates with bread and salt, with as much awe as if the Queen had been present; when they had waited there a little while, the Yeomen of the Guard entered, bare-headed, cloathed in scarlet, with a golden rose upon their backs, bringing in at each turn a course of twenty-four dishes, served in plate (silver) most of it gilt; these dishes were received by a gentleman in the same order they were brought, and placed upon the table, while the lady-taster gave to each of the guards a mouthful to eat, of the particular dish he had bought, for fear of any poison. During the time that this guard, which consists of the tallest and stoutest men that can be found in all England, being carefully selected for this service, were bringing dinner, twelve trumpets and two kettle-drums made the hall ring for half an hour together. At the end of this ceremonial, a number of unmarried ladies appeared, who, with particular solemnity, lifted the meat off the table, and conveyed it into the Queen's inner and more private chamber where, after she had chosen for herself, the rest goes to the Ladies of the Court. The Queen dines and sups alone, with very few attendants; and it is very seldom that any body, foreigner or native, is admitted at that time, and then only at the intercession of somebody in power.

Near this Palace is the Queen's park stocked with deer: such parks are common throughout England, belonging to those who are distinguished either for their rank or riches. In the middle of this is an old square tower, called *Ma fleur*, supposed to be that mentioned in the Romance of Amadis de Gaul: joining to it a plain, where knights and other gentlemen used to meet, at set times and holidays, to exercise on horseback.

Appendix VI

THE QUEEN'S WARDROBE, 1600

The following Extracts are copied from a thin folio book in the possession of Craven Ord, Esq. F.S.A. intituled, "A Booke of all suche Garments, Jewells, Silkes, and other Stuffe Garnishments of Golde, Pearle, and Stone, and also of divers Stones of severall natures and workmanship, as are remayninge in the Robes, the daye of Julie, in the 42d yeare of the raigne of our Soveraigne Ladie Elizabeth, by the Grace of God, of Englande, Fraunce, and Irelande, Queene, Defender of the Faith, &c. and now in the chardge of Sir Thomas Gorges, Knight, Gentlemen of the Robes. At which time the Right Honorable Thomas Lorde Buckhurste, Lorde Highe Treasurer of Englande, George Lorde Hunsdon, Lord Chamberlaine of her Majestie's House, Sir John Fortescue, Knighte, Chauncellor and Under-threasorer of Thexchequer, and Sir Jñ Stanhope, Knighte, Threasorer of her Highnes Chamber, by vertue of her Highnes comission, under the Greate Seale of Englande, bearing the date the 4th daie of Julie, in the saide 42d yere of her Highnes raigne, to them, or to any three of them (wherof the Lord Thrēar or Lorde Chamblaine to be allwaies one) in that behalfe directed, did repaire to the saide Garderobe of the Robes, as well within the Courte as at the Tower of London and Whitehall; and there did take a perfecte survey of all such Robes, Garments, and Jewells, and other P'cells as at that tyme were there founde to remaine. Accordinge to whiche S'vey they have caused to be written twoe severall bookes; the one of whiche bookes is subscribed with the handes of the saide Comissioners, and remaineth for a chardge to the saide Office of the Robes; the other is subscribed by the saide Sir Thomas Gorges, Knight, and remaineth with the saide Lorde Threasorer."

It appears from this account, that the Queen's Wardrobe then [1600] consisted , exclusive of her Coronation, Mourning, Parliament Robes, and those of the Order of the Garter, of

Robes	99	Forepartes	136	Saufegards and Juppes		45
Frenche gownes	102	Peticoates	125	Dublettes		83
Rounde gownes	67	Cloakes	96	Lappe Mantles		18
Loose gownes	100	Cloakes and Saufegards	31	Fannes		27

Kirtells   126   Saufegards   13   Pantobles   2

Robes, late Edwarde the VIth

Firste, one robe of clothe of silver, lyned with white satten, of
thorder of the St. Michell, with a border of embrodirie, with a
wreathe of Venice[1] gold, and the scallop shell, and a frenge of the
same golde, and a small border aboute that; the grounde beinge
blew vellat, embrodered with halfe moones of silver, with a
whoode and a tippet of crymsen vellat, with a like embroderie, the
tippet perished in one place with rats, and a coate of clothe of silver,
with demisleeves, with a frenge of Venice golde.

Apparell.

Item, one gowne of purple golde tissue with a brode garde of
purple vellat, embrodered with Venice golde, and with wreathes of
purple of damaske golde, edged with vellat, unlyned.

Item, one gowne of crimsen satten, embrodered all over with
purles of damaske golde, edged with crimsen, with a short stocke
sleeve unlyned.

Item, one frocke of clothe of golde, reized and tissued with golde
and silver with a *billament* lace of Venice golde, lyned with blacke
vellat.

Item, one frocke of clothe of silver, chequered with redd silke
like birdes eies, with demi-sleeves, with a cutt of crymsen vellat,
pursled on with silver, lined with crimsen vellat.

Item, one coate with demi-sleeves of crimson satten, enbrodered
all over with a twisk of golde, and a border of crimson vellat,
enbrodered with golde, *and pulled out with tincell*, lyned with vellat.

Item, one jerkine of clothe of silver, with longe cutts
downeright[2], bounde with a *billament* lace of Venice silver and
blacke silke, lined with satten.

Jewelles.

Item, one brouche of golde, with a small table rubie in it, and
divers psonages[3].

---

[1] '*Venys* gold occurs in the Wardrobe Account of Rich III. communicated by Mr Astle to the
Editor of the Antiquarian Repertory, III. 243
[2] It was slashed.
[3] Figures. One of the finest jewels of this kind belonging to Margaret Countess of Lenox,
grand-mother of James I. was shown by Dr. Combe to the Society of Antiquaries, in 1782.

Item, one poynarde, the halfe ivorie with an open pomell, the halfe striped downe with golde; with a knife, the hafte of golde, the locker and shape of golde, having a pece of the shape broken of, with a tassell of blew silke, and a skaberde of leather.

GOWNES LATE QUEENE MARIE'S.

Item, one Frenche gowne of blacke vellat, with an edge of purle, and pipes of gold, the wide sleeves turned up all over with like *purle and pipes*, lacking parte of the pipes on the border.

KIRTELLS.

Item, one Frenche kirtle, thoutside of rich cloth of golde tissue, the inside of crimsen cloth of golde, edged with a passamaine[1] lace of golde.

Item, one Frenche kirtle of murrey[2] cloth of silver, let downe with murrey satten, edged with vellat, and lined with crimsen taphata.

Item, one foreparte of a kirtle of white vellat, all over enbrodered with Venice golde, and set with small turquesses, garnets, and ragged pearle set in the border.

ROBES.
The Corončon Robes.

Firste, one mantle of clothe of golde, tissued with golde and silver, furred with powdered armyons[3], with a mantle lace of silke and golde, with buttons and tasells to the same.

Item, one kirtle of the same tissue, the traine and skirts furred with powdered armyons, the rest lyned with sarceonet, with a paire of bodies and sleeves to the same.

The Mourning Robes.

Item, one, mantle of purple vellat, with a mantle lace of silke and golde, with buttons and tassells to the same.

Item, one kirtle and sircoate of the same purple vellat, the traine and skirts furred with powdered armyons, the rest lyned with sarconet, with a paire of upper bodies to the same.

---

[1]An open work-edging.   [2]Black   [3]Query Ermines?

The Parliament Robes.

Item, one mantle of crimsen vellat, fur̃ed througheoute with powdred armyons, the mantle-lace of silke and golde, with buttons and tassells to the same.

Item, one kirtle and sircoate of the crimsen vellat, the same traine and skirts furred with powdered armions, the rest lyned with s̃rconet, with a cappe of mainetenance to the same, striped downe right *with passamaine* lace of gold, with a tassell of golde to the same, furred with powdered armyons, with a whoode of crimsen vellat, furred with powdred armyons, with a paire of bodies and sleeves to the same.

Item, one cappe of maintenance, striped downright, with passamaine lace of golde to the same, furred with powdered armyons.

For the Order of the Garter

Item, one mantle of purple vellat, for the Order of the Garter, lyned with white taphata, with mantle-lacs of purple silke and golde, and tassells of the same.

Item, one Frenche kirtle, with bodies of crimsen vellat, laide with a lace of Venice gold.

Item, one mantle of tawnye satten, bordered with an embroderie of Venice golde and silver, and enbrodered all over with *bias*[1] *cloudes* and spangles of like golde, faced with white satten, razed with a border enbrodered with like golde.

Item, one mantle of aish-colour *sleve*[2] *silke* networke and golde, with a traine.

Item, one bale of white networke, flourished with golde twist and spangles.

Item, one mantle of white lawne or networke, striped, set with tufts of blacke silke and spangles of silver.

Item, one mantle of blacke networke, florished all over with golde and spangles like waveworke.

Item, one mantle, without a traine, of tawney networke, richeley florished with Venice golde and silver, like starrs and *crosse billets*, bounde aboute with a lace of Venice golde.

Item, one vale of blacke networke, florished with Venice silver like flagonworke, and enbrodered all over with roses of Venice

---

[1]Crooked or wreathed.   [2]Network of single or parted silke.

golde, silver, and silke, of colours of silke woman's worke.

Item, one mantle, or loose gowne, of aish-colour network, florished with Venice golde and silver plate billetwise, with *owes* of gold and silver, and a threede of like golde and silver like flames.

Item, one mantle, with a traine, of pale pincke coloured networke, florished all over with silver, like esses[1] and branches billetwise.

Item, one mantle of aish-colour taphata, with two *Burgonyon gardes,* enbrodered all over with gold upon lawne, lyned with white taphata šconet, and set throughoute with ragged pearle.

Item, one mantle of blacke stiched clothe, edged with a *bone lace* of small pearle and bugle[2], and fine fishes of mother of pearle, one set with small ermerodes and garnets.

Item, one mantle of white *sipers*[3], tufted with heare-colour silke, with a small passamaine lace of like coloured silke and Venice silver.

Item, one mantle of white lawne[4] cut and turned in, enbrodered alover with workes of silver, like pomegranetts, roses, honiesocles, and acornes.

Item, one mantle of silver tincell, *printed* and bounde aboute with a *passamaine* lace of silver.

FRENCHE GOWENS.[5]

Item, one Frenche gowne of blacke clothe of golde bordered rounde aboute with a brode border indented-wise, enbrodered within the same like wilde fearnebrakes, upon lawne and golde plate.

---

[1]SS.　　　　[2]Bugles　　　　[3]Cyprus work. So roses of Cypers, gold of Cyprus.

[4] Lawnes and cambricks were first brought to England in this reign.

[5]The Queen told Sir James Melvil, that "she had cloaths of every sort; which every day there after (says he) so long as I was at her Court she changed. One day she had the English weed, another the French, and another the Italian, and so forth. She asked me which of them became her best: I answered, in my judgment, the Italian dress: which answer I found pleased her well; for she delighted to show her golden hair, wearing a caul and bonnet as they do in Italy." —Hume says, "Among the other species of luxury, that of apparel began much to increase during this age, and the Queen thought proper to restrain it by proclamation. Her example was very little conformable to her edicts. As no woman was ever more conceited of her beauty, nor more desirous of making impression on the hearts of beholders, no one ever went to a great extravagance in apparel, or studied more the variety and richness of her dress. She appeared almost every day in a different habit; and her cloaths, that she never could part with any of them; and at her death she had in her wardrobe all the different habits, to the number of 3000, which she had ever worn in her life-time,"

Item, one Frenche gowne of clothe of silver, enbrodered with a brode border, like pillars and *essefirms* of Venice of golde.

Item, one Frenche gowne of blacke vellat, enbrodered all over with *wormes* of silke of sondrie colours, cut upon white sarceonet stained.

Item, one Frenche gowne of heare-colour vellat, richlie enbordered with Venice golde, silver, and ragged seede pearle, like a dead tree.

Item, one Frenche gowne of blacke satten, with a verie brode garde, enbrodered with an enbroderie like artichokes, with leaves of blacke satten and Venice golde and silver, upon carnacon satten. Given to Mr. Hide by the Quene, March 7.

Item, one Frenche gowne of clodie colour satten, garded with heare colour vellat, enbrodered with knotts and *galtroppes*[1] of Venice golde onlie before, covered with blacke taphata cutte.

Item, one frenche gowne of murrey-satten, cut with a skallop cut, and laide with a lace of Venice golde chevernewise all over.

Item, one gowne of horse-fleshe-colour satten, enbrodered all over with owes cut with small cuts, with a brode lace aboute it of Veniceet. golde, the longe sleeves lined with clothe of golde, the gowne lined with orenge-colour s̃rconet.

Item, one Frenche gowne of tawney sattin, embrodered all over with knotts, sonnes and clouds, of golde, silver, and silke, furred with *luzarnes*[2].

Item, one covering for a Frenche gowne of lawne, enbrodered all over with fountains, snaikes, swordes, and other devises, upon silver chamblet prented.

Item, one Frenche gowne of russet stiched cloth, richlie florished with golde and silver, lyned with orenge-colour taphata, and hanginge sleeves, lyned with white taphata, enbrodered with *antiques*[3] of golde and silke of sonderie colours, called china work.

Rounde Gownes.

Item, one rounde gowne of white cloth of silver, with workes of yellow silke, like flies, wormes, and snailes.

Item, one rounde gowne, of the Irish Fashion, of orenge tawney satten, cut and snipte, garded thicke overthawarte with aish-colour vellat, enbrodered with Venice golde and spangles.

---

[1] Caltrops are iron spikes fixt in balls, to throw in the way of the enemy's cavalry.
[2] Luzarn or lucern, a sort of lynx, a Russian animal of the size of a wolf.
[3] *Antics*. Men in fantastical postures, like morris-dancers.

Item, one rounde gowne of *Isabella*-colour[1] satten, cut in snippes and raised up, set with silver spangles.

Item, one rounde gowne of beasar-colour[2] satten, with workes of silver like *Gynney* wheate[3] and branches.

Item, one rounde gowne of lawne, cut and snipt, with small silver plates upon aish-colour silver chamblet.

Item, one rounde gowne of dove-colour *caph'a*[4], with workes of golde and orenge-colour silke, like rainebowes, cloudes, and droppes and flames of fire.

Item, one rounde gowne of hear-coloured raised mosse-worke, enbrodered all over with *leaves, pomegranets, and men*.

Loose Gownes.

Item, one gowne of blacke satten, embrodered all over with roses and *pauncies*[5], and a border of oken leaves, roses, and pauncis, of Venice golde, silver, and silke, with a face likewise embroderen.

Item, one loose gowne of white satten, faced with orenge-colour satten, embrodered all over with *Friers' knotts* and roses, in branches of Venice golde and tawney silke, and cut, with a slight border of Venice silver and orenge-colour sylke.

Item, one loose gowne of *drakes colour* satten, cut and tufted, laide on the seames and rounde aboute with twoe laces of Venice silver, faced and edged with white plushe.

Item, one loose gowne of *ladies-blushe* satten, laide with a bone-lace of Venice golde and silver, with spangles, with buttons downe before of the same lace.

Item, one loose gowne of aish-colour tufte taphata, the grounde silver, furred *with callaber*.

Item, one loose gowne of blacke taphata, with *compas lace* of blacke silke and silver, with a braided lace, with a plate on either side.

Item, one loose gowne of *white curle*, laide with golde lace.

Item, one loose gowne of white *tillyselye*, like grograme, bounde aboute with a small lace of golde, the hangings sleeves beinge cutt and bounde with like lace and tufts of golde threede, and some golde spangles.

---

[1] Or flax-seed colour.
[2] Q. *beafer*, bearer. Or it may be of the *bezoar* stone, which is of a brownish hue.
[3] Indian Wheat
[4] A kind of tiffany. Q. Caffoy, a sort of velvet. Or perhaps only *tapta, for taphata*.
[5] Pansies

KIRTELLS[1]

Item, one kirtle of aishe-colour[2] cloth of golde, with workes of snails, wormes, flies and spiders.

Item, one rounde kirtle of white clothe of silver chevernd, with *bluncket*, with lace of golde, and spangles, buttons, and loopes.

Item, one rounde kirtle of white cloth of sylver, bounde with a lace of Venice golde, and seaven buttons, like the *birdes of Arabia*[3], embrodered down before.

Item, one Frenche kirtle of white satten cutt, all over enbrodered with *hopes*[4], flowers, of Venice golde, sylver, and sylke.

Item, one rounde kirtle of *claie-colour satten, or terr' sigillata,* enbrodered all over with flowers of Venice silver and blacke silke.

Item, one rounde kirtle of white satten, enbrodered with a slight border like a *ryver of the sea,* and slightlie enbrodered all over with plate, *esses*[5] of plate golde, with a deepe golde frenge.

Item, one rounde kirtle of white satten, enbrodered all over with the work like flames, pescods, and pillars, with a border likewise enbrodered with roses. Given by hir Majestie the 16th Apr. 1600.—A. Walsingham.

Item, one rounde kirtle of *beasar*-colour silver chamblet, with embrodered golde buttones downe before.

Item, one rounde kirtle of hear-colour tufte taphata, the ground silver, with workes like pomegranets and artichoques.

FOREPARTES[6].

Item, one foreparte of clothe of sylver, enbrodered all over with rainebowes, cloudes, flames of fyer, and sonnes, of sylke, lyned with greene sarconet.

Item, one foreparte and a dublet of white satten, enbrodered all over with rainebowes, of Venice golde and spangles.

Item, one fore parte of white satten, embrodered all over with bugles, made like flowers upon stalkes, within knotts.

Item, one fore parte of white satten, embrodered with daffadillies of Venice golde, and other flowers.

---

[1]The garment under the mantle. The mantle was a loose cloak, covering the arms, and [4] fastered at the neck or breast. [2]Ash-colour.
[3] Birds of Paradise.
[4] hoops, circles. [5]SS.
[6] Stomachers.

Item, one fore parte of satten, of sondrie colours, embrodered with the twelve signes, of Venice golde, silver, and silke of sondrie colours, unmade.

Item, one fore parte of white satten, embrodered verie faire with borders of the Sonne, Mone, and other Signes and Planetts, of Venice golde, silver, and silke of sondrie colours, with a border of beastes beneath, likewise embrodered.

Item, one fore parte of white satten, embrodered all over with a runninge worke like potts, and within them jelleflowers, lined with yellowe šconett.

Item, one fore parte of white satten, embrodered all over verie faire like seas, with dyvers devyses of rockes, shippes, and fishes[1], embrodered with Venice golde, sylver, and silke of sondrye colours, garnished with some seede pearle.

Item, one fore parte of white satten, embrodered all over with paunceis, little roses, knotts, and a border of mulberies, pillers, and pomegranets, of Venice golde, sylver, and sylke of sondrye colours.

Item, one fore parte of peach-colour satten, embrodered all over verie faire with dead trees, flowers, and a lyon in the myddest, garded with manye pearles of sondry sortes.

Item, one fore parte of white satten, embrodered all over with spiders, flies, and roundells, with cobwebs, of Venice golde and tawnye silke.

Item, one fore parte of greene satten, embrodered all over with sylver, like beastes, fowles, and fishes.

Item, one fore parte of lawne, embrodered with bees and sondrie wormes, lyned with white taphata.

PETTICOATES.

Item, one peticoate of watchet, or blew satten, embrodered all over with flowers and beasts, of Venice golde, silver, and silke, like a wildernes.

Item, one peticoate of tawney satten, razed all over with fower borders of embroderie of Venice silver, and with *lypes,* lyned with orenge-colour šconet.

Item, one peticoate of white satten, embrodered all over with blacke flies, with a border of fountaines and trees, embrodered rounde aboute it, and waves of the sea.

Item, one peticoate of white satten, embrodered all over slightlie with snakes of Venice golde, silver, and some *owes,* with a faire border like seas, cloudes, and rainebowes.

Item, one peticoate of white Turquye satten, embrodered all over with a twiste of Venice golde, and *owes* like knotts.

Item, one peticoate of white satten, enbrodered all over with Venice golde, silver, and silke of divers colours, with a verie faire border of pomegranetts, pyneaple trees, frutidge[1], and the nyne Muses, in the same border.

Item, one peticoate of white s͂conet, quilted all over with a small threede of Venice golde and silke of colours, with flowers and feathers, embrodered with Carnac͂on watchet and grene silke, with three borders rounde aboute, embrodered with pauncies, roses, and pillars.

Cloakes.

Item, one Dutche cloake of blacke vellat, embrodered all over with flowers and grashoppers, of Venice golde, silver, and silke, lyned with tawnie s͂conet, furred with sables.

Item, one cloake of blacke taphata, laide aboute and striped with lace of Venice golde and sylver, wrought wtth *pipes* and ple[2], with a jagge[3] wrought *byas*[4], with *passamanie* lace of Venice golde and silver, lyned with greene cloth of golde and sylver.

Item, one shorte cloake of perfumed leather[5], embrodered with three small borders of Venice golde, sylver and crimsen silke, faced and edged with sables, and furred with *callaber*.

Item, one cloake of heare-colour raized mosseworke, embrodered like stubbes of dead trees, set with fourteen buttons embrodered like butterflies, with fower pearles and one emerode in a pece, lyned with cloth of sylver, prented.

Cloakes and Saufegardes.

Item, one cloake, a saufegarde, and a hatt, of blacke taphata, enbrodered all over with droppes of Venice golde, blacke silke, and spangles.

Item, one cloak and a saufegarde of gozelinge-colour taphata.

Item, one cloake and a saufegarde of taphata, called *pounde cythrone* colour bounde with a lace and buttons of Venice sylver and watchet silke.

---

[1] *Fruitage*, clusters of fruit. [2] Q.*Pearle.* [3] Jagged.
[4] Worked in crooked or waving lines.
[5] Another cloake of perfumed leather occurs.

SAUFEGARDES.

Item, one saufegarde and a dublet of dove-colour of golde, bounde aboute and garnished with buttons and loopes, of plate lace of Venice silver.

Item, one saufegarde of blacke vellat, spotted all over with little knotts and cynques[1] of small seede pearle the border embroidered with pillers and butterflies, of like seede pearle.

SAUFEGARDES AND JUPPES.

Item, one juppe and a saufegarde of brasell-colour cloth of silver, with lace of gold and silver, with spangles upon carnacon satten.

Item, one juppe and saufegarde of orenge-colour, or marigolde-colour vellat, cut and uncutt, the sleeves and downe before garnished with a lace of Venice sylver, like *essefirms*, and laide aboute with twoe plate laces of Venice silver.

Item, one juppe and saufegarde of heare-colour *capha*, like golde flames of fire, and garnished with buttons, loupes, and lace of Venice silver, lyned with white plushe.

DUBLETTES.

Item, one doublet of blacke clothe of golde, with dogges of silver.

Item, one dublett of straw-colour satten cut, and lyned with cloth of silver embrodered upon with knotts, roses, and sonnes, of Venice golde and silver.

Item, one dublet of white satten, embrodered like seas, with fishes, castles, and sonne-beames, of Venice golde, silver, and silke of sondrie colours.

Item, one dublett of *camerike*[2], wrought with Venice golde, silver, and silke of sondrie colours, with white networke, striped with sylver.

LAPPE MANTLES.

Item, one compasse lappe-clothe of white taphata, embrodered all over with sondrie antiques, lined with orenge-colour plushe.

[1] Q. Cinqfoils.
[2] A sort of stuff made of camel's hair. In the wardrobe account of Hen VIII, a doublet set on with camerike.

Item, one mantle of white plush, with a *pane*[3] of redd swanne-downe in the middest.

SILKES.

Item, towe remnants of blacke *burrell*[1], conteyninge both together 12 yardes.

Item, one peece of tawney networke florished with golde, called[2] birds in the cage, conteyneing 23 yardes.

Item, two handekercheifes like barbers aprones.

Item, three peeces of *baudekin*[3] of sondrye colours, each peece contayninge vii yardes. 21 yardes.

Item, 19 remnants of white silke *curle,* contayninge in the whole 104 yardes.

FANNES.

Item, one fanne of white feathers, with a handle of golde, having two snakes wyndinge aboute it, garnished with a ball of diamondes in the ende, and a crowne on each side within a paire of wings garnished with diamondes, lacking 6 diamondes.

Item, one fanne of feather of divers colours, the handle of golde, with a bear and a ragged staffe on both sides, and a lookinge glasse on thone side.

Item, one handle of golde enameled, set with small rubies and emerodes, lacking 9 stones, with a shipp under saile on thone side.

Item, one handle of christall, garnished with sylver guilte, with a worde within the handle.

Item, one handle of elitropia[4], garnished with golde, set with sparks of diamondes, rubies, and sixe small pearles, lackinge one diamonde.

PANTOBLES.[5]

Item, one paire of pantobles of cloth of silver, embrodered with a mill.

---

[3] A breadth.

[1] *Burra,* or *Borra,* is a sort of stuffing or wadding.
[2] Q. *Gold-coloured.*
[3] Gold borocade. The richest cloth.
[4] *Heliotrope.* A precious stone of green colour, with red spots, or veins.
[5] *Pantoufles.* Fr. Slippers.

Item, one paire of pantobles of orenge-colour vellat, enbrodered upon with *essefirmes* and other knotts of seede pearle, and some ragged ple.

SONDRIE P'CELLS.

Item, one little bearinge sworde, with a pommell and hilts of iron, guilte.

Item, one sworde, with a pomell *sanguimarie*.

Item, one canapie of crimson capha damaske to carrie over one, striped with lace of Venice golde and sylver, the handle mother-of-ple.   Item, fower lazarnes skines.

JEWELLS.

Item, in colletts of golde, in everie collet one *ballas*[1], one being broken, 23.

Item, one small jewell of golde, like a white lyon, with a flie on his side, standing upon a base or foote, garnished with twoe opalls, twoe verie little pearles, fyve rubies, one rubie pendaunt, and twoe little shorte cheines on the backe of the lyon.

Item, one fearne braunche of golde, having therin a lyzard, a lady cow[2], and a snaile.

Item, one jewell of golde, with a flie and a spider in it upon a rose.

Item, in buttons with camewes[3], 18.

Item, one jewell of golde, like an *Irish darte*, garnished with fower small diamondes.

Jewells receaved by Sir Thomas Gorges, Knight, of the charge of the ladie Katherine Howarde, Countesse of Nott.

Item, in greate rounde buttons of golde, enameled with sondry colours, each set with small sparks of rubies, and pearle in the middest called *greate bucklers,* 72.

Item, one jewell of golde like a frogg, garnished with diamondes.

Jewells receaved by Sir Thomas Gorges, (Knight), of Mrs. Mary Radcliffe.

[1] A species of ruby of a vermeil rose-colour.
[2] Q. A Lady-bird, an insect so called.   [3] Cameos.

Item, in buttons of golde like tortoyses, in each one a pearle, 454.

Item, one jewell of golde like a dasye, and small flowers aboute it, garnished with sparks of diamondes and rubies, with her Majestie's picture graven within a garnet, and a sprigge of three branches, garnished with sparks of rubies, one pearle in the topp, and a small pendaunte of sparks of diamondes.

Memorand. All the jewells before menc̃oned we receved by Sir Thomas Gorges Knight, of Mrs. Mary Ratcliffe, were by him delivered over unto the charge of the said Mrs. Ratcliff the 28th of Maye, 1603, in the presence of us,

EDW. CARYE. THO. KNYVETT.

FRA. GOTTON.

BIBLIOGRAPHY

For any study of the Progresses of Elizabeth I the most important source is the collection of contemporary descriptions, accounts, lists, entertainment scripts and poems compiled by John NICHOLS (1788 - 1821) entitled *Progresses And Public Processions Of Queen Elizabeth.* The edition used was that of 1828, in three volumes. Other contemporary writing consulted included STOW, John, *Annals of England* (1601); HARRISON, William, *Description of England* (1587); *CAMDEN*, William, *Britannia* (1586), together with Elizabethan poetry, essays and plays. Also John Aubrey's *Brief Lives.*

More recent books and compilations of documents
AUERBACH, Erna, and Kingsley Adams, C.
  Paintings and Sculpture at Hatfield house (Constable 1971)
BATH, Daphne *Longleat from 1566 to the Present Time* (The Longleat Estate, 1949)
BINDOFF, S.T. *Tudor England* (Penguin, 1950)
BURTON, Elizabeth *The Elizabethans at Home* (Longman, 1958)
BUXTON, John *Elizabethan Taste* (Macmillan, 1963)
BYRNE, M. St Clere *Elizabethan Life in Town and Country* (Methuen, 1926)
CECIL, Lord David *The Cecils of Hatfield House* (Constable, 1973)
COCKS, A.G. Somers (introduction by) *Princely Magnificence* (catalogue) (Victoria & Albert Museum)
DOVER-WILSON, J. *Life in Shakespeare's England* (C.U.P., 1911)
DOWSING, James *Forgotton Tudor Palaces of Elizabeth I* (Sunrise Press, no date)
DUNLOP, Ian *Palaces and Progresses of Elizabeth I* (Cape, 1962)
DUNLOP, Sir John *The Pleasant Toen of Sevenoaks* (published by the author, 1964)
FALKUS, Christopher (edited by) *Private Lives of the Tudor Monarchs* (reprints of original documents) (Macmillan, 1962)
FEDDEN, Robin, and KENWORTHY-BROWNE, John *The Country House Guide* (Cape, 1979)
FEDDEN, Robin, and JEEKES, Rosemary *National Trust Guide* (National Trust, 1973)
GIROUARD, Mark *Life in the English Country House* (Yale, 1978)
GIROUARD, Mark *Hardwick Hall* (National Trust, 1976)

GIROUARD, Mark *Robert Smythson and the Elizabethan Country House* (Yale, 1983)

JENKINS, Elizabeth *Elizabeth the Great* (Gollancz, 1958)

MORRIS, Christopher *The Tudors* (Batsford, 1955)

NEALE, J.E. *Queen Elizabeth* (Cape, 1934)

NICOLSON, Nigel *Great Houses of Britain* (National Trust & Weïdenfeld & Nicolson, 1978)

PLOWDEN, Alison *Mistress of Hardwick* (B.B.C., 1972)

ROWSE, A.L. *The England of Elizabeth* (Macmillan, 1950)

SACKVILLE-WEST, V. *Knole and the Sackvilles* (Ernest Benn, 1922)

SITWELL, Edith *Fanfare for Elizabeth* (Macmillan, 1949)

SITWELL, Edith *The Queens and the Hive* (Macmillan, 1962)

STRAUSS, Sheila *A Short History of Wollaton and Wollaton Hall* (Nottinghamshire C.C 1978)

STRONG, Roy *The Cult of Elizabeth* (Thames & Hudson, 1977)

STRONG, Roy *The English Icon* (Thames & Hudson, 1969)

STRONG, Roy (introduction by) *Artists of the Tudor Court* (Catalogue) (Victoria and Albert Museum, 1983)

STRONG, Roy, and OMAN, Julia Trevelyan *Elizabeth R* (Secker & Warbury, 1971)

TURNER, E.S. *The Court at St James's* (Michael Joseph, 1959)

USHERWOOD, Stephen (editor) *The Great Enterprise* (Folio Society, 1978)

WILLIAMS, Neville *Life and Times of Elizabeth I* (Weidenfeld & Nicolson, 1972)

WOOLF, Virginia *Orlando* (Hogarth Press, 1928)

YATES, Frances A. *Astraea; the Imperial Theme in the Sixteenth Century* (Routledge & Kegan Paul, 1975)

Also the guide-books to the country houses mentioned.

INDEX
Numerals in *italics* refer to captions

Agas, Ralph: map of Oxford, 1578 *63*
Alençon, Duc d' 82, 83, 145
Amyce, Israel 171
Amyot, Thomas 186n
Anjou, Duc d'
  see Alençon, Duc d'
Anne Boleyn, Queen 23, 25, 100, 167
  gives birth to Elizabeth 23
  miscarries of male child 25
  suffers execution, 1536 25
Anne of Cleves, Queen 32, 85n
Arnold, William 176
Arthur Tudor, Prince 23
  tomb 49
Arundel, Earls of 82, 104
  Howard
Ascham, Roger 28, 30, 34, 54
  on Elizabeth's educational accomplish-
    ments 30
  The Schoolmaster 30
Ashley, Anthony 69
Ashley, Kat 27, 29
Ashridge, Herts 32
Astraea, pagan goddess 17, 94
Aubrey, John: *Brief Lives* 73

Bacon, Sir Francis 140
  'Of Building' 148, 160
Bacon, Sir Nicholas 72-3
  entertains QE, 1577 73-4
Barber, Dr Richard 69
Barlow, Robert 150
Bath, second and fourth Marquises of 129
Bedford, John Duke of 141
Beauvoys la Noude, Monsieur 69
Bedingfield, Sir Henry 33
Bedington, Surrey 94
  QE visits, 1599 85
Bennet, John: madrigal in praise of QE 18
Bodley, Dr Thomas 71
Boonen, William 44
Bourchier, Thomas, Archbishop of Canter-
  bury 132, 133

Brackenbury, Richard 69
Bristol: QE's visit to, 1574 48-9
Brouncker, Lord 156
Brown, 'Capability' 130
Browne, Henry 88
Browne, Sir Anthony 85n
Browne, Sir George 88n
Bryane, Lady 25, 26
Buckhurst, Lord, *see* Sackville, Sir Thomas
Buckingham, Stafford Dukes of 142
Burbage, James 185n
Burghley House 104, 117, 119-21
  Old Kitchen *121*
  West Front *118*
Burghley, Sir William Cecil, Lord 44, 46,
    61, 64, 65, 72, 73, 82, 104, 163, 173-4
  cost of entertaining QE 19, 20, 123
  forebears 117
  High Chancellor of Cambridge Univer-
    sity 54
  life and career: birth, c. 1520 117; education
    117; first and second marriages 117;
    serves Henry VIII and Edward VI 117-18;
    imprisoned in Tower, 1552 118; serves
    Mary I 119; QE's visit to Cambridge,
    1564 55-6, 57; created baron, 1571 120;
    builds Burghley House 120-2; death,
    1598, and tomb 123-4
  portraits *39*, *119*
  Principal Secretary to QE, 1558 36, 104
  QE's consideration towards 38-9, 69
Buxton, John 160
Bysshop, Thomas 173

Calfhill, James
  Progue (play) 65
  verses to QE 60-1
Cambridge
  King's College 55, 56, 57
    Chapel *55*, 57, 58
  QE's visit, 1564 54-9
  Queens's College 57
  St John's College 54, 56, 117

Sidney Sussex College 142
Trinity College 56
Camden, William
 Annals of Queen Elizabeth 37
 Britannia 130
Campion, Edmund 63
Canterbury: QE's visit, 1573 45
Capgrave, John 141n
Carew, Peter 61, 64
Carew, Sir Francis 85
Carey, Sir Robert 96
Carvell, Sir John 88n
Carye, Edward 213
Catherine Howard, Queen 14
Catherine of Aragon, Queen 23, 25
Catherine Parr, Queen 28, 116, 198n
 marries Thomas Seymour after Henry
 VIII's death 29
 relations with Elizabeth 28-9
 suffers death in childbirth 29
Cave, Sir Ambrose 104
Cavendish, Sir William 150
Cecil, Anne 47, 117, 122, 122n
Cecil, Elizabeth 117, 122n
Cecil, Robert, later Earl of Salisbury 104,
 117, 122, 176
 becomes Earl of Salisbury 104
 death, 1612 105
 exchange Theobalds for Hatfield 105
Cecil, Sir William, *see* Burghley, Lord
Cecil, Thomas 104, 117, 122
Champernowne, Katherine, *see* Ashley,
 Kat
Chandos, Lord 33
Chapuys, Eustace 100
Charles I 15
Chatworth 150
Christian IV of Denmark 104
Christ's Hospital 45
Churchyard, Thomas 10, 171
 entertainments for QE in Norwich, 1578
 50, 52-3
 'Few Plaine Verses . . .' 67
Clinton, Lord 104
Cobham, Lord 45
Colt, Maximilian 105
Coningsby, Sir Thomas 69

Cordell, Sir William 72, 168, 169
 entertains QE, 1578 72, 171
Coryat, Gregory 61
Coventry, QE's visit to 21
Courtenay, Edward 31, 31n, 32, 34
Cowdray Castle, Sussex 85n, 173
 Buck Hall 85n
 QE's visit, 1591 85, 87-8
Cowdray, forest Viscount 173
Cowper, Henry 47-8
Cranmer, Thomas, Archbishop of Canter-
 bury 24, 26, 59, 133
Cromwell, Thomas 25, 100
Cuer, Cornelius 134
Cuff, Henry 68
Cumberland, George Clifford, Earl of 69
Curzon, Lord 178

Darcy, Edward 69
Darnley, Lord 153
Davies, Sir John: *Hymn of Astraea I* 17
De Clinton, Geoffrey 108
De Heere, Lucas 167
De l'Orme, Philibert: *Nouvelles Inventions
 pour bien bastir* 120
De Montfort, Simon 109
De Penchester, Sir Stephen 139
De Pulteney, Sir John 139, 140
Derby, Dowager Countess of 95
Devereux, Penelope 145
Devereux, Sir John 140
Devereux, Robert, *see* Essex, Earl of
Dimmock, Sir Edward 41
Donne, John 166
Dormer, Sir Robert 88n
Dorset, Margaret Grey, Marchioness of 24,
 25, 150
Dorset, Thomas 132
Drake, Sir Francis 145
Du Cerceau: *Livre d'Architecture* 120
Dudley, Ambrose, *see* Warkwick, Earl of
Dudley, John *see* Northumberland
Dudley, Lord Guildford 31, 32n, 108, 143
Dudley, Lord Henry 174
Dudley, Robert, *see* Leicester, Earl of
Dudley, Thomas 38
Dungan, Richard 134

Edrick, Mr, Oxford Greek Reader 65
Edward III 139
Edward V 142
Edward VI 14, 29, 30, 101, 118, 142, 143,
    167, 173
  at Siege of Hampton Court 14
  life and reign: birth 26; education 27-8,
    100-1; succeeds to throne, 1547 29;
    illness and death, 1553 31
Edwards, Richard 61n, 64, 65
  Damon and Pythias 64
  Palamon and Arcite 61n, 61-4 *passim*
Egerton, Sir Thomas 94, 95
  entertains QE 94, 95-6
Elizabeth I
  appearance in portraits 37
  Armada portrait *10*
  beautiful hands 37, 38
  belief in power based on love of subjects
    15, 21
  coaches 44
  composition of royal trian 44-5
  consideration for others 38-9, 40
  coronation 41-2
  cost of entertaining 19, 20, 74, 183-9
  death-mask *97*
  depicted in old age *95*, 121
  Ditchley portrait, *see* colour plate
  enjoyment of travel and pageantry 18
  Ermine portrait *106*
  expenses of teble, 1576 180-2
  funeral 98-9
  fulfils subjects' desire for female deity
    16-17
  illness and death, 1603 96-7, 98
  letter to Edward VI 102-3
  life as princess: birth, 1533 23;
    christening 24-5; early care of 25; lose
    favour on mother's execution, 1536 25-
    6, 100; attends christening of Prince
    Edward 27; educated with Prince
    Edward 27-8, 100-1; protrait aged c.
    thirteen *27*; lives with Catherine Parr
    29; wooed by Thomas Seymour 29, 30,
    in danger from Lord Protector Somerset
    30; educational accomplishments 30, 37;
    hazardous life under Mary I 31-4, 103;
  life at Hatfield 103-4; recognised as
    Queen Mary's heir 34; visits Queen
    Mary 34-5; becomes queen, 1558 35-6,
    104
  looks 37, 93, 97
  madrigals in praise of 18
  musical ability 38
  new year gifts to, 1577-8 190-6
  pre-coronation procession 40-1
  prevarication re marriage 34, 42, 81-2
  progresses 15, 16, 19, 20, 21, 43-96
    passim
  Rainbow portrait 21, 106
  receives one of Gascoigne's works *78*
  suitors 34, 81-2
  Tilbury speech, 1588 11-12
  travels to avoid plague 19
  Triumphal Procession *13*, 18
  vanity 38, 93
  wardrobe 18, 200-13
Elizabethan Lute Songs 91n
Eltham Palace 19
Elvetham, Hants 94
  QE's visit, 1591 88-92, *94*
England, Elizabethan
  architecture 139
  extortions by QE's purveyors 45-6
  introduction of coaches 44
  ruinous state of roads 43-4
English and British sovereigns
  present-day 'progresses' 15
  seclusion from subjects 14, 15
Eric of Sweden 34, 81
Essex, Lettice Knollys, Countess of 80, 111
Essex, Robert Devereux, Earl of 83, *84*, 174
  entertainments for QE's accession day,
    1595 83, 85
  fall from favour and execution, 1601 93
Exeter, fifth Earl of 121
Exeter, Marchioness of 24, 25, 31

Fane, Sir Ralph 142
Farnham Castle QE's visit to 94
Faversham, Kent: QE's visit, 1573 45
Field of the Cloth of Gold 14, 117
Fiennes, James, Baron Say and Sele 132

Fiennes, William 132
Firebrace, Sir Cordell 169
Fletcher, Christopher 49
Fortescue, Sir John 200
Foxe, Jonh: *Acts and Monuments* 198n

Gamage, Barbara 147
Gardiner, Bishop 32
Gascoigne, George *78*
  entertainments for QE at Kenilworth,
    1575 77-80
  Princely Pleasures at the Court of Kenilworth
    76n
Gaunt, Adrian 127
George IV 15
Gheeraerts, Marcus
  portrait of QE 121
  See also colour plate at end of book
Girouard, Mark: *Robert Smythson and the*
  Elizabethan Country House 127n
Glenham, Sir Henry 88n
Gloucester, Humphrey, Duke of 23, 141,
  141n
  inherits Penshurst Place 141
Godwyn, Dr 60
Goldwell (or Goldingham), Henry 82n
Goodman, Geoffrey: sees QE in Strand,
  1588 13-14
Gorges, Sir Thomas 200, 212, 213
Gorhambury House, Herts 73
  QE's visit, 1577 73-4
Goring, Sir Henry 88n
Gotton, Francis 213
Greenwich Palace (Placentia) 14, 15, 23,
135
  QE's court at, 1598-9 197-9
  Queen's House 15
Gresham, Richard 126
Gresham, Sir Thomas 136
Greville, Sir Fulke 47, 82, 96, 123
Grey, Lady Jane 31, 32n, 108, 118, 143, 150,
  176
Grindal, William 28, 54

Habingdon, Thomas 50
Hampton Court 19, 26, 33, 34, 35, 143, 168

Hardwick Hall, Derbyshire 148-57
  High Great Chamber 156
  Long Gallery 155
  New Hall 154, 155
  Old Hall 153
  profusion of glass 148
  south-west view *149*
Hardy, Thomas: *The Mayor of Casterbridge*
  178n
Harefield Place, nr Uxbridge: QE's visit
  95-6
Harington, Lady: conversation with QE 15
Harington, Sir John 15, 81
  papers 15n
Harris, Thomas 61
Harrison, William: *Description of England*
  72, 139, 148, 158
Hatfield House 25, 34, 35, 36, 100-6
  Cecil's building work 105
  Ermine portrait of QE 106: *see also*
    colour plate at end of book
  exchanged for Cecil's Theobalds, 1603
    105
  gardens laid out 105
Hatfield House - *continued*
  Great Hall 103. *See also* colour plate at
    end of book
  memorabilia of QE 105-6. *See also* colour
    plate at end of book
  Old Palace *28*
  Parry's account 101-2
  presented to Elizabeth by Edward VI 30,
    101
  Rainbow portrait of QE 20, 106, *See also*
    colour plate at end of book
Hatton, Sir Christopher 67, 117, 123, 128,
  155-6, 161, *162*, 167
  builds Kirby Hall and Holdenby 162-4
  in debt to QE 164
Hawford, Dr 56
Hawstead 72, 73; QE's visit, 1578 72
Heneage, Sir Thomas 163
Henry III 109
Henry IV 15, 109
Henry V 15, 109
Henry VI 23, 141
Henry VIII 14, 26, 31, 109, 133, 142, 166,

198n
death, 1547 29
divorces Catherine of Aragon 23
extravagance 19
marries Anne Boleyn 23
marries Jane Seymour 26
visits Princess Elizabeth at Hatfield, 1534 100
Henry, Prince of Wales 174
Hentzner: describes QE's court at Greenwich, 1598-9 197-9
Herbert, Lord 93
Hertford, Catherine Grey, Countess of 88, 90, 150, 151
Hertford, Edward Seymour, Earl of 20, 94, 128, 129, 151, 156
entertainment for QE, 1591 88, *89*, 89-92
imprisonment for secret marriage 88
Hever Castle, Kent 133
Hilliard, Nicholas 37
QE portrait at Hatfield attributed to 106
See also colour plate at end of book
Hofnagel, Joris 106
Holbein, Hans 166
Holdenby, Northants 117, 129, 161, 163-4
Holinshed, Raphael 33, 142
Howard, Lord, of Effingham, Earl of Nottingham 46, 65, 94, 122
Howes, Edmund: *Annals* 44n
Humphrey, Dr 56
Hunsdon 26
Hunsdon, George, Lord 123, 200
Huntingdon, Earl of 46

Isaacson, Paul 135

James I (and VI of Scotland) 15, 98, 100, 134, 153, 166, 167, 176
exchanges Hatfield for Theobalds 105
Jane Seymour, Queen 26
dies after giving birth to Edward VI 26
John, King 49, 109, 125
John of Gaunt 109
Jonhson, Edward 91
Jonson, Ben: *To Penshurst* 139, 147

Kenilworth Castle 20, *75*, *107*, 107-13
fame revived by Scott's novel 111-12
comes into hands of John of Gaunt 109
given to Leicester by QE, 1563 110
given to Simon de Montfort by Henry III 109
lake 74, 75, 76, 109
Leicester's work on 110
QE's visit of 1572 47
QE's visit of 1575 74-80, 110, 111, 112-13
Gascoigne's entertainments 77-80
rendered indefensible in Civil War 111
site 109
Kennall, Dr 60
Kildare, Countess of 87
Kingsmill, Mr, Oxford Orator 60
Kirby Hall, Northants *161*, 161, 162-3
Knevet (or Knyvett), Thomas 69, 213
Knole *131*, 131-7
becomes royal property, sixteenth c. 133
early owners 132-3
furniture 135
made over to Sackville family, 1566 134
Painted Staircase *135*
Park 131
QE's visit, 1573 136-7
Knollys, Sir Francis 65, 66
Knollys, Lettice, *see* Essex, Countess of
Knollys, Sir William 69

Lake, Thomas 69
Laneham, Robert 74
Lanham, John 185n
Lawrence, Mr, Oxford Professor of Greek 60
Leicester, Amy Robsart, Countess of 82, 108, 112
Leicester, Robert Dudley, Earl of 20, 38, 44, 46, 47, 50, 63, 67, 72, 107-8, 122, 127, 134, 174
Chancellor of Oxford University 59, 65
commands expedition to Low Countries, 1585 111
created Earl of Leicester, 1564 108
criticises Oxford University 59, 70

death, 1588 67, 111, 116n, 147,
death of first wife 82, 108
debts 111
entertains QE at Kenilworth, 1572 47
entertains QE at Kenilworth, 1575 74-80,
  110, 111, 112-13
entertains QE at Wanstead, 1578 80
finances 110
made QE's Master of Horse 108
master of ceremonies at QE's visit to
  Cambridge, 1564 55, 56, 59
new year gifts to QE 114-16
portrait *66*
secret marriage to Lady Sheffield 110,
  111
secret marriage to Lettice Knollys, 1578
  80, 111
wish to marry QE 79-80, 108
Lennard, John 136
Lennox, Lady Margaret 153, 201n
Lichfield: cost of entertaining QE, 1575
  183-5
Limbert, Stephen 52
London
  Baynard's Castle 43
  Cecil House, Strand 122, 123
  QE's pre-coronation procession 40-1
  Sir John Soane's Museum 168
Longleat *125*, 125-30
  alterations since 1580 129
  building of 126-7
  cost of building 128
  derivation of name 126
  fire of 1567 126-7
  gardens 129-30
  plan of 127
  QE's visit, 1574 129
Loseley Park, Surrey 165-7
  North Front *165*
  QE's visits 166, 167
Lyminge, Robert 105

Marbeck, Roger 67
Marlborough, Sarah, Duchess of 33n
Martin, Humphrey 74n
Mary I 14, 35, 72, 100, 103-4, 118, 119, 143,

comes to throne, 1553 31
disinherited while princess 25
false pregnancy 34
godmother to Edward VI 26
marries Philip II of Spain 32
recognises Elizabeth as heir 34
reinstates Roman Catholicism 31-2
suspicions of Elizabeth 32-3
unhappy in death, 1558 35
Mary Queen of Scots 33, 37, 38, 134, 151,
  153, 156, 166, 167, 174
Master, William 58
Mathew, Toby 65
Mauditor, Monsieur 69
Maynard, Alan 127, 128
Melford Hall, Suffolk 168-9, *169*, 171
  Garden Pavilion *170*
  QE's visit, 1578 72, 171
Melville, Sir James 37, 38, 204n
Montacute House, Devon 19, *39*, 176-9
  Nine Worthies statues 177
  North-east view *177*
Montague, Anthony Browne, Viscount 85n
Montague, Lord: entertains QE, 1591 85,
  87-8
More, Ann: elopes with John Donne 166
More, Sir Christopher 165
More, Sir George 166
More, Sir Thomas 167
More, Sir William 165-6, 167
Morley, Thomas 90
Morton, Cardinal 100, 133

Naunton, Sir Robert 107
Neale, Thomas 61
Nichols, John: *Progresses & Public Processions
  of Queen Elizabeth* 43, 45n, *89*, 114n
Nine Worthies 177n
Noel, Henry 69
Nonsuch Palace 19, 44, 94, 168
Norfolk, Mary Howard, Duchess of 24
Norice, Ralph 133
North, Lord: extracts from Household Book,
  1575 186-9
Northampton, Marchioness of 99
Northumberland, John Dudley, Duke of

31, 108, 110, 118
Norton, Thomas 134
Norwich 51
    plague in, 1578-80 52
    QE's visit, 1578 50-3
Nottingham, Lord, *see* Howard, Lord of
    Effingham

Oatlands Palace 19, 94, 96
Oliver, Isaac 106, 174
    See also colour plate at end of book
Ord, Craven 200
Ormond, Thomas Butler, Earl of 65
Overton, Dr 61
Ovid: *Metamorphoses* 16
Oxford
    All Souls College 67, 70
    Baliol College 70
    Bodleian Library 71, 74n
    Brazen Nose (Brasenose) College 70
    Christ Church 60, 61, 63, 65, 68, 70
      Hall 62, *62*, 65
    Christ Church Cathedral 61, 65
    Corpus Christi College 70
    Exon (Exeter) College 70
    Jesus College 70
    Lincoln College 70
    Magdalen College 63, 70
    map, 1578 *63*
    Merton College 63, 70
    New College 70
    Oriel College 70, 141n
    Papistry in 59, 67
    Pembroke College 70
    plague of 1577 67
    QE's visit, 1566 67-69
    QE's visit, 1592 67-70
      cost 70
    Queen's College 70
    St John's College 70
    St Mary's Church 64-6 *passim*, 68, 69
    Trinity College 70
    Wadham College 70
Oxford, Edward de Vere, Earl of 46, 47, 65,
    122n

Palmer, Robert 173
Palmer, William 173
Parham Park, Sussex 173-5
    Great Chamber 173, *174*
    possible visit by QE, 1593 173
    South Front *172*
Parker, Sir Nicholas 88n
Parma, Duke of 11, 12
Parry, Blanche 123
Parry, Sir Thomas 34, 35, 104
    Hatfield accounts 101-2
Peake, Robert 175
Pearson, Hon. Clive 173
Peck: *Desiderata Curiosa* 123n
Pembroke, Earls of 43, 69, 104, 145
Pembroke, Mary, Countess of 94, 143, 145
Penshurst Place, Kent 139-47
    Barons' Hall 140, *141*
    early owners 139-42
    granted to Sidney family by Edward VI
    142
    President's Tower 146
    South Front *138*
Perkyn, John 185n
Petowe, Henry 98n
Peyton, Sir Edward: *Divine Catastrophe of
    the Kingly Family of the House of
    Stuarts* 93
Phelips family 19, 176, 178
Phelips, Richard 176
Phelips, Sir Edward 176, 179
Philip II, of Spain 14, 33, 34, 35, 143
    marries Queen Mary I 32
Piers, Dr John 65
Poinyz, William 69
Pope, Sir Thomas 34, 35, 104
    entertains Princess Elizabeth at Hatfield
    103-4
Portinton, William 134
Poynes, Maximilian 35

Raleigh, Sir Walter 123
Rebecca, L.B. 145n
Renard, Simon: on young Princess Elizabeth
    23, 31
Reynolds, William 61

Richard II 140
Richard III 142
Richmond, Duke of 25
Richmond Palace 96,97,168
Robsart, Amy, *see* Leicester, Countess of
Rodes, John and Christopher 154
Rogers, Sir Edward 104
Russell, Anne 93
Rutland, Earl of 46

Sackville, Sir Richard 104, 134
Sackville, Sir Thomas (Lord Buckhurst) 67,
    134, *135*, 137, 200
    Gorboduc 67, 134
Sackville-West, Victoria 136
    Knole and the Sackvilles 131
Sadler, Sir Ralph 104, 120
St Loe, Sir William 150
Salisbury, Margaret, Countess of 85n
Sandwich, Kent
    QE's visit, 1573 45
    Royal Lion in Guildhall, *see* colour plate
    at end of book
Savile, Dr 68
Scott, Sir Walter 111
    Kenilworth 112, 112n
Seymour, Edward, *see* Somerset, Duke of
Seymour, Sir Henry 129
Seymour, Thomas, Lord Admiral
    conspires against Protector Somerset 29,
    30
    marries Catherine Parr 29
    relations with Princess Elizabeth 29
    suffers execution, 1549 30
Shakespeare 16
    Hamlet 16n
    Love's Labour's Lost 177n
    Midsummer Night's Dream, A 17, 54
    Richard II 14n
    Romeo and Juliet 73
    Winter's Tale, A 97
Sheffield, John, Lord 65
Sheffield, Lady 110, 111
Shelton, John 25
Sherborne Castle *13*, 18
Shrewsbury, Elizabeth, Countess of ('Bess
    of Hardwick') 96, 149-50, *151*, 155, 156,
    157

ambitions for grand-daughter Arbella
    Stewart 153-4
    buys Hardwick Hall, 1583 153
    construction work at Hardwick Hall 154-5
    first three marriages 150
    imprisoned in Tower 153
    marries sixth Earl of Shrewsbury, 1568
    151
    relations with Mary Queen of Scots 151,
    153
    separates from husband, 1584 153
Shrewsbury, George Talbot, sixth Earl of
    150
    custodian of Mary Queen of Scots 151,
    153
Sidney family 142-7
Sidney, Frances 142
Sidney, Lady mary 143, 145, 146
Sidney Papers 94n
Sidney, Sir Henry 142-3, 145, 146
    children 143
    insignia 143
Sidney, Sir John Shelley 145n
Sidney, Sir Philip 80, 82-3, 111, 143, *144*,
    145, 146
    death in Low Countries, 1579 146
Sidney, Sir Robert 83, 111, 143, 146-7
    becomes Earl of Leicester 147
    QE's visit to, 1600 81
Sidney, Sir William 142
Smith, Abraham 156
Smythson, Robert 127, 128, 154, 155, 159
Somerset, Edward Seymour, Duke of
    ('Protector') 14, 29, 117, 118, 126
    at christening of Edward VI 26
    attempts to implicate Elizabeth in brother's
    plots 30
    executed, 1552 126
Southampton, William FitzWilliam, Earl of
    85n
Southampton, Wriothesley Earls of 166,
    166n
Spanish Armada 11
    defeated 12
Spicer, William 127
Spurs, Battle of the 14
Stafford, Edward, Lord 65, 69
Stafford, Lady 123
Stanhope, John 69

Stanhope, Michael 69
Stanhope, Sir John 200
Stevenson, William 186n
Stewart, Arbella *152*, 153, 154, 156,
    death in Tower, 1615 154n
Stewart, Charles 153
Strange, Henry, Lord 65
Stretes, Guillem 173
Stringer, Philip 68
Strong, Roy: *The Cult of Elizabeth* 18n
Suffolk, Henry Grey, Earl of 19, 176
Surrey, Earls of 52, 174
Sussex, Earl of 46

Tamworth, John 65
Thames defences, 1588 11
Theobalds, Cheshunt 19, 104, 117, 122, 129
    exchanged for Hatfield 105
    QE's visits 123
Thomas, William: on young Princess
    Elizabeth 23
Thorpe, John 123, 134, 162, 168
    Les plus fameux bâtiments 162n
Thorpe, Thomas 162
Throckmorton, Sir Nicholas 65
Thynne family 125-6
Thynne, Sir John I 125
    building of Longleat 126-7, 128
    entertains QE, 1574 129
    imprisoned after fall of Somerset, 1552
    126
Thynne, Sir John II 129
Tilbury, Essex 11
Tothill, Richard 40
Tradescant, John 105
Tritton, Veronica 173
Triumphs of Oriana, The (madrigals) 18
Tudor, Margaret 153
Tudor rose 48n
Turberville, George: *Book of Hunting* 75
Tyrwhitt, Sir William and Lady 30

Unton, Sir Henry: banquet and masque
    Memorial Picture of *87*

Vennard, Richard: *The Miracle of Nature* 94

Verney, Elizabeth 173, 174
Victoria, Queen 15
Virgil: Fourth *Eclogue* 17
Virgin Mary 16

Walpole, Horace: on respect shown to QE
    198n
Walsingham, Frances 145
Walsingham, Sir Francis 44, 146
Wanstead, Essex: QE's visit, 1578 80
Warwick
    Castle *46*, 111
    QE's visit, 1572
        destruction caused by mock battle 47-8
Warwick, Ambrose Dudley, Earl of 20, 46,
    50n, 65, 122, 147, 174
Warwick, Lady 46, 47
Wedel, Lubold von 44
Wentworth, Lord 122n
Westminster Abbey: Elizabeth's coronation,
    1558 41-2
White, Rowland 83, 147
Whitehall Palace 19, 96
    tiltyard show, 1581 82-3
Whitgift, Archbishop 98
Whyte, Dr Thomas 60
Whyte, Mrs Mary 94
Whyte, Rowland, *see* White, Rowland
William III 15
Williams, Lord 33
Willoughby family 158-9
Willoughby, Sir Francis 159, 160
Willoughby, Sir Hugh 159
Windsor, Lord 82
Wingfield, Sir Anthony 167
Wingfield, Sir John 69
Wollaton Hall, Nottingham 154, 155, *158*,
    158-60
Wolsey, Cardinal 19
Wood, Anthony: on The Queen's Enter-
    tainment at Oxford, 1566 59
Wood, Sir Robert 50
Woodstock Palace 60
    Princess Elizabeth's Lodgings 33, 33n
Woolf, Virginia: *Orlando* 136-7
Worcester: QE's visit, 1575 20, 49-50
Worcester, Edward, Earl of 69, 99
Wurtemberg, Duke of 123

Wyatt, Thomas 32
    Rebellion 19, 31, 32, 32n
Wyatville, Sir Jeffrey 129

Yates, Frances A.: *Astraea: the Imperial
    Theme in the Sixteenth Century* 17n
    106n
Young, Sir John 48

Zouche, Lady 149, 150
Zouche, seventeenth Baroness 173